Karen Brown's California

Charming Inns & Itineraries

Written by

KAREN BROWN, JUNE BROWN, and CLARE BROWN

Illustrations by Barbara Tapp
Cover Painting by Jann Pollard

Karen Brown's Guides, San Mateo, California

Karen Brown Titles

Austria: Charming Inns & Itineraries
California: Charming Inns & Itineraries
England: Charming Bed & Breakfasts
England, Wales & Scotland: Charming Hotels & Itineraries
France: Charming Bed & Breakfasts
France: Charming Inns & Itineraries
Germany: Charming Inns & Itineraries
Ireland: Charming Inns & Itineraries
Italy: Charming Bed & Breakfasts
Italy: Charming Inns & Itineraries
Portugal: Charming Inns & Itineraries
Spain: Charming Inns & Itineraries
Switzerland: Charming Inns & Itineraries

Dedicated with Love and Hugs

To

Our Little Ones

Who are so quickly growing up

Clare, Alexandra, Richard, Christian, Georgia, & Claire

The painting on the front cover is of San Francisco

Editors: Clare Brown, June Brown, Karen Brown, Kim Brown Holmsen, Iris Sandilands.

Technical support: William H. Brown III.

Illustrations: Barbara Tapp; Cover painting: Jann Pollard.

Maps: Susanne Lau Alloway—Greenleaf Design & Graphics; Back cover photo: William H. Brown.

Copyright © 1985, 1986, 1992, 1994, 1996, 1997, 1998, 1999 by Karen Brown's Guides.

This book or parts thereof may not be reproduced in any form without obtaining written permission from the publisher: Karen Brown's Guides, P.O. Box 70, San Mateo, CA 94401, USA, email: karen@karenbrown.com.

Distributed by Fodor's Travel Publications, Inc., 201 East 50th Street, New York, NY 10022, USA.

Distributed in the United Kingdom by Random House UK, 20 Vauxhall Bridge Road, London, SW1V 2SA, phone: 44 171 973 9000, fax: 44 171 840 8408.

Distributed in Australia by Random House Australia, 20 Alfred Street, Milsons Point, Sydney NSW 2061, Australia, 2066, phone: 61 2 9954 9966, fax: 61 2 9954 4562.

Distributed in New Zealand by Random House New Zealand, 18 Poland Road, Glenfield, Auckland, New Zealand, phone: 64 9 444 7197, fax: 64 9 444 7524.

Distributed in South Africa by Random House South Africa, Endulani, East Wing, 5A Jubilee Road, Parktown 2193, South Africa, phone: 27 11 484 3538, fax: 27 11 484 6180.

A catalog record for this book is available from the British Library.

Library of Congress Cataloging-in-Publication Data

Brown, Karen, 1956–
    Karen Brown's California: charming inns & itineraries / written by Karen Brown, June Brown, and Clare Brown ; illustrations by Barbara Tapp ; cover painting by Jann Pollard.
       p. cm. -- (Karen Brown's country inn series)
   Includes index.
   ISBN 0-930328-71-X (pbk.)
    1. Bed and breakfast accommodations--California--Guidebooks.
2. Hotels--California--Guidebooks.   3. California--Guidebooks.
I. Brown, June, 1949– . II. Brown, Clare   III. Title.
IV. Series.
TX907.3.C2B756 1999
  647.94794'01—dc21

98-16862
CIP

Contents

INTRODUCTION
    Introduction   1
    About Driving Itineraries   2–4
    Map of Driving Itineraries   3
    About Hotels and Inn Travel   5–12

ITINERARIES
    San Francisco to Los Angeles via the Coast   13–34
    Leisurely Loop of Southern California   35–50
    Wandering through the Wine Country   51–72
    Yosemite, the Gold Country, & Lake Tahoe   73–88
    San Francisco to the Oregon Border–and a Bit Beyond   89–110

PLACES TO STAY
    Inns Listed Alphabetically by Town   111–280

MAPS
    Key Map   281
    Maps Showing Places to Stay   282–288

INDEX   289–300

Introduction

San Francisco Cable Car

California, the Golden State, is fascinating with its diverse regions, dramatic scenery, exciting places to visit, and appealing places to stay. There is almost too much—it can be confusing to decide the most important sights to see and the most special inns to choose. This book is written to help you through the maze: we have done your homework for you. The first section of the book presents five detailed driving itineraries that spider-web across the state. The second section features our personal recommendations of places to stay, written with the sincere belief that where you lay your head each night makes the difference between a good and a great vacation.

About Driving Itineraries

Five driving itineraries map and describe a route through the various regions of California so that you can choose one that includes the area you have your heart set on visiting. Each itinerary is preceded by a map that shows the routing and all the towns in which we have a recommended inn. Each routing can easily be tailored to meet your own specific needs by leaving out some sightseeing if time is limited, or linking several itineraries together if you wish to enjoy a longer vacation.

CAR RENTAL

The itineraries are designed for travel by car. If you are staying in San Francisco at the beginning of your trip, it is not necessary to pick up a rental car until you leave the city since the public transportation system is so convenient and this is a wonderful town for walking. However, if your vacation begins in Los Angeles, you will need a car within the city to get from place to place and should pick it up on arrival at the airport.

DRIVING TIMES

California is a large state, approximately 1,000 miles from tip to toe. If you stay on the freeways, you can quickly cover large areas of territory, but if you choose to savor the beauty of the coast along California's sensational Highway 1 or dip into the countryside along scenic back roads, plan on traveling about 30 miles in an hour and remember to allow extra time for stopping to enjoy countryside vistas.

MAPS

Each itinerary has a map outlining the suggested routing and detailing sightseeing and overnight stops. Alternate places to stay are also marked. The maps are an artist's renderings and do not show every road and highway—you need to supplement them with more comprehensive commercial maps.

PACING

At the beginning of each itinerary we suggest our recommended pacing to help you decide the amount of time to allocate to each one. The suggested time frame reflects how much there is to see and do. Use our recommendation as a guideline only, and choreograph your own itinerary based on how much leisure time you have and whether your preference is to move on to a new destination each day or settle in and use a particular inn as base.

WEATHER

At the beginning of each itinerary a brief note is given on what you can expect to encounter weather-wise in the various regions. In California a whole new climate emerges in just a short distance. The idea that the entire state is sunny and warm year-round can all too quickly be dispelled when the summer fog rolls into San Francisco or 3 feet of winter snow falls in the High Sierras.

About Hotels and Inn Travel

We use the term "inn" to cover everything from a simple bed and breakfast to a sophisticated resort. A wide range of inns is included in this guide: some are great bargains, others very costly; some are in cities, others in remote locations; some are quite sophisticated, others extremely simple; some are decorated with opulent antiques, others with furniture from grandma's attic; some are large hotels, others have only a few rooms. The common denominator is that each place has some special quality that makes it appealing. The descriptions are intended to give you an honest appraisal of each property so that you can select accommodation based on personal preferences. The following pointers will help you appreciate and understand what to expect when traveling the "inn way":

BATHROOMS

It is not standard that every inn recommended in this book has a bathroom for each bedroom. Some inns will offer guestrooms that share a bath with other guestrooms, or rooms that have private baths down the hall. We specify under each description how many of the guestrooms have private bathrooms. We do not detail whether the bath is equipped with shower, tub-shower, tub, or Jacuzzi. Inquire as to what the term "with bathroom" means when making your reservation.

BREAKFAST

A welcome feature and trademark of many inns is their morning repast—many cookbooks have been authored and inspired by innkeepers. Breakfast is almost always included in the room rate, but we definitely mention if it is NOT. Although innkeepers take great pride in their delectable morning offerings, know that breakfast can range from a gourmet "waddle away" feast (as proudly described by one innkeeper-chef) to muffins and coffee. Sometimes breakfast is limited to a Continental in the privacy of your room or a hot breakfast with others in the dining room, and sometimes both. Breakfast times vary as well—some innkeepers serve a hot breakfast at a specified time, while others replenish a buffet on a more leisurely schedule. Breakfasts are as individual as the inns themselves and are something to look forward to.

CANCELLATION POLICIES

Although policies vary, inns, by necessity, are usually more stringent than large chain hotels in their cancellation policies: understand their terms when securing a reservation.

CHARM

It is very important to us that an inn has charm—ideally an inn should be appealing, perhaps an historic building, beautifully decorated, lovingly managed, and in a wonderful location. Few inns meet every criterion, but all our selections have something that makes them special and are situated in enjoyable surroundings—we have had to reject several lovely inns because of a poor location. Many are in historic buildings, but remember that California is a relatively young state, so anything over 50 years in age is considered old—few inns date back further than the mid-19th century and many are new or reproduction-old buildings. Small inns are usually our favorites, but size alone did not dictate whether or not a hostelry was chosen. Most are small (a few have only three guestrooms), but because California offers some splendid larger establishments of great character and charm (one has 198 guestrooms), a few of these are also included.

CHECK-IN

Inns are usually very specific about check-in time—generally between 3 and 6 pm. Let the inn know if you are going to arrive late and the innkeeper will make special arrangements for you, such as leaving you a door key under a potted plant along with a note on how to find your room. Also, for those who might arrive early, note that some inns close their doors between check-out and check-in times. Inns are often frequently staffed only by the owners themselves and that window of time between check-out and check-in is often the one opportunity to shop for those wonderful breakfasts they prepare in addition to running their own personal errands.

CHILDREN

Many places in this guide do not welcome children. They cannot legally refuse accommodation to children, but, as parents, we really want to know and want to stay where our children are genuinely welcome. Under each description we have indicated the general policy of each inn, i.e., whether it is, or is not appropriate for children—but these are only guidelines. Many places will accept children with certain stipulations such as if they have the proper room available, if the children are of a certain age, if other families are going to be in residence, or if it is a slow period.

COMFORT

As influential as charm, comfort plays a deciding role in the selection of inns recommended. Firm mattresses, a quiet setting, good lighting, fresh towels, scrubbed bathrooms—we do our best to remember the basics when considering inns—the charming decor and innkeeper will soon be forgotten if you do not enjoy a good night's sleep and comfortable stay. Also, do remember, however, that parts of California can be hot during the summer months and that many inns are in older buildings and do not have the luxury of air conditioning.

CREDIT CARDS

Whether or not an establishment accepts credit cards is indicated at the bottom of each description—AX (American Express), MC (MasterCard), VS (Visa), all major, or none accepted. Even if an inn does not accept plastic payment, it will perhaps take your credit card number as a guarantee of arrival.

FOOD

The majority of places featured in this guide do not have restaurants but innkeepers are usually very knowledgeable and happy to recommend local favorites. However, almost all of the inns do serve breakfast: quite often a sumptuous one. Frequently, in addition to breakfast, tea or wine and hors d'oeuvres are served in the afternoon. Sometimes, if you request in advance, a picnic lunch can also be prepared.

If you have any special dietary requirements most innkeepers will gladly try to accommodate your needs. Not having the stock a restaurant would have, innkeepers usually plan a menu that features one entree and have those ingredients on hand. Therefore, it is best to mention any special requests at the time of making your reservation both as a courtesy and from a practical point of view so that they can have on hand items such as special low-fat dairy products, egg substitutions, sugar-free syrups, etc.

PHYSICALLY CHALLENGED ACCOMMODATION

If an inn has *at least* one guestroom that is wheelchair accessible, it is noted as *Wheelchair Friendly* in details listed under the hotel description.

PROFESSIONALISM

The inns we have selected are run by professional innkeepers. There are many homes that rent out extra bedrooms to paying guests but this was not what we were looking for and they are not included in our guide. We have recommended only inns that have privacy for the guests and where you do not have to climb over a tricycle to reach the bathroom.

RESERVATIONS

The best way to make a reservation is to just pick up your phone and call. It is very satisfactory and helpful to be able to personally discuss the various differences in available accommodation and policies of the inn. As a courtesy to the innkeepers, however, keep in mind that staff is often limited, and during certain periods of the day, such as the breakfast hour, they are busier than others—flipping pancakes, checking out guests, helping plan activities. Also, inns are often homes, and you might be waking up the innkeeper if you call late evenings or early mornings. Another convenient and efficient way to request a reservation is by fax: if the inn has a fax, we have noted the number in the information line next to the telephone number. Also quickly becoming a widely accepted and inexpensive means of communicating is by computer modem and the use of E-mail—where only local, rather than long-distance phone charges are incurred. For the computer-savvy, included in this 1999 edition are E-mail addresses whenever available for the individual inns. As a final note: When planning your trip be aware that the majority of inns in this guide require a two-night stay on weekends and over holidays.

RESPONSIBILITY

Our goal is to outline itineraries in regions that we consider of prime interest to our readers and to recommend inns that we think are outstanding. All of the inns featured have been visited and selected solely on their merits. Our judgments are made on the charm of the inn, its setting, cleanliness, and, above all, the warmth of welcome. Each property has its own appeal, and we try to present you with a very honest appraisal. However, no matter how careful we are, sometimes we misjudge an inn's merits, or the ownership changes, or unfortunately sometimes inns just do not maintain their standards. If you find an inn is not as we have indicated, please let us know, and accept our sincere apologies.

ROOM RATES

It seems that many inns play musical rates, with high-season, low-season, midweek, weekend, and holiday rates. We have quoted the 1999 high season, general range of rates from the lowest-priced bedroom for two people (singles usually receive a very small discount) to the most expensive suite, including breakfast. The rates given are those quoted to us by the inn. Please use these figures as a guideline and be certain to ask at the time of booking what the rates are and what they include.

We have not given prices for "special" rooms such as those that can accommodate three people traveling together. Discuss with the innkeeper rooms and rates available before making your selection. Of course, several inns are exceptions to our guidelines and whenever this is the case we mention the special situation (such as breakfast not being included in the rate). Please be aware that taxes are not included in the rates quoted and usually inn taxes are very high—frequently around 10%.

SMOKING

In addition to the fact that California has recently passed a law that prohibits smoking in any public places, most inns have had extremely strict non-smoking policies all along. A few inns permit smoking in restricted public areas or outside, and so at the bottom of each hotel description, whether a hotel allows "Smoking" or "No smoking" is in reference specifically to their policy about smoking in the garden, on the deck or in a specially designated public area. Ask about smoking policies—it is best to be forewarned.

SOCIALIZING

Inns usually offer a conviviality rarely found in a "standard" hotel. The gamut runs all the way from playing "cozy family" around the kitchen table to sharing a sophisticated, elegant cocktail hour in the parlor. Breakfast may be a formal meal served at a set hour when the guests gather around the dining-room table, or it may be served buffet-style over several hours where guests have the option of either sitting down to eat alone or joining other guests at a larger table. Then again, some inns will bring a breakfast tray to your room, or perhaps breakfast in the room is the only option.

After check-in, many inns offer an afternoon refreshment, such as tea and cakes or wine and hors d'oeuvres which may be seen as another social opportunity. Some inns set out a buffet where guests are invited to meander in and out mixing or not mixing with other guests as they choose and then others orchestrate a more structured gathering, often a social hour, with the innkeeper presiding. Choose the inn that seems to offer the degree of togetherness or privacy that you desire.

TELEPHONES

California attracts not only a lot of visitors but people who decide to settle here as well—evidenced by the fact that as this edition of the book goes to press, we have just learned that certain area codes will be changed in 1999 to accommodate the increasing population. Actually in the next five years, thirteen new area codes will be introduced in California, doubling the current count.

Telephone numbers referenced throughout this guide, both for sightseeing and hotel contacts, reflect the current (i.e., 1999) area codes. Although there will be a six-month permissive dialing period where both the old and the new area codes will operate, and afterwards a recording to advise customers of the reassignment, we thought it best to bring the fact that the numbers will change to your attention.

WEBSITE

We are constantly changing and updating the Karen Brown Website, wanting it to be an enhanced extension of our guides with a desire to provide you with even more information on the properties and destinations that we recommend. A number of hotels that we work very closely with are featured on our website and their web address is detailed on their description page. In 1999 we will continue our efforts to add pictures for as many properties as possible and, when available, it will be possible to link directly to the properties' individual websites for their personal photos and information. We also plan to share comments, feedback, and discoveries from you, our readers, and will keep you informed on the latest updates and special offerings of our guides. We want our website to serve as a valuable and added dimension to our guides. Be sure to visit our website at www.karenbrown.com.

San Francisco to Los Angeles via the Coast

San Francisco to Los Angeles via the Coast

Golden Gate Bridge

You can drive between San Francisco and Los Angeles in a day or fly in an hour. But rather than rushing down the freeway or hopping aboard an airplane, drive leisurely along the coast between these two metropolises and enjoy the quaintness of Carmel, the charm of Santa Barbara, the splendor of the Big Sur coastline, the opulence of William Randolph Hearst's hilltop castle, and the fun of experiencing a bit of Denmark in Solvang. Also intertwined in this itinerary are stops to appreciate a piece of California's colorful heritage—her Spanish missions. This routing roughly follows the footsteps of the Spanish padres who, in the 1700s, built a string of missions (about a day's journey on horseback apart) along the coast of California from the Mexican border to just north of San Francisco. Today many of these beautiful adobe churches and their surrounding settlements have been reconstructed and are open as museums, capturing a glimpse of life as it was lived by the Spaniards and the Indians in the early days of colonization.

Recommended Pacing: We recommend a minimum stay of two or three nights in San Francisco, affording two full days for a quick introduction to the city, and definitely more time if your schedule allows. San Francisco is a beautiful city and there is much to explore and enjoy. From San Francisco, if you take the direct route, you can easily drive to Carmel in about three hours. However, located just south of San Francisco is the Año Nuevo Reserve, where you can observe the enormous elephant seals in their natural habitat. It takes several hours to walk around the secluded beaches where the seals congregate, so if you want to visit the reserve en route to Carmel, we recommend an early start from the city—or use Karen's own Seal Cove Inn, located just south of San Francisco, as a more leisurely stopping point. Plan on at least two to three nights (or again, if possible, more) in the Carmel, Pacific Grove, or Monterey area. One day can easily be devoured exploring the Monterey Bay Aquarium, Cannery Row, and the wharf. Another full day is needed to drive the gorgeous Seventeen-Mile Drive, walk the spectacular Point Lobos State Park, visit the beautiful Carmel Mission—and we have yet to even discuss shopping in downtown Carmel. From Carmel, you can drive the dramatic coastline of Big Sur and on to Santa Barbara in four to five hours, but plan to overnight in Cambria if you want to include even just one of the tours of Hearst Castle and visit the cute artist's town of Cambria—it's too much to do in one day. Santa Barbara is a beautiful, charming city with an expanse of lovely beach. You'd be disappointed if you didn't plan at least two nights in the area before continuing on to Los Angeles.

Weather Wise: San Francisco and the coast are often foggy during June, July, and August. The farther south you go, the earlier in the day the fog burns off. The northern California coast is cool and rainy during the winter. In southern California the weather is warmer year-round and traditionally less rain falls during the winter. Smog is a problem in certain parts of the Los Angeles area during the summer.

When you ask travelers around the world, "What is your favorite city?" many times the answer is "San Francisco." And it is no wonder: **San Francisco** really is special, a magical town of unsurpassed beauty—spectacular when glistening in the sunlight, equally enchanting when wrapped in fog. But the beauty is more than skin deep: San Francisco offers a wealth of sightseeing, fabulous restaurants, splendid shopping, and a refreshing climate.

There are many large, super-deluxe hotels in San Francisco and we recommend a marvelous selection of small, intimate inns. Study our various recommendations to see what most fits your personality and pocketbook. Be advised that hotel space is frequently tight, so make reservations as far in advance as possible.

A good way to orient yourself in San Francisco is to take a half-day city sightseeing tour (brochures on these tours should be available at your hotel) and then return to the destinations that most catch your fancy. If you like to study before you arrive, there are entire guidebooks devoted to San Francisco and the Visitors' Bureau will send you an information packet on what to see and do. San Francisco Visitors' Bureau, P.O. Box 6977, San Francisco, CA 94101, (415) 391-2000. To keep you on the right track the following is an alphabetical listing of some of our favorite sights:

Alcatraz: A visit to the abandoned prison island in the middle of San Francisco Bay is a fascinating excursion and affords a magnificent view of the city skyline—if you don't have a friend with a yacht, this is the next best thing! The lonely, concrete, fortress-like structure of Alcatraz was deemed escape-proof until a couple of prisoners (yet to be found) dug their way out with a spoon. The tour of the prison involves lots of walking, so be sure to wear sturdy, comfortable shoes and don't forget your camera or woolly sweater because the views are gorgeous and it is cold on this windswept rocky island. This excursion is very popular. For further information call: (415) 705-5555.

California Palace of The Legion of Honor: Without a doubt, this is our favorite museum in San Francisco—we just love the exhibits and the spectacular setting on a bluff in Lincoln Park overlooking the ocean. The original of Rodin's famous Thinker welcomes you to the San Francisco replica of the Palais de la Légion d'Honneur in Paris where Napoleon first established his new government. A self-guided audio tour is available to steer you through the galleries which include one devoted to medieval art (there's a ceiling from a 15th-century Spanish palace), a British gallery with paintings by Gainsborough and Constable, and 19th- and 20th-century galleries with their popular works by Monet, Renoir, and Picasso. Located at 34th Avenue and Clement Street, for more information call (415) 750-3600.

Cable Cars: You cannot leave San Francisco without riding one of the colorful little trolleys that make their way up and down the breathtakingly steep city hills. Rather than touring by cab or bus, plan your sightseeing around hopping on and off cable cars. You can travel easily from the shopping district of Union Square past Chinatown and the "crookedest street in the world"—Lombard, and on to the Ghiradelli Square-Fisherman's Wharf area. For a behind-the-scenes look at this charmingly antiquated transit system visit the Cable Car Museum at the corner of Washington and Mason Streets. Here you can view the huge cables that pull the cars from below the streets and a historical display that includes the first cable car.

Chinatown: Just a few short blocks from Union Square enter beneath the dragon arch (at the corner of Bush Street and Grant Avenue) into another world with street signs in Chinese characters, tiny grocery stores displaying Chinese vegetables and delicacies, apothecary shops selling unusual remedies, spicy aromas drifting from colorful restaurants, older women bustling about in traditional dress, and the surrounding hum of unfamiliar phrases. Of course the streets are jammed with tourists and locals and there is a plethora of rather tacky, but fun-to-explore souvenir shops. Don't limit your exploration of Chinatown to the main thoroughfare of Grant Avenue: poke down the intriguing little alleys and side streets. Plan a visit to 56 Ross Alley, the Golden Gate Fortune Cookie Factory. Down another alley, at 17 Adler Place, is the Chinese Historical Society of America—a small museum portraying the story of the Chinese immigration. The Chinese Cultural Center, housed in the Holiday Inn at Kearny and Washington streets, offers fascinating docent-led heritage and culinary walks affording a glimpse of the "real Chinatown." For information call (415) 986-1822. The Cultural Center also has a wonderful small museum which offers an ever-changing schedule of exhibits.

Coit Tower: Coit Tower, located at the top of Telegraph Hill, is a relic of old San Francisco and fun to visit—not only because of the great view, but because its story is so very "San Francisco." The money to construct the watch tower, which resembles the nozzle of a fire hose, was willed to the city by the wealthy Lillie Hitchcock Coit, a volunteer fireman (or should we say firewoman) who dearly loved to rush to every blaze wearing her diamond-encrusted fire badge. A mural on the ground floor provides a vivid depiction of early California life.

Fisherman's Wharf to Ghiradelli Square: This portion of the waterfront is very popular with tourists. **Pier 39** is lined with New England-style shops; nothing authentic, but a popular shopping and restaurant arcade complete with street performers and a beautiful two-tier carousel. Pier 39 is also home to a new aquarium and some very boisterous and amusing sea lions. (415) 981-7437. Pier 41 is where you purchase tickets for the popular excursion to Alcatraz (see listing). **Fisherman's Wharf** where fishermen haul in their daily catch, has long been a favorite with tourists. It is difficult to find even the heart of Fisherman's Wharf behind all the trinket-filled souvenir shops and tourist arcades, but look carefully and sure enough, you will see the colorful fishing boats bobbing about in the water at the waterfront between Jones and Taylor Streets. Nearby, Fish Alley, a small pier extending out into the harbor, affords a good view of the fishing fleet and the aroma of fresh fish mingling with the salty air. At the corner of Leavenworth and Jefferson **The Cannery**, formerly a fruit cannery, is today an attractive shopping complex. At the foot of Hyde Street **Hyde Street Pier** is home to the Maritime Museum's fleet of historic ships, several of which can be boarded and explored. Our favorite is the *Balclutha* (1886) a three-masted merchant ship typical of the hundreds that came round the Horn to San Francisco. Inspect the comfortable captain's quarters and cramped crew's quarters and exhibits of nautical gear. Just beyond the **Hyde Street cable car turnaround** lies **Ghiradelli Square**, a lovely brick building that used to house the Ghiradelli chocolate factory, now a complex of attractive stores and restaurants. The ship-shaped building in Aquatic Park (in front of Ghiradelli Square) is the land base of the **Maritime Museum**, full of displays on the history of water transportation from the 1800s to the present, including marvelous photos of old San Francisco. (415) 556-3002.

Golden Gate Bridge and **Fort Point:** San Francisco's symbol is the Golden Gate Bridge with its graceful orange arches. The visitors' viewing area on the San Francisco side offers stunning views (if the fog is not in) and access to the pedestrian walkway that enables a walk across the bridge (2½ miles round trip, wear warm clothing). At the base of the Golden Gate Bridge's south pier, Fort Point, built in 1861 as one of the west coast's principal points of defense, provides a fascinating insight into military life during that period. (415) 556-1693.

Golden Gate Park: You will need to take a bus or taxi to Golden Gate Park, but don't miss it. The park encompasses over 1,000 acres, so large you really cannot hope to see it all, but many attractions are located near each other. Wander through the traditional **Japanese Tea Garden** and enjoy tea and cookies Japanese-style at the tea house. (415) 831-2700. The **De Young Museum** is primarily devoted to American art while the adjacent **Asian Art Museum** contains one of America's finest collections of Asian art. (415) 750-3600. The **Museum of Natural History** offers dioramas of wildlife from African to Californian (along with an impressive collection of gems and minerals), while the neighboring **Steinhart Aquarium** has all things fishy from a tropical swamp with alligators and turtles to a fish roundabout—an enormous donut-shaped fish tank. (415) 750-7145. Just a short walk from the museums lies the **Conservatory of Flowers**, an immense Victorian wooden greenhouse full of plant life varying from a humid rain forest to colorful displays of seasonal flowers. (415) 831-2700. If you are hungry, you might want to consider the **Beach Chalet**, a restaurant on the ocean side of the park near the Dutch Windmill. The menu offers good, simple fare matched with their list of brewery selections. The building once served as the changing rooms for Ocean Beach. On the first floor are beautifully restored murals of San Francisco in its early days and the guest tables enjoy unobstructed views of the surf from the second floor expanse of window. Tel: (415) 386-8439.

Lombard Street: Lombard is an ordinary city street—except for one lone, brick-paved block between Hyde and Leavenworth where the street goes crazy and makes a series of hairpin turns as it twists down the hill. Pretty houses border each side of the street, and banks of hydrangeas add color. Start at the top and go down what must be the crookedest street in the world: it is lots of fun. The Hyde Street cable car makes a stop at the top of the hill and from here you can easily walk down to Fisherman's Wharf.

Lombard Street

Mission San Francisco De Assisi: This mission at Dolores and 16th Streets is frequently referred to as the Mission Dolores. If you are interested in Californian missions, you will find a visit here worthwhile. It was on this spot that San Francisco was born when Father Francisco Palou founded his mission here in 1776. At one time this was a large complex of warehouses, workshops, granaries, a tannery, soap shop, corrals, Indian dwellings, and even an aqueduct. Today, all that is left is the chapel and next to it the garden where gravestones attest to the fragility of life. Although small, the chapel is beautiful in its simplicity with 4-foot-thick adobe walls and massive redwood timbers. (415) 621-8203.

Museum of Modern Art (MOMA): A cylindrical, striped turret rising from blocks of red bricks gives a hint of what lies within this futuristic building at 151 Third Street. To help you appreciate the exhibits, an audio cassette can be rented in the lobby to guide you through the museum's permanent collection of abstract expressionistic paintings and avant-garde photography. Even if you are not a fan of modern art, you will be awed by the building's interior: the space soars upwards from the lobby for seven stories to a broad catwalk that runs below the cylindrical glass skylight. (415) 357-4000. Just across the street from the MOMA lie the **Yerba Buena Gardens and Galleries**. The gardens are an oasis of tranquillity where a broad expanse of grass leads to a cascading sheet of water—a perfect place to relax and people-watch. The galleries offer changing exhibits that showcase the San Francisco Bay Area's cultural diversity. On the top floor encircled by windows and a spectacular view of the city skyline is a new ice-skating rink. Open daily 1 pm to 5 pm and evenings with some limitations. (750 Folsom Street between 3rd and 4th, [415] 777-3726.) Just round the corner (678 Mission Street) a turn-of-the-century hardware store houses the **California Historical Society** with its bookstore and changing exhibits of photographs, paintings, and objects documenting California's growth and change. (415) 357-1848.

Sausalito and **Tiburon:** An enjoyable excursion is to take the ferry from Pier 43½ in San Francisco to Sausalito or Tiburon, small towns just across the bay full of intriguing shops, art galleries, and wonderful restaurants. As a bonus, en route you enjoy wonderful vistas of San Francisco and the Golden Gate Bridge. For information call the Red and White Fleet at (415) 705-5555.

Theater: For theater buffs, San Francisco offers an excellent variety of entertainment. Most theaters are located in the heart of the city within walking distance of Union Square. In addition, San Francisco has fine opera and ballet. The San Francisco Visitors' Bureau, (415) 391-2000, can send you a packet with information on what is going on. You can also call the "hot line" at (415) 391-2001 for a recording of all current events.

Union Square: In the center of the city sits Union Square, hallmarked by a small park around which tower deluxe hotels and fancy department stores. Do not tarry too long at the "biggies" because just beyond the square lies every specialty shop imaginable from FAO Schwartz's toy emporium to any number of "designer" boutiques. San Francisco's own exclusive and elegant Gumps at 135 Post Street merits a visit. The Crocker Galleria at 50 Post houses collections from top names in international design and many fine specialty stores and restaurants.

Union Street: Union Street (between Laguna and Steiner), lined with lovely restored Victorian houses, offers a wonderful variety of quaint gift shops, elegant boutiques, beautiful antique stores, small art galleries, excellent restaurants, and a multitude of intriguing little shops hidden down tiny brick-paved lanes.

It's a 3 hour drive south from San Francisco to Carmel taking the scenic Highway 280 to San Jose and Highways 17 and 1 on to Carmel. But rather than head directly to Carmel, we suggest you meander down the coast, following the contours of the spectacular coastline, enjoying a number of sights en route—a journey that will deserve a couple of days.

Leave San Francisco to the south on 19th Avenue to Highway 280 and take Highway 1 through Pacifica where the freeway ends and the road narrows to meander around the precipitous rocky promontory known as Devil's Slide. Just south of Devil's Slide is **Moss Beach**, a suburban coastal town home to Karen Brown and her inn, **Seal Cove**, named after the nearby crescent of golden sand. Seal Cove Inn and the colorful restaurant, the **Moss Beach Distillery**, (650) 728-5595, known for its ghosts and beautiful ocean setting, are neighbors to the **Fitzgerald Marine Reserve** and park, where you can walk along the bluffs and investigate the tidepools at low tide. (650) 728-3584.

Just to the south of Moss Beach, **Princeton harbor**, with its mass of fishing vessels and sailboats, is one of California's last true commercial fishing harbors. Sport-fishing and whale-watching boats leave early mornings from Princeton. Bookings can be made through Huck Finn Sport Fishing, (650) 726-7133.

Detour off the Coastal Highway to the east at Highway 92 and take it for one block, making a right on **Half Moon Bay's** Main Street. Park just across the bridge and visit

Half Moon Bay Feed and Fuel, an authentic country store that sells saddles, rabbits, chickens, animal feed, and farm implements. Poke your head in the variety of shops, restaurants and art galleries that line Main Street. (Another detour, traveling past Main Street farther east on Highway 92, is to the **Half Moon Bay Nursery**, nestled off the road just before it begins its climb up the mountain. An attraction in its own right with its wood-burning fireplace and classical music, the nursery also offers a bounty of reasonably priced plants.) Leaving Half Moon Bay, continue down Main Street to rejoin Highway 1 to the south of town.

Lengthy expanses of sandy beach are accessible from the many state parks along the coastline. **Pigeon Point Lighthouse** is one of the tallest lighthouses on the west coast. Tours are given only on Sundays between 10 am and 3 pm.

Thirty miles south of Half Moon Bay is the **Año Nuevo State Reserve**, home to elephant seals whose huge males with their trunk-like snouts reach a whopping 6,000 pounds. From mid-December to the end of March docents conduct a 3-mile round-trip hike to the breeding grounds of these car-size mammals. Reservation lines open in October for the following season: (800) 444-7275. If you are not able to book several months in advance, call the park directly, (650) 879-2025, and they may be able to advise you if last-minute tickets are available. We have, in the past, secured tickets by arriving at 8:30 am and queuing at the entrance booth for tickets for tours that day. Outside of the breeding season obtaining permits to view the seals (there are often also a great many sea lions in residence) is not a problem: tickets are issued on arrival and you follow the well-marked path out to the distant beach where the seals are found. The best time to visit outside of the breeding season is during July and August when the males return for their summer molt.

Ten miles to the south of Año Nuevo you come to the cluster of houses that makes up the town of **Davenport**. Fronting Highway 1 is the **New Davenport Cash Store** which sells everything from handmade jewelry to local pottery and whose restaurant offers a varied and healthful menu with excellent soups and tasty vegetarian dishes. (831) 426-4122.

Downtown **Santa Cruz**, 11 miles south of Davenport, was badly damaged in the 1989 earthquake, but a newly revived Pacific Avenue demonstrates all the laid-back charm the town is noted for, with outdoor cafés, a variety of shops and galleries, and numerous street performers. Years ago this busy seaside town, with its bustling **boardwalk** and amusement park bordering a broad stretch of white sand beach, was a popular day trip for workers in San Francisco. In recent years the rides and attractions have received a face-lift, making it a pleasure to visit, particularly since it is so clean and well maintained. The rides include a heart-stopping wood-en roller coaster and a wonderful old-fashioned carousel.

If you enjoy riding trains, you may want to take the old-fashioned diesel that departs from the boardwalk twice a day during the summer months for the 60-minute ride to Felton to board an old stream train of the **Roaring Camp Railroad**, a train that winds along narrow-gauge tracks up into a redwood forest. The train leaves several times a day from its main station in **Felton** (except on Christmas) along narrow-gauge tracks built to carry lumber out of the forest. The conductor tells stories of the old days as the train circles up through the trees, making a brief stop at the "cathedral," a beautiful ring of redwoods that form a natural outdoor church, before heading back to the depot. It is possible to take a picnic with you, alight at the top, and take the next train back. Call for schedules and directions: (831) 335-4400.

Roaring Camp Railroad, Felton

Leaving Santa Cruz, take Highway 1 south for about 20 miles to Highway 129 where you head east. Continue on the 129 for approximately 16 miles through small farms and rolling hills to **San Juan Bautista** and its most attractive **mission**. There is far more to see here than just an old church, for an area of the town has been restored to the way it was 150 years ago with the mission as its focus. Facing the square is the restored Plaza Hotel, now a museum where tickets are sold for admission to the attractions in the park. The focal point of the sightseeing is, of course, the mission, but do not end your touring there. Directly across from the mission is a most interesting house, nicely restored, and furnished as it must have looked many years ago. Adjacent to this is a blacksmith's shop and stables where there is a colorful display of old coaches. Next door to the Plaza Hotel is another home now open as a museum with period furnishings. Also, be sure not to miss San Juan Bautista which still maintains its 19th-century, small-town ambiance.

Follow Highway 156 west for a couple of miles until it merges with Highway 101 going south to the Monterey Peninsula. As you pass through Prunedale, begin to watch for signs indicating a sharp right-hand turn on Highway 156 west to the Monterey Peninsula. Along the way, fields of artichokes dominate the landscape as you near Castroville, the artichoke capital of the world. When you begin to smell the sea air, stay in the left lane following signs for Highway 1 south to the Monterey Peninsula. As you approach Monterey, dunes lining the sweep of the bay come into view.

The main sightseeing attractions in **Monterey** are in two areas: old town and the marina, and Cannery Row and the Monterey Bay Aquarium. A bayside walking and biking path runs from the Marina beside Cannery Row to the Aquarium and beyond to the adjoining town of Pacific Grove. A fun way to explore Monterey is to rent a side-by-side tricycle near the aquarium and pedal to the Marina.

Kayaking lets you enjoy another perspective of Monterey—looking back at the town and gorgeous beaches from the Bay. Open deck kayaks make the sport easy even for the inexperienced and paddling out amongst the seals and otters is quite memorable. All equipment, loose-fitting rain gear (although plan on getting wet), life jackets and instruction is included in the price. We rented from **A B Seas Kayak** and found owner,

Geoff Hand, and his team to be very helpful and accommodating. Geoff has generously offered any of our readers a 20% discount on the $25 per person, 3 hour rental package if they mention our guide. A B Seas Kayak is conveniently located at 32 Cannery Row (on the coastguard pier), tel: (831) 647-0147, www.kayak.idsite.com.

In **Old Town** a 3-mile walking tour links the restored buildings of early Monterey. The old adobes are interesting and a sharp contrast to the bustle of nearby **Fisherman's Wharf**, a quaint wooden fishing pier lined with shops and restaurants. At the end of the pier huge sea lions vie for the fish cast off the fishing boats.

Cannery Row, once the center of this area's thriving sardine industry (the fish are long gone), and brought vividly to life by John Steinbeck in his novels featuring Doc and the boys, is now filled with small stores and tucked into an old warehouse are some outlet stores. The premier attraction in Monterey is the adjacent **Monterey Bay Aquarium**. The centerpieces of the Aquarium are the huge glass tanks that showcase the underwater world of the local offshore marine habitat from the diverse tidepools to the multitude of life in the Monterey Bay: one tank is populated by huge sharks and colorful schools of fish while another contains a mature kelp forest teeming with fish. A recent addition, the Outer Bay exhibit, a vast tank of water representative of the outer ocean, brings a new dimension to the Aquarium and leaves the visitor with a memorable impression of just how little is known about that massive body of water. Tel: (831) 648-4888.

Monterey is all hustle and bustle (especially in summer) and it is nice to continue on to the neighboring, much quieter town of **Pacific Grove**. To reach Pacific Grove, follow the road in front of the Aquarium up the hill and make a right turn onto Ocean View Boulevard, a lovely drive lined on one side with gracious Victorian homes and splendid views of the sea on the other. Besides being an affluent residential community, Pacific Grove is famous for the Monarch butterflies that return faithfully each October and cluster in the grove of trees next to Butterfly Grove Inn on Lighthouse Avenue.

Carmel lies just a few miles beyond Pacific Grove and there is no more perfect way to arrive than along the famous Seventeen-Mile Drive which meanders around the Monterey Peninsula coastline between the two towns. The route is easy to find as the road that leads to the "drive" intersects Lighthouse Avenue and is appropriately called The Seventeen-Mile Drive.

The Seventeen-Mile Drive loops through an exclusive residential area of multi-million-dollar estates and gorgeous golf courses. Because the land is private, $7 per car is levied at the entrance gate, where you'll receive a map indicating points of interest along the way. The scenic drive traces the low-lying shore, passes rocky coves where kelp beds are home to sea lions, sea otters, cormorants, and gulls (remember to bring your binoculars), and meanders through wood-lands where Monterey pines gnarled by the wind stand sentinel on lonely headlands. Along the drive is the famous **Pebble Beach Golf Course**, site of the National Pro-Am Golf Championship each January.

Carmel—filled with Hansel-and-Gretel-style cottages nestled under pines and surrounded by flower-filled gardens—is one of California's most appealing towns. Tourists throng the streets lined with appetizing sweet shops, beckoning bakeries, a wonderful selection of restaurants enticing boutiques, pretty gift stores, and attractive art galleries. We are especially partial to a gallery that features the work of Jann Pollard, the very talented water-colorist who is responsible for our gorgeous cover paintings. **The Cottage Gallery** is located in the heart of town at the corner of 6th and Mission.

San Francisco to Los Angeles via the Coast

The picturesque combination of fairy-tale cottages and a sparkling blue bay makes Carmel so very special. Its main street slopes gently down the hill to a glorious white sand beach crested by windswept dunes.

Just south of town is the **Carmel Mission**, established in 1770 by Father Junipero Serra. Beautifully restored and fronted by a pretty garden, the mission was Father Serra's headquarters. It is from here that the stalwart little priest set out to expand the chain of missions. A small museum shows the simple cell in which Father Serra slept on a hard wooden bed. The church itself, with its Moorish tower, star-shaped window, and profusion of surrounding flowers, has a most romantic appearance.

Located just south of Carmel on Highway 1, **Point Lobos State Reserve** is, in our estimation, the premier place to enjoy the California coast. A small admission fee entitles you to day use of the park. Walk along the coastal trails and venture down wooden steps to secluded sandy beaches. Rocky coves are home to sea lions, harbor seals, and sea otters. Between December and May migrating gray whales surface and dive offshore. Bring your binoculars and head for Sea Lion Point and the headland on Cypress Grove Trail, the best places to see the whales. Walking trails and picnic areas are well marked and the times of guided nature walks are posted at the entrance gate. (831) 624-4909.

Believe everything you ever read about the beauties of the **Big Sur Coastline**: it is truly sensational. However, hope for clear weather, because on foggy or rainy days an endless picture of stunning seascapes becomes a tortuous drive around precipitous cliff roads. (If the weather is inclement, you may wish to take the inland route to Cambria by following the picturesque Carmel Valley road east to Highway 101 where you then head south. When you come to Highway 46, turn west. The road intersects with coastal Highway 1 just south of Cambria.) As you drive south on Highway 1, you have an indication that you are approaching Big Sur when you see the road sign "Hill Curves—63 miles," which is exactly what the road does as it clings precipitously to the edge of the cliff. While the road is quite narrow, there are plenty of turnouts and opportunities for taking photos.

If you have a luxury of time, you might want to consider a very scenic ten mile detour east off Highway 1 following the **Old Coast Road** that journeys through beautiful redwood groves and country ranchland. To access the Old Coast Road, turn left just before crossing the dramatic span of Bixby Creek Bridge. You'll be on your own for most of the journey and the road will deposit you back on Highway 1, across from the entrance to the wonderful **Andrew Molera State Park**. Allow approximately one hour for the adventure, and know that the road is not passable after heavy rains.

If opting to remain on scenic Highway 1, its passage is dramatic over the much-photographed, long concrete span of **Bixby Creek Bridge**. A few miles later the rocky volcanic outcrop topped by the Point Sur lighthouse appears. About 40 miles south of Carmel is the **Pfeiffer Big Sur State Park** with its camping facilities and many miles of hiking trails among coastal redwood groves.

If you choose only one place to stop along the Big Sur drive, make it **Nepenthe**, about 3 miles south of the entrance to Pfeiffer Big Sur State Park. Nepenthe is a casual restaurant, with a 60s-style decor, perched on a cliff high above the ocean offering unsurpassed views (on a clear day) of the coast to the south. (831) 667-2345. Below Nepenthe, **The Phoenix Shop** has a wonderful offering of clothes, artwork, books and gifts. (831) 667-2347. Interestingly, at the heart of the complex is a cottage that Orson Welles bought for his then wife, Rita Hayworth.

Another stop along the way where you can gain a closer view of this magnificent coastline is at the **Julia Pfeiffer Burns State Park**. The parking area is to the left of the road. Leave your car and take the short walk leading under the highway and round the face of the cliff that overlooks a superb small cove with emerald-green water and a white sand beach. From the rocky bluff a waterfall drops directly into the ocean and the restless sea beats against a craggy point. After the Ragged Point Inn, the bends become less frequent, and as the cliffs give way to the coastal plain, the driving becomes less arduous.

After the road begins to flatten out, watch for **Hearst Castle** impressively crowning the coastal hills. In 1919, William Randolph Hearst commissioned California's famous architect Julia Morgan to design a simple vacation home atop a hill on his estate overlooking the California coastline. Twenty-eight years and $10,000,000 later, he moved to Los Angeles and left his 100-room retreat, La Cuesta Encantada (the enchanted hill), which has never been completed. Hearst Castle continues to delight its millions of visitors: next to Disneyland, Hearst Castle is the most popular visitor attraction in California.

The number of visitors allowed on the hill during any one day is limited, so it is essential that you make reservations in advance. Hearst Castle is open every day except Thanksgiving, Christmas, and New Year's Day. Several different one-hour and forty-five-minute tours are available. On certain days an evening tour that combines the highlights of the castle is offered—this tour is tremendously popular and must be booked well in advance. Tickets for all tours are available for purchase eight weeks in advance by calling (800) 444-4445. Plan on arriving at the visitors' center at the foot of the hill at least half an hour before your scheduled departure, as the tours depart with clockwork-like precision and do not wait for stragglers. If you arrive early, you can browse through the small museum located next to the departure depot where groups assemble by number for their turn to be taken up the hill by bus.

Tour 1, the overview of the castle, is the one recommended for first-time visitors. You walk through the gardens to the main house, La Casa Grande, to tour the rooms on the lower level. The sheer size and elaborate decor of the assembly room where Hearst gathered with his guests before dinner sets the opulent mood of this elegant establishment. In the adjoining refectory Hearst and his guests dined in a re-created medieval banquet hall—the bottles of Hearst's favorite ketchup on the table seem rather out of place. In the theater a short home movie of Hearst and some of his celebrity friends gives you an idea of life at the castle during the 1930s. A feeling for the opulence of the guest accommodation is given as you tour the guesthouse, Casa del Sol.

The indoor Roman pool has over half a million Italian mosaic tiles, vast amounts of gold leaf, and took over five years to complete. Tour 2 views suites of bedrooms, the kitchen, and the swimming pools. Tour 3 visits the guest wing of the castle, a guesthouse, and the pools. Tour 4, offered only in summer, does not go into the main house, but focuses on the gardens.

From the Hearst-San Simeon State Historical Monument it is just an 8-mile drive south to Cambria. **Cambria** was once a whaling station and a dairy town that shipped butter and cheese to San Francisco. Now the main town lies away from the coast and encompasses two streets of art galleries, gift shops, antique stores, and restaurants.

Hearst Castle

Leave Cambria on Highway 1 going south. The road leaves the coast and travels through low-lying hills to **San Luis Obispo**, merging with Highway 101 traveling south. If you want to visit every mission en route, when you reach San Luis Obispo take the Broad Street exit and follow signs to the **mission** which lies at the heart of this busy town.

About 10 miles south of San Luis Obispo Highway 101 returns to the coast at Pismo Beach where you take the exit for Highway 1 and **Pismo Beach**, a 12-mile arc of white-sand beach backed in part by dunes. This is the home of the famous Pismo clam which has unfortunately in recent years become rather scarce. As you travel south on Highway 1, views of the beach are blocked by apartments and motels, but do not despair: 2 miles south of town, leave the freeway by turning right into **Pismo Beach State Park**. After paying the entrance fee, pass quickly over the soft sand. Once your tires hit the well-packed, damp sand, your way feels more secure as you drive along the beach, paralleling the crashing waves. From this vantage point you can really appreciate the beautiful sweep of this white-sand bay. While it is possible to drive about 5 miles south on the beach, the auto exit ramp lies 1 mile to the south.

Leaving Pismo Beach, follow Highway 1 south, passing flat wide fields of vegetables and eucalyptus groves through Guadalupe, a rather poor agricultural town. The road becomes a divided two-lane highway as Highways 135 and 1 merge. After passing the gates of Vandenburg Air Force Base (on the approach to Lompoc), take a left turn onto Mission Purisma Road which leads to **Mission La Purisma Concepcion** founded in 1787 and now carefully restored and maintained by the state park system. A self-guided tour offers you the opportunity to see how the Indians practiced mission crafts such as leather working, candle making, and building. The simply decorated church with its sparse furnishings, rough floors, and stenciled walls is typical of Spanish and Mexican churches of the period. One of the nicest aspects of La Purisma Concepcion Mission is its lovely setting—far in the countryside amidst rolling hills and meadows filled with flowers.

Leaving the mission, follow signs for **Buelleton** which has the redoubtable fame of being the home of split-pea soup—you come to **Andersen's Pea Soup Restaurant** just before Highway 246 crosses Highway 101. The menu has more to offer than soup, but it is still possible to sample a bowl of the food that put this little community on the map.

From Buelleton it is just a short drive into **Solvang,** a town settled originally by Danish immigrants which has now become a rather Disneyfied version of how the perfect Danish village should look—a profusion of thatch-like roofs, painted towers, gaily colored windmills, and cobble-stoned court-yards. The shops house a plethora of calorific bakeries and fudge and candy stores interspersed with lots of nifty-gifty Scandinavian craft shops. Interestingly, a large portion of the town's residents truly are of Danish descent. Even if you are not a shopper, the town merits a bakery stop.

Leaving Solvang, rejoin Highway 246 and follow signs for Santa Barbara. Just outside Santa Inez, Highway 246 merges with Highway 154 and the lush green valley gives way to hills as the road climbs through the mountains up the San Marcos Pass. Rounding the crest of the pass, you see **Santa Barbara** stretched out below, hemmed between the mountains and the sea. The red-tile roofs and abundance of palm trees add an affluent look to this prosperous town.

Solvang

Santa Barbara is one of California's loveliest cities. The homes and public buildings show a decidedly Spanish influence and make such a pretty picture—splashes of whitewashed walls, red-tiled roofs, and palm trees snuggled against the Santa Ynez mountains to the east and stretching to the brilliant blue waters of the Pacific to the west.

A pleasant introduction to Santa Barbara is to follow the scenic driving tour that is outlined in the brochure published by the Chamber of Commerce. You can probably pick up a brochure at your hotel or by calling the Chamber of Commerce at (805) 965-3023. The route is well marked and gives you an overall glimpse of the city as you drive by beaches, the wharf, the old downtown area, and affluent suburbs. The brochure also outlines what is called the "Red-Tile Walking Tour" which guides you through the beautiful streets of Santa Barbara. It will take discipline to stay on the path as you pass the multitude of shops filled with so many tempting things to buy, but do continue on, because Santa Barbara is a beautiful city whose public buildings are lovely. The highlight of the tour is the **Santa Barbara County Courthouse**, a magnificent adobe structure with a Moorish accent.

You definitely must not leave town without visiting the splendid **Mission Santa Barbara** which is located at the rise of the hill on the northern edge of town. This beautiful church with two bell towers faces a large park laced with rose gardens. As in many of the other missions, although the church's main purpose is for religious services, a museum is incorporated into the complex with examples of how life was lived when the Spaniards first settled in California.

When your allotted stay in Santa Barbara draws to a close, it is a little less than a 100-mile drive to the Greater Los Angeles area. The vast, often smog-filled **Los Angeles** basin is criss crossed by a mind-boggling network of freeways which confuses all but the resident Southern Californian. Frustrating traffic jams during the morning and afternoon rush hours are a way of life. Therefore, plot the quickest freeway route to your destination and try to travel during the middle of the day in order to avoid the worst traffic. Los Angeles does not offer a wide selection of inns, but there are many attractive, modern hotels where you can stay. The Greater Los Angeles area has an incredible wealth of places to visit and things to do—something to suit every taste. Sightseeing suggestions are described in the following *Leisurely Loop of Southern California* itinerary.

Leisurely Loop of Southern California

Disneyland

Los Angeles and San Diego are popular destinations, attracting travelers from around the world to a wealth of sightseeing treats. But in addition to visiting these justifiably famous cities, we hope to entice you to venture out into the countryside to explore lesser-known sightseeing gems: quaint Balboa Island with its handsome yachts, charming La Jolla with its idyllic beaches, picturesque Julian exuding its Gold Rush heritage, secluded Idyllwild nestled in the mountains, glamorous Palm Springs where movie stars still steal away, beautiful Arrowhead with its crystal-clear lake. Perhaps nowhere else can you discover within only a few short miles such a rich tapestry of places to visit—all so different, all so appealing. White sand beaches, forests with towering pines, deserts rimmed with snow-peaked mountains, bountiful orchards, historical mining towns, and shimmering blue lakes all await your discovery.

Recommended Pacing: Greater Los Angeles is an enormous metropolis of cities and suburbs connected by an overwhelming maze of very busy freeways—during the commuter rush hours it can take hours to get from one side of the city to the other. Choose a hotel or motel close to the principal attraction you are visiting in Los Angeles and use it as a base for your other sightseeing. If you are just visiting Disneyland, stay in the area for two nights—the more attractions you want to include, the longer the recommended stay: if you include San Diego or La Jolla, add two nights; if you visit Palm Springs, add another and possibly include one additional night for Lake Arrowhead.

Weather Wise: The weather along the coast is warm year round and there is very little winter rain. Julian has a more temperate climate—though sometimes in the summer it has the odd very hot day and in the winter the occasional snowfall. Palm Springs can be boiling hot, but with a dry heat, during the summer, and is ideal in the winter, with warm days and cool mountain-desert nights. Lake Arrowhead is a mountain resort with warm summer weather and snow in winter.

If you are going to be staying for an extended period of time in **Los Angeles**, supplement this guide with a book totally dedicated to what to see and do. There is also a wealth of free information available from the Los Angeles Visitors' Bureau: (213) 624-7300—they will send you a very useful packet of information. We are not going to attempt to detail all of Los Angeles' sightseeing possibilities, but just briefly mention a few highlights.

Disneyland: The wonderland created by Walt Disney needs no introduction. What child from two to ninety-two has not heard of this Magic Kingdom, home to such lovable characters as Mickey Mouse, Donald Duck, Pluto, and Snow White? The park is a fantasyland of fun, divided into various theme areas. You enter into Main Street USA and from there it is on to Tomorrowland, Fantasyland, Frontierland, and Adventureland, each with its own rides, entertainment, and restaurants. Disneyland is open every day of the year. The park is located at 1313 Harbor Boulevard in Anaheim. For further information call (714) 781-4565.

Huntington Library, Art Gallery, and Botanical Gardens: The home and 207-acre estate of the late Henry Huntington are open to the public and should not be missed by any visitor to the Los Angeles area. Huntington's enormous home is now a museum featuring the work of French and English 18th-century artists. What makes the museum especially attractive is that the paintings are displayed in a homelike setting surrounded by appropriately dramatic furnishings. Nearby, in another beautiful building, is the Huntington Library—a real gem containing, among other rare books, a 15th-century copy of the Gutenberg bible, Benjamin Franklin's handwritten autobiography, and marvelous Audubon bird prints. The gardens of the estate merit a tour in themselves and include various sections such as a rose garden, a Japanese garden, a camellia garden, a cactus garden, an English garden, and a bonsai garden. Located at 1151 Oxford Road in San Marino, the estate is open Tuesday through Friday noon—4:30 pm, and Saturday and Sunday 10:30 am–4:30 pm. For information on special events and shows call (626) 405-2281.

The Getty Center: Opened in December 1997, the 110 acre arts and cultural campus of the Getty Center dominates the foothills of the Santa Monica Mountains. Conceived and built by Getty, the center unites its museums, institutes and grant program on one magnificent site. From the front entrance, visitors ascend the hill by electric tram to the central plaza where six buildings house the museum, dining facilities, an auditorium, library and exhibition halls. From the eighty-six acres of landscaped gardens one can enjoy sweeping views of Los Angeles. Collections from the J. Paul Getty Museum in

Malibu have been relocated to the new center and so the Villa is closed until the year 2001 when it will reopen as a center for comparative archaeology and cultures. Closed Mondays and holidays, the center will be open weekends 10 am to 7 pm and weekdays 11 am to 7 pm or 9 pm. For information call (310) 440-7300.

NBC Television Studios: Los Angeles is the television capital of the world. To get an idea of what goes on behind the screen, visit the NBC Television Studios and take their one-hour tour that gives you a look at where the stars rehearse, how costumes are designed, how stage props are made, and what goes into the special effects. The tour also visits some of the show sets. The studios are located at 3000 West Alameda Avenue in Burbank. For further information call (818) 840-3537.

The Norton Simon Museum of Art: The Norton Simon Museum of Art is without doubt one of the finest private art museums in the world, set in a beautiful Moorish-style building accented by a reflecting pool and manicured gardens. Norton Simon and his actress wife, Jennifer Jones, share their incredible collection of art including paintings by such masters as Rubens, Rembrandt, Raphael, Picasso, and Matisse. The museum, open Thursday through Sunday noon–6 pm, is located at 411 West Colorado Boulevard in Pasadena. For further information call (626) 449-6840.

Pueblo de Los Angeles: With all the tinsel of modern-day Los Angeles, it is easy to forget that this city grew up around a Spanish mission. You catch a glimpse of the town's history in Pueblo de Los Angeles, a little bit of Mexico where Hispanic people sell colorful Mexican souvenirs and operate attractive restaurants. The 42-acre complex of old buildings (some dating back to the 1780s) has been restored and is now a state park. Pueblo de Los Angeles is located at 130 Apse de la Plaza, Los Angeles. For further information call (213) 628-1274.

The *Queen Mary*: If you take Highway 710 west to Long Beach, the freeway ends at the waterfront with the *Queen Mary* docked alongside: you can go aboard and wander through the biggest ocean liner ever built. A portion of the ship is a hotel, the rest a museum, re-creating the days of splendor when the *Queen Mary* was queen of the seas.

Universal Studios: Visiting Universal Studios, the biggest, busiest movie studio in the world, is like going to a vast amusement park and there is so much to see and do that you must spend a whole day here. Included in the admission price is a two-hour tram journey which takes you around the 420-acre lot, out of the real world and into make-believe: along the way you encounter the howling fury of King Kong and tremble in a terrifying 8.3 earthquake. Water World, a live sea war spectacular, Back to the Future, a time-travel ride from the age of the dinosaurs to 2015, and Backdraft's raging 10,000 degrees firestorm thrill you with their excitement, while the animal actors' stage show and the re-creation of the zany Lucille Ball sitcoms give you comic relief from adrenaline rushes. The studios are just off the Hollywood Freeway at the Universal Center Drive exit in Universal City. For further information call (818) 508-9600.

It takes only a couple of hours to whip down the freeway between Los Angeles and San Diego, but, instead, follow our sightseeing suggestions and dawdle along the way to enjoy some of southern California's coastal attractions en route.

Drive south from Los Angeles on Highway 405, the San Diego Freeway, until you come to Highway 73, the Corona del Mar Freeway, which branches to the south toward the coast. Take this, then in just minutes you come to Highway 55, Newport Boulevard. Exit here and stay on the same road all the way to **Newport Beach**. Soon after crossing the bridge, watch for the sign to your right for Newport Pier. (In case you get off track, the pier is at the foot of 20th Street.) Try to arrive mid-morning so that you can capture a glimpse of yesteryear when the **Dory Fleet** comes in to beach, just to the right of the pier. The dory fleet, made up of colorfully painted, open wooden fishing boats, has been putting out to sea for almost a hundred years. It is never certain exactly what time the fleet will come in (it depends upon the fishing conditions), but if you arrive mid-morning, the chances are you will see the fishermen preparing and selling their catch-of-the-day from the back of their small boats. If seeing all the fresh fish puts you in the mood for lunch, walk across the street to the **Oyster Bar & Grill**—the food is excellent and the clam chowder truly outstanding. If you want to overnight in Newport Beach, **Doryman's Inn**, just steps from the pier, is recommended.

From Newport Beach, continue south along the long, thin peninsula: the next community you come to is **Balboa**. In the center of town there is a clearly signposted public parking area next to Balboa Pier: leave your car here and explore the area. The beach is beautiful, stretching the entire length of the peninsula, all the way from the southern tip to beyond Newport Pier. Stroll along the beach and then walk across the peninsula (about a two-block span) to the Balboa Pavilion, a colorful Victorian gingerbread creation smack in the center of the wharf. Next to the pavilion are several booths where tickets are sold for cruises into the harbor. One of the best of these excursions is on the *Pavilion Queen* that makes a 45-minute loop of the bay. Buy your ticket and, if you have time to spare until the boat leaves, wander around the nostalgic, honky-tonk boardwalk with its cotton candy, Ferris wheel, saltwater taffy shops, and penny arcade. But be back in time to board your boat because the Balboa harbor cruise should not be missed. The trip is a boat fancier's dream: over 9,000 yachts are moored in the harbor. Also of interest are the opulent homes whose lawns stretch out to the docks where their million-dollar cruisers are moored.

A block from the Balboa Pavilion is the ferry landing—you cannot miss it. After your cruise, retrieve your car and follow signs to the Balboa Ferry. You might have to wait in line a bit because the little old-fashioned ferry only takes three cars at a time. When your turn comes, it is just minutes over to **Balboa Island**, a delightful, very wealthy community. Park your car on the main street and poke about in the pretty shops, then walk a few blocks in each direction. The homes look quaint and many seem quite small and simple, but looks are deceiving—the price tags are very high.

From Balboa Island there is a bridge across the harbor to the mainland. Almost as soon as you cross the bridge, turn right, heading south on Highway 1 through the ritzy community of **Corona del Mar**. Although there is still a quaintness to the area, exclusive boutiques, expensive art galleries, palatial homes, and trendy shops hint at the fact that this is not the sleepy little town it might appear to be.

From Corona del Mar, Highway 1 parallels the sea which washes up against a long stretch of beach bound by high bluffs. The area seems relatively undeveloped except for its beach parks. About 11 miles south of Corona del Mar the road passes through **Laguna Beach**, famous for its many art galleries, pretty boutiques, and miles of lovely sand. In summer, from mid-July through August, Laguna Beach is usually packed with tourists coming to see the Pageant of the Masters, a tableau in which town residents dress up and re-create paintings. Two dozen living paintings are staged each evening and viewed by spectators in an outdoor amphitheater.

Continue south along the Coastal Highway. Soon after passing Dana Point, take the turnoff to the east on Highway 5 to **San Juan Capistrano**. Watch for signs directing you off the highway to **Mission San Juan Capistrano** (just two blocks from the freeway). This mission, founded by Father Junipero Serra in 1776, has been carefully restored to give you a glimpse of what life was like in the early days of California. Although located in the center of town, the mission creates its own environment since it is insulated by lovely gardens and a complex of Spanish adobe buildings. Another point of special interest at San Juan Capistrano is that the swallows have chosen it as "home," arriving every March 19th (Saint Joseph's Day) and leaving October 23rd. Visit the mission and then retrace your route to Highway 1 and continue south about an hour to **San Diego.**

The San Diego Visitors' Bureau—(619) 232-3101—will send you a packet of valuable information for touring its many attractions. A recently completed train line makes it easier and more fun than ever to get around San Diego and its environs. You can actually board the train in Old Town and journey to the Mexican border. San Diego offers a wealth of attractions and amusements—we feature some of our favorites.

Balboa Park: Balboa Park is without a doubt one of the highlights of San Diego. One of the most famous attractions within the park is the **San Diego Zoo**, one of the finest in the world. For a good orientation of the zoo take either the 40-minute bus tour or the aerial tramway. Most of the more than 3,000 animals live within natural-style enclosures with very few cages. The Children's Zoo is especially fun, with a nursery for newborn animals and a petting zoo. But Balboa Park offers much more than its splendid zoo. There are fascinating museums and exhibits within the 1,400-acre park: the Museum of Man, the Aerospace Museum, the San Diego Museum of Art, the Timken Art Gallery, the Natural History Museum, the Reuben H. Fleet Space Theater and Science Center, the Hall of Champions, the Museum of Photographic Arts, the Lily Pond, and the Botanical Building. Most of the museums are housed in picturesque Spanish-style buildings. For information call (619) 239-0512.

Coronado: While in San Diego take the bridge or the ferry over to Coronado, an island-like bulb of land tipping a thin isthmus that stretches south almost to the Mexican border. Here you find not only a long stretch of beautiful beach, but also the Del Coronado Hotel, a Victorian fantasy of gingerbread turrets and gables. The Del Coronado, locally referred to as "The Del," is a sightseeing attraction in its own right and makes an excellent choice for a luncheon stop.

The Embarcadero: The Embarcadero is the downtown port area located along Harbor Drive. From here you can take a harbor cruise or visit one of the floating museums tied up to the quay, such as the *Star of India*, built in 1863, a dramatic tall-masted ship that carried passengers and cargo around the world and the *Medea*, a turn-of-the-century luxury yacht. For information call (619) 234-9153.

Heritage Park: Just adjacent to **Old Town** is Heritage Park, where some of San Diego's Victorian heritage is preserved. Next to the spacious village green, a street lined with fabulous Victorian houses slopes gently uphill. The houses were moved here from other areas of San Diego to save them from the bulldozers and now these intricate creations house small shops and offices (do not miss the doll shop with a wonderful collection of doll houses and antique toys).

La Jolla: Be sure to visit La Jolla, "The Jewel," a sophisticated town just north of San Diego. Classy shops line the streets and spectacular homes, secluded behind high walls, overlook the ocean. La Jolla is home to a branch of the University of California and within its Scripps Institution of Oceanography is an excellent aquarium and museum featuring marine life from California and Mexico. However, what really makes La Jolla so special are her beautiful white sand beaches sheltered in intimate little coves. You may prefer to stay here rather than in San Diego.

Mexico: Mexico lies just south of San Diego. Do not judge Mexico by its border town of **Tijuana**, but if you would like to have a *taste* of Mexico, take one of the "shopping and sightseeing" tours that leave from downtown for the short drive to the border. You can drive across the border, but the bus tour removes the hassle from the trip. United States citizens need only carry identification such as a driver's license if they are staying in Mexico for less than 72 hours. For further information call Gray Line Tours at (619) 491-0011.

Mission San Diego de Alcala

Mission San Diego de Alcala: The oldest of the chain of missions that stretches up the coast is Mission San Diego de Alcala. The mission was originally closer to San Diego but was moved to its present site (10818 San Diego Mission Road) in 1774. To reach the mission, head east on Highway 8; it is signposted to the north of the highway beyond the intersection of Highway 15. For information call: (619) 281-8449.

Old Town: Old Town is where San Diego originated. Just southeast of the intersection of Highways 5 and 8 you see signposts for the oldest sections of San Diego. The area has been designated as a city park and several square blocks are accessible to pedestrians. Make the Historical Museum your first stop and orient yourself by viewing a scale model of San Diego in its early days. Although small in area, Old Town is most interesting to visit as many of the buildings are open as small museums, such as the Machado-Steward Adobe, the Old School House, and the Seeley Stables (an 1860s stage depot with a good display of horse-drawn carriages). If you are in Old Town at mealtime, you can choose from many attractive restaurants. For further information call (619) 291-4903.

Seaport Village: Just a little way south of the Embarcadero is Seaport Village, a very popular tourist attraction and fun for adults and children alike. Situated right on the waterfront, it has little paths that meander through 23 acres of a village of shops and restaurants built in a colorful variety of styles from Early Spanish to Victorian. Street artists display their talents to laughing audiences. An old-time merry-go-round (an import from Coney Island) jingles its gay melody, irresistibly beckoning the child in all of us to climb aboard.

Sea World: San Diego's marine display is in Mission Bay Park. Set in a 150-acre park which includes a 1-acre children's playland, Sea World features one of California's famous personalities, Shamu, the performing killer whale who delights children of all ages with her wit and aquatic abilities. Penguin Encounter is a particularly fun exhibit where you watch comical penguins waddling about in their polar environment, while Shark Encounter presents one of the largest displays of sharks in the world and provides the terrifying thrill of being surrounded by these efficient killing machines as you walk through an acrylic tube. For further information call (619) 226-3901.

Wild Animal Park: This is a branch of the San Diego Zoo 30 miles north of the city near Escondido—truly a zoo on a grand scale. The animals roam freely in terrain designed to match their natural habitat. You feel as if you are on a safari in Africa as you watch for lions and other animals while you tour the park on the Wgasa Bushline Monorail tour. There are also several open theaters where animal shows are presented. For further information call (619) 234-6541.

Leaving San Diego, Highway 8 takes you east and winds through shrub-filled canyons dotted with ever-expanding housing suburbs. About 30 minutes after the highway leaves the city, watch for the sign for Highway 79 where you turn north toward Julian. The road weaves through an Indian reservation and the scenery becomes prettier by the minute as you climb into the mountains and enter the **Cuyamaca Rancho State Park**. There are not many opportunities to sightsee en route, but if you want to break your journey, you can pause at the park headquarters and visit the Indian museum or the museum at the **Old Stonewall Mine**. Leaving the park, the road winds down into Julian.

Julian is a small town that can easily be explored in just a short time. What is especially nice is that, although it is a tourist attraction, the town is not "tacky touristy." Rather, you get the feeling you are in the last century as you wander through the streets and stop to browse at some of the antique shops, visit the small historical museum in the old brewery, and enjoy refreshment at the soda fountain in the 1880s drug store. If you want to delve deeper into mining, just a short drive (or long walk) away on the outskirts of town is the **Eagle Mine**, founded by pioneers from Georgia, many of them soldiers who came here after the Civil War. Tours are taken deep into the mine and a narration gives not only the history of the mine, but the history of Julian.

If you are in Julian in the fall, you can enjoy another of Julian's offerings—apples. Although you can sample Julian's wonderful apples throughout the year (every restaurant has its own special apple pie on the menu), the apple becomes king during the fall at harvest time. Beginning in October and continuing on into November, special craft shows and events are held in the Julian Town Hall, and, of course, apples are featured at every meal in every restaurant. You might also want to visit one of the packing plants on the edge of town where you can buy not only apples, but every conceivable item that has apples as a theme.

It is only a short drive north from Julian on Highway 79 to **Santa Ysabel** where you turn right at the main intersection. At this junction you see **Dudley's Bakery**, a rather nondescript looking building that houses a great bakery: loyal customers drive all the way from San Diego just to buy one of their 21 varieties of tasty bread. As you leave Santa Ysabel you come to **Mission Santa Ysabel**, a reconstructed mission that still serves the Indians. This is one of the less interesting missions, but you may want to see the murals painted by the local Indians.

About 7 miles after leaving the mission, Highway 79 breaks off to the east and you continue north on Highway 76. In five minutes you come to Lake Henshaw. Just beyond the lake turn northeast (right) on East Grade Road which winds its way up the mountain to the **Palomar Observatory**. Just near the parking area is a museum where you learn about the observatory through photos and short films. It is a pleasant stroll up to the impressive white-domed observatory that houses the Hale telescope—the largest in the United States. A flight of steps takes you to a glass-walled area where you see the giant telescope whose lens is 200 inches in diameter, 2 feet thick, and took 11 years to polish. You cannot see the telescope in operation because it is used only at night, but it is fun to imagine scientists scanning the heavens.

After viewing the observatory, loop back down the twisting road to the main highway and when it intersects with Highway 76 turn northwest (right), driving through hills covered with groves of avocado and orange trees. In about 12 miles you come to **Pala** and the **Mission San Antonio de Pala**, established in 1810, one of the few remaining active "asistancias" (missions built in outlying areas to serve the Indians). The mission is small, but the chapel holds great beauty in its rugged simplicity enhanced by thick adobe walls, rustic beamed ceiling, and Indian paintings. A bell tower stands alone to the right of the chapel, a picturesque sight; to the left are a simple museum and souvenir shop.

From Pala it is about a ten-minute drive north on S16 to Temecula. Just before you enter town the road intersects with Highway 79 and you head east for 18 miles to Aguanga where Highway 371 takes you northeast for 21 miles to Highway 74. As you head north on 74 the mountain air becomes sweeter and the scenery increasingly prettier as you enter the forest. In about 12 miles you see signs for **Idyllwild** to the northeast. Turn here on Highway 243 and very soon you come to the small resort tucked into the mountains high above Palm Springs. Homey little restaurants, antique stores, and fascinating gift shops make up the town. If you are interested in handmade items, stop at **Kountry Kollectibles**. Originally the store featured handmade items from 15 local artisans—now it has 750 suppliers, not only from every state, but from around the world. There is a Christmas section with a marvelous selection of Santa Claus ornaments. The shop is located in an old six-room house at 54380 North Circle Drive.

Leaving Idyllwild, continue north on Highway 342 to Banning where you turn east (right) on Highway 10. In about 12 miles you come to Highway 111 where you turn right and follow signs to Palm Springs (about a ten-minute drive). **Palm Springs** was first discovered by the Indians who came to this oasis to bathe in the hot springs which they considered to have healing qualities. The same tribe still owns much of Palm Springs and rents their valuable real estate to homeowners and commercial enterprises. The hot springs are still in use today.

During the winter season the town is congested with traffic and the sidewalks are crammed with an assortment of people of every age, size, and shape dressed in colorful sporty clothes. Palm Springs used to be deserted in summer when the days are very hot. However, more and more tourists are coming in June, July, and August, attracted by the lower hotel rates. Although the temperature in the summer months is frequently well above 110 degrees, it is a dry heat and not unbearable in the mornings and balmy evenings. In fact, due to the altitude, evenings often require a sweater. So if your visit is in summer, plan your sight-seeing for early and late in the day and spend midday in the comfort of your air-conditioned inn.

Aerial Tramway, Palm Springs

In addition to the pleasures of basking in the sun or playing on one of the many golf courses in the area, Palm Springs offers a variety of sightseeing. The most impressive excursion is to take the **Aerial Tramway** (located just north of town off Highway 111) from the desert floor up 2½ miles into the San Jacinto Mountains. In summer you go from sizzling heat to cool mountain forests, while in winter you go from desert to snow. The weather atop the mountain is often more than 40 degrees cooler than in Palm Springs, so remember to take the appropriate clothing. At the top are observation decks with telescopes, a restaurant, and miles of hiking trails.

If you enjoy deserts, be sure not to miss the **Living Desert Outdoor Museum** (closed in summer) where 6 miles of trails wind through different types of desert found in the United States. Tour booklets are available at the entrance to assist you along the trails. If you are interested in the rich and famous, join a bus tour that takes you by the outside of their magnificent homes—many movie stars have second homes in Palm Springs.

Palm Springs is a convenient place to end this itinerary because it is a quick, easy freeway-drive back to Los Angeles. But, if time permits, squeeze in one more contrasting destination, the exclusive Alpine resort of Lake Arrowhead.

Leave Palm Springs and head north on Highway 111 for about 10 miles to Highway 10 and turn west for Banning. Approximately 20 miles past Banning at Redlands, exit from the freeway on Highway 30 and drive north for a few minutes until Highway 38 travels into the hills. As the road begins to climb up from the valley the scenery becomes prettier with every curve—the dry desert brush is gradually left behind, replaced by evergreen trees. At the town of Running Springs turn west on Highway 18. This is called the "**Rim of the World Highway**," a road where sweeping vistas of the valley floor can be glimpsed through the clouds. Be aware that fog often hovers around this drive and then, instead of admiring beautiful views, you creep along in thick gray mist.

Lake Arrowhead village is a newly built cluster of restaurants and shops along the lakefront. The lake is bordered by magnificent estates of the wealthy from southern California. The magnet of Lake Arrowhead is not any specific sightseeing, but rather the out-of-doors experience: although lakefront and beach access is restricted and private, you can take leisurely walks through the forest, picnic in secluded parks, explore the lake by paddle boats, or rent bicycles for a bit of fresh-air adventure. You also must take the hour-long ride on the nostalgic steamer that circles the lake.

When it is time to complete your itinerary, retrace your path back to the valley and follow Highway 10 back into Los Angeles. Unless you encounter unexpected traffic, the trip should take about two hours.

Wandering through the Wine Country

The Napa Valley

The Napa and Sonoma Valleys, just north of San Francisco, have earned a well-merited reputation for the excellence of their wines. Happily for the tourist, many of the wineries are open to the public for tours and tasting. But it is not only visiting the wineries that makes this area so special—these valleys are also memorable for their beauty. A visit to the wine country makes a pleasant excursion any time of year. In summer the days are long and warm, perfect for bike rides, picnics, music festivals, concerts, and art shows. As summer days give way to the cooler afternoons and crisp evenings of fall, the lush foliage on the thousands of acres of grapevines turns to red, gold, and yellow—a colorful reminder that it is time for harvest. You can sense the energy of the crush as vintners work against the clock and weather to pick grapes at their prime. In winter, cool days are often washed by rain, but this is also an excellent time to visit since this is "off season" and the winery tours will be almost private as you travel from one winery to the next. Spring is glorious: mustard blossoms paint the valley yellow, contrasting dramatically with the dark bark of the vines laced with the delicate green of new leaves.

Recommended Pacing: The Napa and Sonoma wine regions can possibly be squeezed into a day's journey from San Francisco with time to visit one or two wineries. It requires only about an hour to drive from San Francisco to the southern boundaries of either valley. Running north and south, Napa Valley spans a territory of approximately 35 miles while the Sonoma Valley stretches about 17 miles. However, since the primary attraction in either valley happens to be its vineyards, and wine tasting is offered at almost every one, it is most restful to investigate a few in an afternoon's time, sample their wines and then incorporate a nap or a laze by a pool into the day's schedule. Since the prospect of returning to San Francisco and battling traffic at rush hour is not a welcome notion, we recommend that you plan to leisurely spend a minimum of one to two nights in the Napa Valley and one to two nights in the Sonoma Valley. With the distance between the valleys being only about 10 to 12 miles, you can also use either valley as a base from which to explore both wine regions.

Weather Wise: The Napa and Sonoma Valleys have a very similar climate. Summer days can be scorching hot and roads are often clogged with visitors. Autumn gives way to mild, sunny days, cooler afternoons, and crisp evenings. From autumn to spring you can expect some rain although many days will be sunny. In winter temperatures are mild yet several degrees cooler than in the nearby San Francisco Bay Area.

Note: We have tried to be as accurate as possible when giving information about touring wineries, but things change, so be certain to give each winery a call in advance to see whether or not they are open and whether you need an appointment for a tour or tasting.

This itinerary which wends up the Napa Valley and down the Sonoma Valley is an introduction and a sampling of what the wine country has to offer. This itinerary is not intended to be strictly adhered to in its exact routing. Rather, it is meant as an overall plan from which you can pick and choose what sounds most interesting to you. Use it as a framework to plan your own holiday, taking various segments as they fit in with your time frame. The featured wineries have been chosen for a variety of reasons such as their historical interest, the excellence of their wines, the appeal of their tour, and their special ambiance. Some wineries offer wine tasting free of charge, others charge a fee.

From San Francisco, travel east on Highway 80 across the San Francisco-Oakland Bay Bridge. After crossing the bridge, stay in the left-hand lane and follow signs for Highway 80 in the direction of Sacramento. Approximately 5 miles after crossing the Carquinez Bridge, watch for the Marine World Parkway (Highway 37) turnoff. Take the Parkway that takes you right past the exit to **Marine World, Africa USA**, a wonderful park and family attraction. If traveling with children you might want to allocate a day here. On an expanse of 160 acres, there are numerous theaters that stage a multitude of shows to include both marine and African life: tigers, elephants, lions, killer whales, dolphins, seals, and sharks, to name a few. Many rides and new attractions were added in 1998. Admission to the park covers the cost of all shows and attractions. Shows are staggered throughout the day and it is feasible to see them all if you want to. Food service is available throughout the park, but you can also pack a picnic and enjoy the expanse of tables set under trees next to the children's playground. For additional information and their calendar, telephone (707) 643-6722.

After Marine World, continue on the parkway for 2 miles and turn north on Highway 29 which travels in the direction of Napa. The road widens and the scenery improves dramatically as the road nears the base of the Napa Valley. There are two parallel roads that stretch the length of the valley—Highway 29 and the Silverado Trail. Highway 29 is the busier road and the address for many of the valley's larger wineries and all the towns. The Silverado Trail, the more scenic, less commercial route, hugs the eastern hills, and twists and winds amongst smaller vineyards, often offering a welcome escape from the summer crowds and traffic. This itinerary suggests a route north through the Napa Valley, criss crossing back and forth between Highway 29 and the Silverado Trail, and then travels west to follow a route south through the Sonoma Wine Valley.

For our first suggested winery stop, the Jarvis Winery, continue on Highway 29. When the road divides, take the east (right) fork, Highway 121, which goes to Napa and on to Lake Berryessa. To reach the Jarvis Winery, stay on Highway 121, continuing to follow signs to Lake Berryessa. When Highway 121 makes a turn to the east and leaves the valley floor, it begins to climb into the wooded hills and assumes the name Monticello Road. After the turnoff, continue toward Lake Berryessa for about 4 miles. Watch for a gate on the left marking the Jarvis entrance at 2970 Monticello Road. The gates will automatically open after you give your name and say you have a reservation for the tour.

A tour of the **Jarvis Winery** necessitates a reservation well in advance. If you are watching your pennies, you can bypass this tour (which costs $10 per person) and proceed on to the next stop. However, the structure of the Jarvis Winery is different than any other winery you will see in the Napa Valley. It also produces excellent wines (Cabernet Franc, Cabernet Sauvignon, Chardonnay, and Merlot) and offers a fun tour. All you see as you approach are two massive doors built into the hillside—it looks like an entrance into a bunker. But inside, another world opens up as you find yourself in a giant cave. Tour groups are limited to a very small number, which makes the tour very personal. You follow a path that forms a loop around the cave, passing by an underground stream and a waterfall, and visiting the Crystal Chamber, a grand reception hall. The tour ends in an intimate room where guests sample fine wines at a small table surrounded by gilded chairs with blue velvet upholstery. Tours are offered on a reservation basis, seven days a week at 1:30 pm. Based on demand, additional tours are sometimes added. For information and reservations call (707) 255-5280.

Leaving the Jarvis Winery, retrace your route back down the hill until Highway 121 (Monticello Road) intersects the Silverado Trail. Turn right (north) on the Silverado Trail until you come to Oak Knoll Avenue. Turn west on Oak Knoll, a beautiful drive bounded by walnut trees and vineyards, and watch for a small signpost on your right marking the entrance of **Trefethen Vineyards** at 1160 Oak Knoll Avenue. Surrounded by its own grapevines, Trefethen Vineyards is housed in the oldest wooden winery in the Napa Valley. Pumpkin in color with a brown roof, this handsome complex recently celebrated its one hundredth birthday and there was much reason to celebrate, as the Trefethen family fortunately rescued and lovingly restored the property. This wonderful old winery was designed by the same architect responsible for the Niebaum-Coppola and Beaulieu wineries. Trefethen Vineyards is a delightful small winery, family-owned and operated, which has proved that size is in no way a factor in excellence. The Trefethens have converted a bulk winery to the production of fine estate-grown Chardonnay, Riesling, and Cabernet Sauvignon. Trefethen wines are featured in some of the finest restaurants. Old farming implements border the parking area and a brick walk encircles a handsome oak in front of the winery where you can sample the wines. The winery is open to the public and tours are available each day at 10:30 am and 2:00 pm, but you must make an appointment: call (707) 255-7700.

After a visit to the Trefethen Vineyards, continue west on Oak Knoll Avenue and in a few minutes you come to Highway 29 where you turn right and continue north up the valley. When you come to the small town of **Yountville**, take the first exit, keep to your right, then turn left at the first street which is Washington. You will see on your left **Vintage 1870**, a wonderful complex of 40 shops and restaurants housed in a quaint old brick winery. Even non-shoppers will enjoy a stroll through this lovely building: the old brick, heavy beams, and tiled and cobbled floors are dramatic against a meticulously groomed backdrop of green lawn and flowers. A variety of specialty shops make any purchase possible: toys, antiques, handmade sweaters, books, kitchenware, jewelry, or art. An assortment of restaurants will appease most appetites whether you desire a gourmet salad, pastries, or simply a refreshing ice cream cone. You can also arrange for an early-morning balloon ride—the office for **Adventures Aloft** is located in Vintage 1870, next to the Pacific Blues Café. The telephone number is (707) 255-8688. Departures are at sunrise, the best possible time as the winds are gentle and the air is cool. The flights are expensive, but memorable.

Drive south from Yountville on California Drive, crossing under Highway 29 in the direction of the Veterans' Home. Just after passing under the freeway, turn right onto the property of **Domaine Chandon** at One California Drive. When the proprietors of Moët & Chandon first came to the valley with the intention of making sparkling wine following the principles and rigid process of true French champagne, *methode champenoise*, they contracted to use Trefethen Vineyards. Successful in their venture, their sparkling wine was well received and they moved to the present location and established their own winery, Domaine Chandon. Roses front the vineyards, a French tradition, copied both for its practicality as well as for its aesthetic value. The roses add a grace and beauty to the planted fields, but they are also susceptible to the same root diseases and insect problems. If the roses are blemished, vintners know to investigate the vines closely.

Although the winery is relatively new, mature oak trees shade a lovely lawn and a series of terraced ponds with fountains. A wooden footbridge spans the creek-fed ponds to the stone winery tucked back into the hillside. Tours are offered daily on the hour between 11 am and 5 pm. The visitors' center is closed on Mondays and Tuesdays from January through April: for further information call (707) 944-2280. Reservations can be made online at www.dchandon.com. The tours are hosted by courteous guides who are well informed about the aspects of *methode champenoise*. Visitors see first the traditional storage of the wine in polished stainless-steel tanks and then continue on to observe the additional steps involved in making champagne. In the cellar, bottles of sparkling wine are aged and riddled (turned). In the bottling room you see the process of freezing then disgorging the sediment, corking, cleaning, and labeling the bottles. After the tour visitors are invited back to the salon where Domaine Chandon's sparkling wines may be purchased by the glass. From the salon it is possible to view through a glass partition Domaine Chandon's elegant restaurant. A visit to Domaine Chandon shows French and Californian vintners sharing expertise and working side by side.

From Domaine Chandon, return to Highway 29 heading north a few miles to the roadside town of **Oakville**. A few buildings comprise this town, the principal one being the original **Oakville Grocery**. If you plan to picnic, stop here for supplies and gourmet treats to accompany your wine-tasting purchases.

Just to the north of Oakville, on the right of Highway 29 you soon come to **Opus One** (the address is 7900 Saint Helena Highway, Highway 29). This winery is a masterpiece which is the showplace of Robert Mondavi and the Rothschild family. The purpose of their joint venture was to combine the talents of the best French wine-makers with the know-how of California's Mondavi family to produce some of the world's finest wines. The gleaming white, circular structure looks a bit like a luxurious, futuristic, coliseum—it is totally different in ambiance from the typical Napa Valley winery. It certainly makes a statement, which is just want the owners wanted to do. As you enter the impressive building, it is immediately obvious that no expense was spared: everything is of the finest quality. Visitors are treated as honored guests and wait in an elegant lounge before the tour begins. You must sign up two to four weeks in advance for Opus One's complimentary tour. The tasting of premium wines costs $20, and the tasting room is open daily from 10:30 am to 3:30 pm. The telephone number is (707) 944-9442.

Your next stop, the **Robert Mondavi Winery** (the same Robert Mondavi who is a partner in the Opus One which you have just visited), is just a little bit farther north, on the left side of the highway (7801 Saint Helena Highway, Highway 29). This modern winery with an original Bufano statue of Saint Francis at its entrance was styled after the Franciscan missions, with an open-arched entry framing an idyllic view of vineyards. The one-hour tour is extensive, extremely informative, and provides a good general introduction to the essence of wine making. By special arrangement, you can also make reservations for an advanced wine growing tour ($15 per person), touring the fields and studying the grapes as well as the winery. After each tour guests are invited into the tasting room to sample the wines. The lovely lawn at the back is the site of summer concerts and art shows. Reservations are advisable. For further information call (707) 259-9463.

After visiting the Robert Mondavi Winery, your next stop is another real winner, the **Niebaum-Coppola Winery**. Continue north on Highway 29 for a few miles beyond the Robert Mondavi winery. Just past Niebaum Lane on the left, you will see the entrance to the winery. In the late 1870s a Finnish sea captain, Gustave Niebaum, retired from shipping to invest his fortune in the Napa Valley, envisioning a winery that would produce magnificent wines, even surpassing the finest French wines. After his death, Niebaum's property was divided, but in 1995 the Coppola family (owners of the Niebaum-Coppola Winery since 1975) purchased the adjacent Inglenook château and its vineyards, thus uniting once again the original historic estate. Francis Ford Coppola (world-renowned movie director) and his wife, Eleanor, have great respect for wine and the enormous potential of the land. They carry on the Niebaum tradition by growing, producing, and bottling all on the estate—a rare occurrence in today's viticultural world. Niebaum-Coppola is a handsome winery which enjoys a superb setting nestled against the western foothills of the Napa Valley. Since the winery dates back to the 19th century, it is able to offer what the valley's new wineries cannot—character achieved with age and time. At a cost of $20, one can enjoy a historic tour through the original stone aging cellar containing some magnificent large German oak casks. The tour includes the tasting of four wines. The magnificent château has been restored to its original splendor, and a museum both to commemorate Gustave Niebaum and to explore the creative workings of film and the work of Francis Ford Coppola was opened. Reservations are required to tour the winery and visit the château. There is a $7.50 charge for tasting of four wines. For further information call (707) 963-9099.

Niebaum-Coppola Winery

From Niebaum-Coppola cross over Highway 29 to Rutherford Road, directly opposite. On the corner is a clustering of buildings forming **Beaulieu Vineyards**. Referred to as BV, Beaulieu is known for some excellent wine and now offers both a tour and wine tasting. The tour is free. Complimentary tasting is offered in the Main Visitor's Center and one can also request the Private Reserve Room and sample four to six reserve wines at a flat rate of $12.50. For additional information call (707) 967-5200.

Rutherford Road affords a scenic drive shaded by an archway of oak trees. Travel the short distance to its end, past the Louis Honig Winery, and then turn north on Conn Creek Road which then intersects with the Silverado Trail. Turn north on the Silverado Trail, but drive slowly as you want to take the first right turn onto Rutherford Hill Road which winds up past the Auberge du Soleil, to the Rutherford Hill Winery.

Although relatively new, the **Rutherford Hill Winery** is housed in a stunning building of weathered redwood in the shape of a chalet-barn, draped with Virginia creeper and wisteria and bounded by grass and flowers. The winery crowns a plateau and enjoys a spectacular valley view. Paths lead down the hillside to picnic tables set under olive trees where the views will tempt you to wile away an afternoon. Rutherford Hill is the dream of a number of independent vintners who together purchased what was once the Souverain Winery (now located in the Sonoma Valley) in order to process and control the production of their limited quantities of grapes into wine. By now, Rutherford Hill Winery is widely considered the leading producer of Merlot in the Napa Valley. The owners also constructed what was at the time the largest expanse of underground caves in the valley—these maintain a constant natural temperature of 58 degrees, minimizing evaporation far more successfully than when temperatures are controlled by air conditioning. The tour of Rutherford Hill includes a visit to these caves. Guides at Rutherford Hill are friendly and quite proud of (as well as knowledgeable about) the winery and visitors are encouraged to ask questions. Although all wine-making procedures are basically the same, Rutherford Hill is a small winery and the guide's explanation of the step-by-step process seems easier to understand than the same explanation at a much grander winery. Wine tasting is $4 per glass. Advance reservations are not needed. For more information call (707) 963-7194.

From Rutherford traveling north on Highway 29 it is just a few miles to **Saint Helena**. Highway 29 becomes this lovely town's Main Street, lined with elegant stores, boutiques, and restaurants. Detour east two blocks off Main Street via Adams Street to Saint Helena's **Library and Museum**. The library has a very interesting section on wine and one wing of the museum is dedicated to Robert Louis Stevenson, the great Scotsman who settled with his new bride in an old miner's shack northeast of Calistoga. It was here that he wrote *Silverado Squatters*, a book romantically promoting the beauty of the Napa Valley. Stevenson buffs can also visit the **Robert Louis Stevenson Park** on Highway 29 between Calistoga and Middletown and also make an appointment to tour Schramsburg Vineyards, the winery Stevenson featured in his chronicles of the wine country.

Also in Saint Helena, at 2555 Main Street (which is also named Highway 29), is the **Culinary Institute of America**, a fascinating place to dine. The prestigious institute, which opened in the fall of 1995, is housed in what has long been a landmark of the Napa Valley—the Christian Brothers Winery. On the second floor of the right wing of the massive old winery is the **Greystone Restaurant**, a super place to eat lunch or dinner. The culinary team is made up entirely of Culinary Institute graduates or advanced students who display their skills at an open-to-view kitchen, set center stage in the room. Greystone's own organic gardens inspire the menu which mingles Mediterranean flavors and textures with the culinary aesthetics of Northern California. The food is delicious and the price is an excellent value. Lunch is served from 11:30 am to 2:45 pm, a light "tasting" menu from 3 to 5:30 pm, and dinner from 5:30 to 9 pm every day except Tuesdays, December to April. For reservations call (707) 967-1010. In the left wing of the Culinary Institute is a museum where you can see many antique tools used for wine making and an extensive display of antique corkscrews.

Before leaving Saint Helena visit the **V. Sattui Winery**, at 1111 White Lane Street. Sattui wine-making history dates back to 1885 when Vittorio Sattui founded the winery in the North Beach district of San Francisco. Great-grandson Daryl Sattui revived the family tradition in 1973 by moving the winery to Saint Helena. Currently 15 vintage-dated wines are produced, all of which are sold exclusively at the winery or by mail order. V. Sattui wines are not available in any stores, wine shops, or restaurants. With a lovely garden setting, this is an attractive winery where you can also purchase picnic supplies—such as over 200 different kinds of cheeses, homemade salads, patés, breads, and desserts. The winery has a wonderful picnic spot with tables set on the lawn beneath shady trees. Tours are self guided and tasting is complimentary. For further information call (707) 963-7774.

As Highway 29 leaves the commercial district of Saint Helena and enters a very exclusive residential district on its northern borders, watch carefully for the gated entry to **Beringer Vineyards** (2000 Main Street, Highway 29), set on a knoll, surrounded by beautifully landscaped grounds of mature trees, lawns, and gardens. What was once the home of the founding Beringer family now houses a wine and gift shop. Reflecting its heritage and standing as a tribute to one of the valley's founding wineries, the dramatic stone and half-timbered building with a slate roof was one of two family homes built as a replica of the German home that Frederick and his brother Jacob left behind when they emigrated. Half-hour tours are offered every day between 9:30 am and 5 pm (November to May the last tour is at 4 pm) and availability is on a first-come basis. Tours emphasize the historical aspect of the winery and include a memorable visit through the tunnels and caverns where the wine is aged in barrels. There is a fee of $2 if you want to sample the reserve wines; otherwise tasting is complimentary. For information call (707) 963-4812.

From Beringer head north another 4 miles and then turn right on Larkmead Lane. The **Kornell Champagne Cellars**, a name synonymous with fine champagne, is located at 1091 Larkmead Lane. Kornell is devoted to the production of traditional, bottle-fermented sparkling wines and a limited amount of handcrafted wines. Visitors are welcome and tours are informal and personalized to suit the group and the production activities of any particular day or hour. The tour is more informative than visual: an in-depth, detailed explanation is offered about the traditional methods of making sparkling wine. For further information call (707) 942-0859.

Schramsberg Vineyards, which offers tours by appointment, (707) 942-4558, is tucked in the western foothills of the Napa Valley just off Highway 29 to the south of Calistoga at 1400 Schramsberg Road. Over 2 miles of tunnels are devoted to the production of sparkling wine in this historic winery. Wine tasting is offered at a charge of $7.50 for three current releases, but only in conjunction with the tour.

Beyond the Schramsberg Vineyards, a large sign on Highway 29 instructs you to turn just a few miles farther north on Highway 29 at Dunaweal Lane to visit **Sterling Vineyards**. Reminiscent of a Moorish castle, Sterling Vineyards enjoys a crowning position on a hill idyllically set in the middle of the valley. From the winery you can savor panoramic views looking down through tall pines to a checkerboard of vineyards. Access to Sterling is possible only by small gondolas. For a fee of $6 (the fee is $3 for children under 18 which includes juice at the top) you can ride the aerial tramway from the parking lot to the winery and back (first tram 10:30 am, last 4:30 pm). Arrows and detailed signs direct you on an informative, but impersonal, self-guided tour through the maze of rooms that comprise the winery. For general information, call (707) 942-3344. By appointment, group tours are available Monday to Friday, call (707) 942-3359. At the end of the tour, a flight of steps leads up to a tasting room with disappointedly limited rather than panoramic views of the valley. However the wines are lovely, and another inviting feature about Sterling is the wonderful melodic sound of bells that ring out every quarter-hour. These bells once hung in London's Saint Dunstan's-in-the-East Church. Wine tasting is complimentary.

Across the street at 1060 Dunaweal Lane you will find Clos Pegase for those who appreciate wine and art. When owner Jan Isaac Shrem, a Paris-based business man and art collector, turned 50, he decided to move to Napa Valley and take up viticulture. Shrem enlisted the help of the San Francisco Museum of Modern Art to help him find an architect to design his winery. That person turned out to be Michael Graves, who designed the structure with influences that range from Ancient Rome to Art Decco. The result is a beautiful building that the Washington Post called "America's first monument to wine as art." Not only will you have the pleasure of touring the winemaking facilities, the winery boasts an abundance of 20th century art and artifacts. Clos Pegase is open daily from 10:30 am-5:00 pm with guided tours at 11:00 am and 2:00 pm. Winetasting of the premium wines is $2.50. For information call (707) 942-4981.

The delightful town of **Calistoga** is just a few miles north from Sterling Vineyards at the intersection of Highway 29 and Highway 128. Bounded by rugged foothills and vineyards, Calistoga is an attractive town servicing local residents and tourists alike. Its main street, Lincoln Avenue, is lined on both sides by attractive shops and numerous restaurants. This charming town has been famous ever since Spanish explorers arrived in 1823 and observed Indians taking mud baths in steamy marshes. Sam Brannan, who purchased a square mile of land at the foot of Mount Saint Helena, gave the town its name: he wanted the place to be the "Saratoga of California" and so called it Calistoga. He bought the land in the early 1860s and by 1866 was ready to open his resort of a few cottages and palm trees. The oldest surviving railroad depot in California, now serving as a quaint and historic shopping mall, received its first train-load of passengers when they came to Calistoga for the much-publicized opening of Sam Brannan's resort. For more than a hundred years, Calistoga has attracted visitors from all over the world, primarily for its hot springs and spas. People came in search of its glorious, healing waters long before the region became a popular destination for its wineries.

There are many spa facilities to choose from—at the eastern end of town look for the **Calistoga Spa and Hot Springs**, 1006 Washington Street. (707) 942-6269. Their facilities are newly renovated, expansive, and modern and the attendants are professional and very nice. Offered are volcanic-ash mud baths, mineral baths, steam baths, blanket wraps, and massage. The entire package, "the works," takes almost two hours and their rates are very competitive.

If you are feeling adventurous, You can take a balloon flight with **American Balloon Adventures**. A sunrise launch is arranged from a selection of wineries. This one-hour balloon fantasy voyage includes a gourmet brunch. For further information call (707) 942-6546. Another adventure is the **Calistoga Gliders**, located at 1546 Lincoln Avenue. To arrange for a glider ride, call (707) 942-5592.

If you have never seen a geyser, travel a few miles farther north from Calistoga on Highway 128 in the direction of Lakeport to Tubbs Lane. Turn right onto Tubbs Lane and in half a mile you see the entrance to the **Old Faithful Geyser** on the left. Old Faithful, one of only three such regularly erupting geysers in the world, erupts at intervals of every 50 minutes with a spume of about 4,000 gallons of water reaching more than 60 feet into the air. This is certainly an interesting phenomenon, although the staging is a bit honky-tonk.

Leaving Calistoga, take the Petrified Forest Road west in the direction of Santa Rosa, forsaking the Napa Valley for the neighboring Sonoma Wine Valley. The road climbs and winds a scenic 10 miles through forest and past pastures where cattle graze next to neighboring vineyards and orchards of apples and almonds. You may wish to stop at the rather commercial **California Petrified Forest**, a grove of redwoods that was petrified by ash from the volcanic eruption of Mount Saint Helena over 6,000,000 years ago. It is this same ash that is responsible for fertile wine-valley soil.

On the residential outskirts of Santa Rosa the Petrified Forest Road merges with

Highway 12 and then turns south (left) toward Sonoma. This highway travels down the center of Sonoma Valley, often referred to as the "Valley of the Moon" after Jack London's famous novel of the same name. London fell in love with Sonoma Valley's magnificent landscape—a wondrous mix of high hills, oak-covered knolls, open pastures, forests of oaks, madrones, fir, and redwood trees, grassy fields, and streams. The author chose the valley as his home—"a quiet place in the country to write and loaf in and get out of nature that something which we all need, only most of us don't know it."

Your first destination in this lovely valley, **Château Saint Jean**, lies about 7 miles south of Santa Rosa on the left, at 8555 Sonoma Highway 12. An extremely pretty road winds up through the vineyards to the strikingly beautiful winery and main house surrounded by lush lawns. With the exception of its mock tower, Château Saint Jean is Mediterranean French in its architecture, its red-tile roofs and arched entries stunning against a backdrop of green hills. The estate is dedicated exclusively to the production of premium wines, but as a visitor you will feel that the winery's chief concern is making visitors feel welcome by outlining a very comprehensive self-guided tour of the wine-making process. After the tour you cross the courtyard to the original "château" for tasting. Questions you have will be answered graciously. For additional information call (707) 833-4134.

Your next stop, **Kenwood Vineyards**, is just beyond Château Saint Jean, but completely different in character. Kenwood occupies an attractive complex of old wooden barns where wine is produced, stored, and tasted. Mini-tours of this small winery are offered by request, and based on the availability of the winemaker, daily between 10 am and 3:00 pm. (707) 833-5891. Weekdays are recommended over weekends.

The next winery you come to (just beyond Kenwood Winery on the same side of the road) is the **Kunde Winery** at 10155 Sonoma Highway 12. The founder, Louis Kunde, settled in the Sonoma Valley in 1904. The present-day winery, which re-creates an 1883 barn that previously stood on the same site, houses a reception area with wine tasting and a small shop where you can find attractive, wine-oriented gift items. In addition to wine tasting, tours are available of the caves which feature half a mile of interconnecting tunnels. Caves are open to the public, Fridays, Saturdays, and Sundays, on the hour, between 11 am and 4 pm. For further information call (707) 833-5501.

As you travel south on Highway 12, take a turnoff to the right marked to Glen Ellen. Travel this main road through Glen Ellen, following signs for Jack London State Park. Before you reach the park, stop to visit the Benziger Winery, which will be on the right.

The **Benziger Winery** is family run in the truest sense of the word—signs warn to watch for children at play. From babies to Goober, the family dog and "official reception committee," everyone at Benziger is warm and friendly. The Benziger family were wine

Trolley at Benziger Winery

importers in New York before moving to the Sonoma Valley to produce their own wines. If it's close to lunch time, take advantage of picnic tables set under redwood trees. The tasting room is quite a hike from the parking lot, so if someone in your party has difficulty with a hilly driveway, continue on to the handicapped area, or circle round to drop them off in the front. The tour here is truly a treat: guests climb onto a trolley, pulled by a cheerful bright red tractor, for a tour of the vineyards. The day we took the tour, Goober climbed aboard and sat on the bench next to the other guests, happily wagging his tail as the tram moved through the fields. Stops are made en route where a guide explains the production of wines. Reservations are not taken, and space on the trolley is limited, so arrive early. Weather permitting, the tours are at 12:30 pm, 2 pm, and 3:30 pm. After the tour, visit the gift shop and stay to taste some of the excellent wines. For further information call (707) 935-3000 or (800) 989-8890.

Continue on to **Jack London State Park** where Jack London is buried. This is a lovely wooded park, established as a tribute to the famous author who has had such an impact on the Sonoma Valley. This strikingly handsome man lived a life of rugged adventure and wrote passionately about life's struggles and how to survive them with integrity. In the 16 years prior to his death at age 40, he wrote 50 novels which were immensely popular and are today considered classics. Two of his more renowned novels are *Call of the Wild* and *Sea Wolf*. This park offers a fitting tribute to Jack London, a courageous, dynamic man, full of life and concern for others. Open all year, admission is $6 per vehicle—for information call (707) 938-5216.

In the park you can visit the ruins of Wolf House (London's dream house which mysteriously burned to the ground the night of its completion), Beauty Cottage (the cottage where London wrote much of his later work), and the House of Happy Walls (the home that Charmian London built after her husband's death). The House of Happy Walls is now an interesting museum that depicts London's life through numerous photographs, writings, and furnishings that belonged to the author. From the museum, paths lead to the other homes and the grave site. From the park return to Arnold Drive and travel south (past the Sonoma State Home) to Madrone where you turn left, crossing over to Highway 12 which takes you into Sonoma. Note: If you're hungry, just a short detour north of Madrone on Highway 12 is the wonderful Garden Court Café and Bakery, great for breakfast, lunch, or gourmet picnics-to-go. (707) 935-1565, open 7 am to 2 pm.

Sonoma is a gem of a town. By simply exploring the boundaries of its main square you will glimpse some of California's most important periods in history. (A small admission price is charged to tour Sonoma's historic buildings.) On the square's northern edge sits the **Sonoma Barracks**, a two-story, adobe building that was the Mexican provincial headquarters for the Northern Frontier under the command of General Vallejo. The adjacent wood-frame **Toscano Hotel** has been restored and on weekends guides lead interesting tours through the rooms. The nearby **Mission San Francisco Solano de Sonoma**, the last Franciscan mission built in California, was restored in the early 1900s. If you visit during the week, you may see elementary-school children, dressed as missionaries with their simple cloaks and rope ties, experiencing history "hands on" as they work with crafts and tools from the days of the missionaries. In one hall of the mission is an unusually beautiful collection of watercolor paintings of many of California's missions. The long, low adobe building across the way, the Blue Wig Inn, originally built to house soldiers assigned to the mission, enjoyed a more colorful existence as a saloon and gambling room during the Gold Rush days.

In addition to the historic sites on Sonoma's plaza, there are numerous shops and boutiques to investigate. There are some wonderful specialty food stores where you can purchase picnic supplies. The **Sonoma Cheese Factory** on Spain Street is interesting to visit and easy to pop into between historic sites. The front of the shop has a deli and at the back, behind a glass partition, you can observe the making of cheese. On First Street East, you can purchase delicious bread at the **Sonoma French Bread Shop** and enjoy a tasty ice cream at the ice cream parlor.

Leaving the Square, go east on Napa Street for 2 miles to Old Winery Road where you turn left to the **Buena Vista Winery**, the region's oldest winery located at 18000 Old Winery Road. Nestled in a wooded glen, the old stone, ivy-covered buildings are very picturesque with arched caverns and stone walls. Picnic tables are set under the trees (it is hard to find a spot in the summer). Wine tasting is offered 10:30 am to 5:00 pm daily in the old press house, and a self-guided tour directs you to cellar building. At 2 pm daily there is a tour guide who gives you a presentation of the historical founding of the winery. For further information call (707) 938-1266.

General Vallejo, the military commander and director of colonization of the Northern Frontier (until the Bear Flag Revolution established California as a free and independent republic), lived nearby with his wife and their 12 children. Vallejo's Home, "**Lachryma Montis**" (translated to mean mountain tear, an adaptation of the Indian name given to a free-flowing spring that surrounds the property), is well signposted on the outskirts of town on Spain Street. In its day this lovely Victorian-style house was considered one of the most elegant and lavishly decorated homes in the area, and is still attractively furnished.

Mission San Francisco Solano de Sonoma

Wandering through the Wine Country

After you leave the Sonoma Valley, one more winery awaits you as you return to San Francisco. When Highway 12 dead-ends at Highway 116, turn right onto Highway 116 (signposted Petaluma) and at the intersection of Highway 121 turn left in the direction of San Francisco. A short drive brings you to the **Gloria Ferrer Champagne Caves**, a fitting grand finale for this wine country itinerary. The Ferrer family, who brought their expertise on Spanish sparkling wines to the Sonoma Valley in 1982, hails from Catalonia, Spain and, consequently, the handsome winery with its stucco walls and tiled roof resembles a small Catalonian village. A wide road sweeps up to the winery through the vineyards. The very informative tours last half an hour and are available daily between 11 am and 4 pm. They start from the tasting room, a spacious room whose windows look out over the vineyards and valley. Most of the narrative is given in a room decorated with wine-making instruments used a half a century ago in the Ferrers' winery in Spain. The riddling of the bottles to capture the sediment is explained, and then you go to the observation room to see the process of freezing then disgorging the sediment, corking, cleaning, and labeling the bottles of sparkling wine. The tour then descends into a maze of interconnected wine storage tunnels. It is awesome to stand next to towering heights of stacked bottles. The tour concludes back in the tasting room next to their beautiful Vista Terrace overlooking the Mayacamas mountains that separate the Napa and Sonoma Valleys. A fee is charged to sample the sparkling wine. For further information call (707) 996-7256.

From the Gloria Ferrer winery it is about an hour's drive back to San Francisco by continuing along Highway 121 to Highway 37 and onto Highway 101 which takes you over the Golden Gate Bridge into the city.

Yosemite, the Gold Country, & Lake Tahoe

Half Dome, Yosemite

This itinerary features two of California's most spectacular natural attractions, majestic Yosemite National Park and beautiful Lake Tahoe, and links them together by one of California's best kept secrets—the spirited, nostalgic, Gold Rush towns which string along the Sierra foothills. These colorful towns date back to 1848 when the cry went up that gold had been found at Sutter Creek, precipitating the rush to California by men eager to make their fortunes. Overnight, boom towns sprang up around every mining camp, with a cluster of similar-style saloons, restaurants, hotels, dance halls, and homes.

Gold Rush fever quickly cooled and many of the towns were left, quietly forgotten, until tourists rediscovered their charm. Today these benignly neglected towns have been spruced up and bustle with activity: antique shops, art galleries, nifty boutiques, attractive restaurants, and appealing inns are tucked into old Victorian houses lining sleepy streets. The highway that runs through the mother lode country is numbered 49 after the gold-seeking miners who were known as the Forty-Niners.

Recommended Pacing: We recommend a minimum of two nights in Yosemite and suggest that you try to stay at accommodation in the park (see page 76). Either before or after visiting Yosemite, you have a perfect opportunity to explore California's Gold Rush Country. Rather than backtracking, plan to progress through the region, spending at least one night in the south and at least one night in the north. From the northern region of the Gold Country it is a logical continuation on to Lake Tahoe. Many people enjoy Lake Tahoe as a resort and will spend at least a week here, basking on its sandy beaches in the summer and skiing down the snow-covered peaks that ring its waters in the winter. If you are visiting Lake Tahoe as a tourist, we recommend a two-night visit.

Weather Wise: Heavy snow is the norm at Tahoe and Yosemite during the winter, while most of the Gold Rush towns are beneath the snow line and experience heavy winter rains. During summer months the days are hot in Yosemite and Tahoe, and several degrees warmer in the Gold Country.

As you read through this itinerary, please be aware that each of the areas featured could well be a destination in itself. Yosemite and Lake Tahoe are especially popular resorts and an entire vacation could easily be dedicated to either one. If that is your desire, just extract from the itinerary the portion that suits your interests. However, the Gold Country is not as well known and makes a super link between Yosemite and Tahoe—or, for that matter, also a great destination in its own right.

Since Yosemite makes a most convenient first-night stop from either San Francisco or Los Angeles, driving directions are given from both so that you can tailor the trip to your own needs. Much of the first day of this itinerary is spent driving to Yosemite National Park, about a four- to five-hour drive from San Francisco or a six- to seven-hour drive from the Greater Los Angeles area. A brief description of what to see and do during your stay in San Francisco is included in *San Francisco to Los Angeles via the Coast*, while the list of attractions of the much larger, more sprawling Los Angeles are included in *Leisurely Loop of Southern California*.

Leave San Francisco east over the Bay Bridge, in the direction of Oakland. Once across the bridge, stay in the middle lane and follow signs for Highway 580, heading east, signposted Stockton. Stay on Highway 580 for about 48 miles until you come to Livermore where Highway 580 meets Highway 205 which you take, continuing east, following signs for Manteca. Near Manteca, take Highway 120 east, directly to the northern gate of Yosemite National Park. Total driving distance is about 200 miles.

Leave Los Angeles heading north on Highway 5 until you come to the junction of Highway 99 which you take north (signposted Bakersfield). Continue on Highway 99 to the north edge of Fresno where you take Highway 41 north, directly to the southern gate of Yosemite National Park. Total driving distance is about 300 miles.

The main attractions of the over 1,000 square miles of **Yosemite National Park** lie within the narrow 7-mile-long **Yosemite Valley** which is where you should try to stay if at all possible. A two- or three-night stay in the park is recommended. From hotels through tented cabins, all accommodations in Yosemite are controlled by the **Yosemite Concessions Services (YCS)** for information call (209) 372-0265. It is necessary year-round to make reservations well in advance by phoning (209) 252- 4848.

From the stately and very expensive **The Ahwahnee Hotel**, through lodges, cabins, tented camps, and regular campsites, Yosemite has accommodations to suit every pocketbook. If your taste in hotels runs to grand, stay at The Ahwahnee. **Yosemite Lodge** provides more moderately priced accommodations in both cabins and motel/hotel-type rooms. Still less expensive are the tented camps that provide canvas tents on wooden board floors (you do not need sleeping bags since beds and linens are provided). The budget choice is regular camping. But please remember—space is very limited in every category and reservations are essential.

While the attractions of staying in the valley cannot be denied, a more relaxed, serene, country atmosphere pervades the **Wawona Hotel**, located within the park, but about a 27-mile drive south of the valley on Highway 41. With its shaded verandahs overlooking broad rolling lawns, the hotel presents a welcoming picture. Bedrooms with private bathrooms are at a premium—most rooms use communal men's and women's bathrooms (sometimes situated quite a distance from your bedroom).

Yosemite Valley, an awe-inspiring monument to the forces of nature, is bounded by magnificent scraped granite formations—**Half Dome**, **El Capitan**, **Cathedral Rock**, **Clouds Rest**—beckoning rock climbers from around the world. And over the rocks, cascading to the valley far below, are numerous high waterfalls with descriptive names such as Bridalveil, Ribbon, Staircase, and Silver Strand. Below the giant walls of rock the crystal-clear River Merced wends its way through woodlands and meadows of flowers. Undeniably, this is one of the most beautiful valleys anywhere in the world.

A first stop should be the information center to obtain pamphlets, books, and schedules. The park service offers a remarkable number of guided walks, slide shows, and educational programs—look over the possibilities and select the ones that most appeal to you.

Once you are in the valley, park your car and restrict yourself to travel aboard the free shuttle buses as you can do most of your sightseeing by combining pleasant walks with shuttle-bus rides. Alternative modes of transportation are on horseback on guided trips and by bike (bicycles can be rented in the park). Because the valley is flat, it has miles of paths for biking—a very unstrenuous, efficient way of getting around.

Be warned that during the summer months Yosemite Valley is jammed with cars and people—spring and fall are much more civilized times to visit.

Within the park, but beyond the valley floor, are many areas of great natural beauty. Situated just inside the park's southern perimeter is the **Mariposa Grove** of giant sequoias. It was here that John Muir, the great naturalist who fathered the idea of the national park system, persuaded President Theodore Roosevelt to add the 250-acre grove of trees to the Yosemite park system. A tram winds through the grove of sequoias as the driver tells the stories of these giant trees—some of the largest in the world.

To the south of the valley Highway 41 climbs for about 10 miles (stop at the viewing point just before the tunnel) to the Glacier Point turnoff. It is a 15-mile drive to the spectacular **Glacier Point**—a vista point over 3,000 feet above the valley floor. From Glacier Point everything in the valley below takes on Lilliputian proportions: the ribbon-like River Merced, the forest, meadows, and waterfalls all dwarfed by huge granite cliffs. Beyond the valley a giant panorama of undulating granite presents itself. The ideal photographic time to visit is early in the morning or evening. Rangers at Glacier Point offer evening interpretive programs.

Leave Yosemite by the northern gate on Highway 120 to **Groveland**, a handsome old town shaded by pines. The nearby town of Big Oak Flat is little more than a couple of houses strung along the road. As Highway 120 drops steeply down 5 miles of twisting road to Highway 49, the shady pine forests of the mountains give way to rolling, oak-studded foothills, the typical scenery of the Gold Country.

Heading north on Highway 49, detour into **Chinese Camp**, home to over 5,000 Chinese miners in the 1850s and now almost a ghost town sleeping under a profusion of delicate Chinese Trees of Heaven.

The main street of **Jamestown** is off Highway 49 and therefore free of thoroughfare traffic. With its wooden boardwalks, balconies, and storefronts, Jamestown has managed to retain much of the feel of the Gold Rush days. Inviting shops, particularly the emporium, merit a browse, the western-style saloons are full of local color, and the **The National Hotel** as well as the **Jamestown Hotel** have been restored to a beauty such as the Gold Rush days never witnessed. Just above Main Street on Fifth Avenue is the **Railtown 1897 State Historic Park** where visitors can see old freight and passenger cars, steam trains, and the roundhouse. The park is open on weekends when tours of the roundhouse are conducted.

Leaving town, continue up the main street and cross Highway 49 onto a peaceful little road that takes you through the countryside to Columbia. Follow signs for Columbia or, wherever a junction is unmarked, continue straight. A 15-minute drive brings you to Parrot Ferry Road on the outskirts of the town.

In the 1850s **Columbia** was one of the largest towns in California, with many saloons, gaming halls, and stores. Today the main street is closed to car traffic and has been restored as a state park to reflect the dusty, raucous days when Columbia was the "gem of the southern mines." The renovated buildings of Main Street are like exhibits that make learning fun. Be sure to visit the Wells Fargo office, fire station, candy store, mining museum, and concession shops where costumed citizens sell goods appropriate to the period. You can enjoy a cold sarsaparilla at the saloon, munch candy rocks at the Candy Kitchen and pan for gold at the mining shack. It is great fun to climb aboard a stagecoach for a ride through the town or take a tour to the Hidden Treasure Mine.

City Hotel, Columbia

Both the **Fallon** and **City Hotel** have been restored (at vast expense) by the state of California to mirror the look of two of Columbia's hotels in Gold Rush days. The City Hotel on Main Street has a less ornate Victorian decor, reflecting the Columbia of the 1860s.

Parrot's Ferry Road leads north from Columbia, crosses the dam and continues through hilly countryside in the direction of Murphys. If you would like to try your hand at rappelling into the largest cavern in California, you have the opportunity at **Moaning Cavern**. (You can, of course, take the saner descent down a spiral staircase into a room capable of holding the Statue of Liberty.) The rappel is exciting, and with outfitting, instruction, and a boost of confidence, you descend through a small opening into the well-lit cavern—a most exhilarating experience.

From the caves a short drive brings you to Highway 4 where you turn east (right) for about a 20-mile drive to **Calaveras Big Trees State Park**, a 6,000-acre preserve of forest including two magnificent stands of sequoia trees. A 45-minute self-guided tour takes you through the North Grove and the nearby visitors' center provides information and history on these mammoth trees. If you have time and interest, you can visit the more distant South Grove of giant sequoias.

Leaving the park, retrace your route down Highway 4 and detour into **Murphys**, a sleepy Gold Rush town sheltered under locust and elm trees where several old buildings and an **Old Timers' Museum** reflect its Gold Rush heritage. Well signposted from the center of town is another cavern complex, **Mercer Caverns**, with rooms of stalactites, stalagmites, and other interesting limestone formations. You might also want to detour a beautiful winery, **Kautz Ironstone,** set on the hill outside Murphys. (Turn off Main Street up the road to the side of Murphy's Hotel, at the stop sign, turn right on Six Mile Road and travel 1 mile). The grounds are absolutely gorgeous in their landscaping and at the end of an extremely informative tour it is a memorable experience tasting wine while listening to the winery's magnificent organ from the old Alhambra Theater. Tours are offered daily at 11 am, 1 pm, and 3 pm, (no 11am tour offered in winter months) the winery is closed Christmas and Thanksgiving. Kautz Ironstone Winery, 1894 Six Mile Road, Murphys, CA 95247. (209) 728-1251.

At the junction of Highways 4 and 49 sits **Angels Camp**, a pleasant town with high sidewalks and wooden-fronted buildings. Today Angels Camp's fame results not from mining, but from the frog-jumping contests held every May. There is even a monument to a frog taking the place of honor on the main street along which almost all the shops sell items carrying a frog motif.

Leave Angels Camp traveling north on Highway 49 through San Andreas where nearly all evidence of Gold Rush days has been obliterated by modern shopping centers and commercial businesses. On the outskirts of the town Highway 49 makes a sharp turn to the east (right) which is signposted Jackson. A 7-mile drive brings you to **Mukulumne Hill** which in its heyday was one of the more raucous mining towns, though now it seems to be quietly fading away. Turn off Highway 49 and loop through town past the impressive (though genteelly shabby) Hotel Leger and turn left in front of the crumbling I.O.O.F building, then through the residential area and back onto the main road.

Jackson still supports roughly the same population as it had during the Gold Rush—consequently, modern shopping centers and sprawling suburbs are the order of the day. Turn right at the first stop sign in town and almost immediately left to the main street. Set above the old town in an impressive Victorian home is the **Amador County Museum**, 225 Church Street. The various rooms have rather eclectic exhibits from the Gold Rush era: for example, the kitchen is full of 19th-century cookware while a small upstairs bedroom displays Indian baskets. Set in an adjacent building is a scale working model of the North Star Stamp Mill which crushes tiny stones.

Retrace your route to where you turned off Highway 49 and turn left on Highway 88 signposted for Lake Tahoe and Pine Grove. Just outside Pine Grove turn left (signposted for your next two destinations, Indian Grinding Rock State Park and Volcano) and follow one of the gold country's prettiest backroads to **Chaw'se Indian Grinding Rock State Park**. A giant slab of limestone has over 1,000 grinding mortars worn into it by Indian women grinding acorn meal. A typical Miwok village has been built nearby with a ceremonial roundhouse and various tree-bark dwellings. The adjacent cultural center, built in the style of an Indian roundhouse, has interesting displays from several local Indian tribes.

Just a short drive takes you past the turnoff for Sutter Creek and into **Volcano**, one of the smallest (population 100), prettiest Gold Country towns which boasted the first lending library and theater group in the state. Now it is a tiny one-street town whose most impressive building is the three-storied, balconied **Saint George Hotel**. Several weathered building fronts give an impression of what the town looked like in more prosperous days. Three miles beyond the town lies **Daffodil Hill** where over 25,000 daffodil bulbs provide a colorful spring display.

Follow the narrow wooded ravine alongside Sutter Creek as it twists down to the town of the same name. **Sutter Creek** rivals Nevada City as the loveliest of the Gold Rush towns. Its main street is strung out along busy Highway 49 but somehow the noisy logging trucks, and commercial and car traffic do not detract from its beauty. False wooden store fronts support big balconies which hang over the high sidewalks of the town. Today many of the quaint wooden buildings are home to antique, craft, and gift shops.

Amador City and **Drytown**, the first two towns you encounter after leaving Sutter Creek as you head towards Placerville on Highway 49, have an old-world charm and are worth exploring. However, following them are a string of commercial towns that offer nothing of attraction to the tourist although the intervening countryside is still most attractive. Follow Highway 49 as it weaves through the commercial sprawl of **Placerville**, crosses Highway 50, and climbs out of town.

It is an 8-mile drive along Highway 49, through apple orchards and woodlands, to Coloma where the Gold Rush began. Or you can make it a 25-mile drive by taking a right turn east just after leaving Placerville onto Highway 193, a narrow road which twists down a thickly forested canyon to Chili Bar (a popular spot for rafters to launch) and then does a spectacular weaving climb out of the valley through Kelsey and into **Georgetown**. Stop to explore Georgetown's shaded streets and then pick up Marshall Road (turn left behind the gas station) which takes you down to Highway 49 where you turn south into Coloma.

Set on the banks of the American River, the scant remains of the boom town of **Coloma** are preserved as **Marshall Gold Discovery State Historic Park**. It all began in 1848 when James Marshall discovered gold at **Sutter's Sawmill**. The remaining historic buildings are scattered over a large area, each separated by expanses of green lawn and picnic places along the banks of the river. The residential part of town is a sleepy little cluster of attractive houses set back from the river—it is hard to believe that there was once a population of over 10,000 here. The museum shows a short film on gold discovery and provides information for a self-guided tour. A duplicate of Sutter's original sawmill, looking like a big shed, sits on the bank of the river. For a change of transportation, a number of companies offer one-day rafting trips on the American River from Coloma.

Auburn lies 20 miles farther north along Highway 49 which weaves through its suburbs, crosses Highway 80, and continues as a fast, wide road for approximately 24 miles into Grass Valley. An alternative, far more attractive, and just a few miles longer route, is to take Highway 80 north to the Colfax-Grass Valley exit and follow Highway 174 through pretty woodlands and orchards into Grass Valley. (The following sightseeing suggestion, Empire Mine State Park, is signposted on your left as you near town.)

Grass Valley has a booming economy and sprawls far beyond its historic boundary. Its old downtown buildings housing everyday stores attest to its prosperity. Save town explorations for adjacent Nevada City and concentrate on Grass Valley's **Empire Mine State Park** at the southern end of town. This hard-rock mine produced $100,000,000-

Nevada City

worth of gold before it closed. An exhibition depicts the mining methods used by miners who came here from the Cornish tin mines in England. Park personnel offer tours of the mine buildings, the most interesting of which is the opulent home of William Bourne, the mine's original owner.

The adjacent town of **Nevada City** is as handsomely quaint as Grass Valley is functional. The old mining stores and saloons have been cleverly converted into pleasant restaurants, antique stores, and the like. It is a most attractive town for wandering around. Many settlers came here from the east bringing with them the deciduous trees of their home states, so Nevada City is one of the few places in California that has the glorious fall foliage.

As a conclusion to your Gold Country explorations, take a 45-mile round trip to **Malakoff Diggins** where high-powered jets of water were blasted at a mountainside to extract gold. The method was very successful, but it clogged waterways for miles and left a lunar landscape where there had once been a forested mountainside. This is a very pleasant summer evening trip, but rather than run the risk of returning down narrow country roads in the dark, make the loop as you leave Nevada City for Lake Tahoe. The route is quite well signposted, but it gives you reassurance to have in hand the map from Nevada City Chamber of Commerce. (530) 265-2692. Leave Nevada City going north on Highway 49, following it through wooded countryside for 11 miles to the marker directing you right to Malakoff Diggins (signposted Tyler Foote Crossing Road). The narrow paved road leads you through the forest and, just as you are beginning to wonder quite where you are going, a signpost directs you right down a dirt road into **North Bloomfield**, a town of white-painted houses and buildings set behind picket fences under forest shade. (The town is being restored by the park service and the museum/ranger station is a useful informational stop.) The road through town leads to the diggins proper, a vast lunar landscape of awesome scars. If the weather is inclement, turn back at this point and return to Nevada City by way of the paved highway. Otherwise, continue along the well-maintained dirt road (forking left and downhill at junctions) which leads you down through some lovely scenery to a narrow wood-and-metal bridge spanning a rocky canyon of the South Yuba River where you pick up the paved road that brings you back to Highway 49 on the outskirts of Nevada City.

Leave Nevada City on Highway 20 east, a freeway which soon becomes a two-lane highway passing through forests and along a high ridge giving vistas of the Sierras. As Highway 20 ends, take Highway 80 towards Truckee, a fast freeway which climbs into the Sierra mountains through ever-more-dramatic rugged scenery.

The freeway climbs over **Donner Pass** and by **Donner Lake**, both named in honor of the group of settlers led by George Donner who in 1846 became snowbound while trying to cross the Sierra Nevada in late fall. Harsh conditions and lack of food took many lives and resulted in the survivors resorting to cannibalism.

Take Highway 89, the Tahoe City exit, and follow it alongside the rushing **Truckee River** to **River Ranch**, an inn where in summertime it is great sport to sit on the patio and watch the river tumbling by.

Follow the Truckee River to its source, **Lake Tahoe**. Tucked in a high valley, Lake Tahoe is a vast, blue, icy-cold lake ringed by pine forests and backed by high mountains. The lake has about 70 miles of shoreline, a maximum depth of 1,645 feet, and a summer temperature of about 65 degrees. When people from the San Francisco Bay Area say they are "going to the mountains," Tahoe is usually where they're heading. While certain enclaves have their share of hot dog stands, McDonald's restaurants, and glitzy gambling casinos, there are many unspoilt areas where you can enjoy the exquisite beauty of the lake and its surrounding stunning scenery. For bikers and joggers, a marvelous, seemingly endless trail traces a path along the lakefront and down the Truckee River.

Tahoe City combines rustic, folksy shops, restaurants, and everyday stores with two quite interesting tourist attractions: Fanny Bridge and the Gatekeeper's Cabin. **Fanny Bridge** is very close: just turn right at the supermarket, and there it is. You will see immediately the derivation of "Fanny" when you see the tourists leaning over the railing to watch the trout gobble up the food tossed to them. On the same side of the bridge where the fish feed, outlet gates are opened and shut to control the level of the lake—the entire flow of water exiting from Lake Tahoe is regulated here as the water runs into the Truckee River. The other attraction of Tahoe City, the **Gatekeeper's Cabin**, sits on the bank of the Truckee. The rustic old cabin, once home to the man who controlled the river level, is now an attractive small museum operated by the local historical society.

Hugging the shoreline, Highway 89 opens up to ever-more-lovely vistas as the road travels south. Nine miles south of Tahoe City brings you to **Sugar Pine State Park** with its many miles of hiking trails, and camping and picnic sites. In summer you can tour the nicely furnished Ehrman Mansion, once the vast lakeside summer home of a wealthy San Francisco family.

You will know by the sheer beauty of your surroundings when you are at **Emerald Bay**. The road sits hundreds of feet above a sparkling, blue-green bay and miles of Lake Tahoe stretch beyond its entrance. Center stage is a small wooded island crowned by a stone tea house. A 1½-mile trail winds down to the lake—it seems a lot farther walking up—and in summer you can tour **Vikingsholm**, the 38-room lakeside mansion built in 1929 and patterned after a 9th-century Norse fortress. It is the finest example of Scandinavian architecture in America and is filled with Norwegian furniture and weavings.

Just below Emerald Bay a trail leads from the parking lot up a ¼-mile steep trail to a bridge above the cascading cataract of **Eagle Falls** which offers fantastic views of Lake Tahoe. A mile farther up the trail is **Eagle Lake**, in an isolated, picture-perfect setting.

A memorable outing from Tahoe is a day trip to Nevada's silver towns, Virginia City and Carson City. Leaving Tahoe City, follow the northernmost shore of the lake across the Nevada state line and take Highway 431 from Incline Village over Mount Rose to the stop light at Highway 395. Cross the highway and go straight ahead up the winding Geiger Grade, Highway 341, to **Virginia City**. Built over a honeycomb of silver mines, in its heyday Virginia City had a population of over 30,000. Its wooden sidewalks, colorful saloons (you must visit the Bucket of Blood Saloon), and false-front buildings with their broad balconies make it a town straight out of a John Wayne movie. The stores sell everything from homemade candy to western boots and several have been reconstructed as museums. You can walk up to the old cemetery, take a steam-train ride, or tour a mine.

Leaving town, travel on through Gold Hill and Silver Hill to Highway 50 where you turn south for the 7-mile drive to **Carson City**, the state capital. The town itself has little of interest except for the **Nevada State Museum**, just across the street from the Nugget Casino on the main road. The highlight of the museum is the re-created silver mine in the basement. You walk along rail car lines in semi-darkness, past exhibits of miners at work and mine machinery—a lot safer than going down a working mine.

To return to Tahoe go south on Highway 395, the main street of town, to Highway 50 west. Turn right and when you come to Lake Tahoe turn right, following the lake to Tahoe City.

Leaving Lake Tahoe it is a fast four- to five-hour freeway drive, via Highway 80, to the San Francisco Bay area. If you are going to Los Angeles, take Highway 80 to Sacramento and Highway 5 south to Los Angeles—a fast eight- to nine-hour drive.

San Francisco to the Oregon Border and a Bit Beyond

San Francisco to the Oregon Border —and a Bit Beyond

Mendocino

If your heart leaps with joy at the sight of long stretches of deserted beaches, rugged cliffs embraced by wind-bent trees, sheep quietly grazing near crashing surf, and groves of redwoods towering above carpets of dainty ferns, then this itinerary will suit you to perfection. Nowhere else in California can you travel surrounded by so much natural splendor. Less than an hour after crossing the Golden Gate Bridge, civilization is left far behind you and your adventure into some of California's most beautiful scenery begins. The first part of this route includes many well-loved attractions: Muir Woods, the Russian River, Sonoma County wineries, the Mendocino Coast, and the Avenue of the Giant Redwoods. Then the route becomes less "touristy" as it reaches the Victorian jewel of Ferndale, the bustling town of Eureka, and the coastal hamlet of Trinidad, and concludes amongst the giant coastal redwoods of Redwood National Park.

Recommended Pacing: You can cover the distance between San Francisco and Mendocino in a day. It is approximately a four-hour drive if you are traveling inland on Highway 101 and then cutting west over at Cloverdale on Highway 128 back to the coast and Highway 1 just south of Mendocino. It is approximately a six-hour journey if you follow Highway 1 as it hugs the coast all the way north. However, if time allows, follow our routing and spend a night just north of San Francisco near Point Reyes National Seashore (more if you want to take advantage of the hiking and biking trails), and a night or two in the Healdsburg/Russian River area before arriving in Mendocino. Allow two nights for the Mendocino area and two nights for the Eureka area before continuing up the coast to Oregon.

Weather Wise: The weather along California's northern coast is unpredictable: beautiful warm summer days suddenly become overcast when the fog rolls in (July and August). The prettiest months are usually June, September, and October. Rain falls during the winter and spring, while fall enjoys beautiful crisp clear days.

San Francisco, a city of unsurpassed beauty, is a favorite destination of tourists and it is no wonder: the city is dazzling in the sunlight, yet equally enchanting when wrapped in fog. The setting is spectacular: a cluster of hills on the tip of a peninsula. San Francisco is very walkable and if you tire, a cable car, bus, or taxi is always close at hand. Enough sightseeing suggestions to occupy several days begin on page 16.

Avoiding commuter hours and congestion, leave San Francisco on the **Golden Gate Bridge** following Highway 101 north. After you cross this famous bridge pull into the vista point for a panoramic view of this most lovely city. For another spectacular detour, take the very first exit after the viewing area, Alexander Avenue, turn left back under the freeway, and continue as if you are heading back onto the Golden Gate Bridge, but, instead, take a quick right to the **Marin Headlands**. Some of the city's most spectacular skylines are photographed from the vantage point of these windswept and rugged headlands looking back at the city through the span of the Golden Gate. The road continues through the park and eventually winds back to Highway 101. Information and maps are available at the visitors' center located in the old Fort Barry Chapel. Signs in the park direct you to the center which is open daily, 9:30 am–4:30 pm. (415) 331-1540. Not to be missed is the **Marine Mammal Center**, where injured seals and other marine animals are nursed back to health by a multitude of volunteers. (415) 289-7325.

After returning to Highway 101, continue on to the Mill Valley exit. Circle under the freeway and follow signs for Highway 1 north. As the two-lane road leaves the town behind and winds up through the trees, watch closely for a sharp right turn to **Muir Woods**. The road takes you high above open fields and down a steep ravine to the Muir Woods entrance and car park. A park volunteer gives out a map and information and there is no charge for admission to the park. Near the park entrance a cross section of a trunk of one of the stately giant coastal redwoods gives you an appreciation of the age of these great trees. Notations relate the tree's growth rings to significant historical occurrences during the tree's lifetime: 1066—the Battle of Hastings, 1215—the Magna Carta, 1492—the discovery of America, 1776—the Declaration of Independence. But this tree was only a baby—some date back over 2,000 years. Your brochure guides you on the walk beneath the redwoods or you can take a guided tour with one of the rangers. Allow about an hour for the park, longer if you take a long walk or just sit on one of the benches to soak in the beauty.

Leaving the park, continue west to the coastal road Highway 1. Turn left and then, almost immediately, right. There is a small sign marked **Muir Beach**, but it is easy to miss. Just before you come to the beach you arrive at the **Pelican Inn**, a charming re-creation of an English pub that fortunately also offers lodging. The adjacent Muir Beach is a small half-moon beach bound at each end by large rock formations.

Return to Highway 1 and head north along a challenging, winding section of this beautiful coastal road. The road descends to the small town of **Stinson Beach** where by entering the state park you can gain access to a fabulous stretch of wide white sand, bordered on one side by the sea and on the other by grassy dunes. This is a perfect spot to stretch and enjoy a walk along the beach.

Leaving Stinson Beach, the road curves inland bordering **Bolinas Lagoon**, a paradise for birds, and then leaves the water and continues north for about 10 miles to the town of Olema. At Olema you leave Highway 1 and take the road marked to Inverness, just a short drive away.

If the weather is fine, allow time to explore **Point Reyes National Seashore**, a spectacular wilderness area stretching along the sea. If you happen to be in the area on a weekend, in addition to the free Ranger programs, call ahead, (415) 663-1200, to inquire about special field trips (such as tidepool studies, bird watching, and sights and sounds of nature) that are offered for a fee. The Ranger Station, located in a handsome redwood building at the entrance to the park, has maps, leaflets, books, a museum, and a movie theater where a presentation gives interesting information on the park. Be sure to stop here before your explorations to obtain a map and study what you want to see and do. A short stroll away from the ranger station is the "earthquake trail" where markers indicate changes brought about by the 1906 earthquake. Also within walking distance is the **Morgan Ranch** where Morgan horses are raised and trained for the park system. If the weather is clear, a drive out to **Point Reyes Lighthouse** is a highlight that should not be missed. As you drive for 45 minutes across windswept fields and through dairy farms to the lighthouse you

Point Reyes Lighthouse

San Francisco to the Oregon Border—and a Bit Beyond

realize how large the park really is. When you arrive, it is a ten-minute walk from the parking area to the viewing area. From there, steps lead down to the lighthouse. Be prepared: it is like walking down a 30-story building and once down, you have to come back up! In late fall and spring it is a perfect place from which to watch for migrating gray whales.

After a visit to the lighthouse, look on your map for **Drakes Bay**, one of the many beaches along this rugged strip of coast, and named for the explorer seeking lands for Queen Elizabeth I of England. He is purported to have sailed into the bay on the *Golden Hinde*, and christened it Nova Albion, meaning New England. If you are hungry, there is a café at Drakes Bay where you can have a bite to eat. Another interesting stop is at the **Johnson Oyster Company** on Sir Francis Drake Boulevard—a sign directs you to it on the left on the drive toward Point Reyes Lighthouse. Stop to see the demonstration of how oysters are cultivated in the bay for 18 months before being harvested.

If you choose to continue on to the northernmost point of the peninsula, travel Pierce Point Road which ends at the Tule Elk Range. Before 1860 thousands of tule elk roamed here but were hunted to extinction, then in 1978 two bulls and eight cows were successfully reintroduced and now the herd numbers about 250. Trails lead through this wilderness and research area to the Tomales Point Bluff or a shorter distance down to McClures Beach and Elephant Rock.

Retrace your route through the park to **Point Reyes Station** where the **Station House Café**, a delightful restaurant with delicious, imaginative food, beckons you into its dining room or tranquil, brick-paved, cottage-garden patio. Continue north on Highway 1 as the road winds through fields of pastureland and creameries and then loops back and follows for a while the northern rim of **Tomales Bay**, providing lovely vistas across the water to the wooded hills and the town of Inverness. About a 20-minute drive brings you to the village of Marshall, and soon after, the road heads inland through rolling ranch land bound by picket fences, passing the towns of **Tomales** (the **Tomales Bakery**, located in the old barbershop and open Thursday through Monday, is worth visiting—rivaling anything you would sample in France) and Valley Ford before turning west to Bodega Bay and the small town of Jenner. From here it is about a 15-minute drive to **Fort Ross**. "Ross" means "Russian" and this is the site where the Russians, in the early part of the 19th century, built a fort to protect their fishing and fur interests in California. After browsing through the museum, follow the footpath through the woods and enter the courtyard bounded by the weathered wooden buildings where the settlers lived and worked. Be sure not to miss the pretty Russian Orthodox chapel in the southeast corner of the compound. When you have finished roaming through the encampment, take the dramatic walk along the bluffs above the ocean. (707) 847-3286.

Leaving the fort, retrace your path to Jenner and follow Highway 116 inland along the banks of the **Russian River**. This is a tranquil stretch of road, passing through dense forests that open up conveniently to offer views of the very green water of the Russian River. (In winter after heavy rains the river can become a rushing torrent—no longer green and tranquil.) On weekends this road is very congested, but midweek and off season this is a very pretty drive. The largest resort along the river is **Guerneville** and just a few miles beyond the town you come to the **Korbel Winery**, a picturesque large building banked with flowers. The last guided tour usually leaves at 3 pm—to be safe, call to double check the schedule: (707) 887-2294. Korbel is famous for sparkling wines and the tour and video presentations are especially interesting. Three Korbel brothers came to this area from Bohemia to harvest the redwoods and ended up harvesting grapes. There is also a tour of the pretty rose garden nestled on the slope to the left of the winery.

Sampling champagne at Korbel will whet your appetite for additional wines from Sonoma County. Leaving the winery, continue for a short distance along River Road, watching for a left-hand turn for Westside Road (if you go over the bridge, you have gone too far). Westside Road winds its way to Healdsburg, past vineyards, meadows with cows grazing, pretty apple orchards, and several wineries, including **Hop Kiln**

Winery and the nearby **Rochioli Winery** which are open for tasting until 5 pm. The architecture at Hop Kiln is very interesting, with whimsical chimneys jutting into the sky. As the name implies, the winery was originally used for drying beer hops. For more information call Hop Kiln Winery, telephone (707) 433-6491 or for the Rochioli Winery, telephone (707) 433-2305. Nearby **Healdsburg** has an attractive main square lined with quaint shops and restaurants.

Leaving Healdsburg, follow Highway 101 north for the half-hour drive to Cloverdale where you take Highway 128 heading northwest toward the coast. At first the road twists slowly up and over a rather steep pass. After the summit, the way becomes more gentle as you head down into the beautiful **Anderson Valley**, well-known for its delicious wines. Whenever the hills spread away from the road, the gentle meadows are filled with vineyards. If time permits, stop at the **Navarro Winery**, housed in an attractive contemporary building where wine tasting is offered. For further information call (707) 895-3686. As the road leaves the sunny open fields of grapes, the sun almost disappears as you enter a majestic redwood forest, so dense that only slanting rays of light filter through the trees. Upon leaving the forest, Highway 128 soon merges with the coastal Highway 1 (about a 60-mile drive from where you left Highway 101). Here you join Highway 1 going north through Albion and Little River, and then on to Mendocino.

Mendocino is an absolute jewel: a New-England-style town built upon headlands that jut out to the ocean. It is not surprising that the town looks as if it were transported from the East Coast because its heritage goes back to adventurous fishermen who settled here from New England, and, upon arrival, built houses like those they had left behind. (In fact, the "New England" setting, seen in the popular television series *Murder She Wrote,* was filmed here.) Tucked into the many colorful wood-frame buildings are a wealth of art galleries, gift shops, inns and restaurants. We recommend a number of inns and a favorite restaurant is the **Café Beaujolais**, tel & fax: (707) 937-5614. (Ironically we met the owners, Margaret Fox and Christopher Kump while researching our Austrian guide and learned of their fabulous castle-hotel, the Schloss Matzen in Brixlegg.) Do not let your explorations stop at the quaint town, but venture out onto the barren, windswept headlands—a visit to Mendocino would not be complete without a walk along the bluffs. In late fall or spring there is an added bonus: spouts of water off the shoreline are an indication that a gray whale is present.

Mendocino makes a most convenient base for exploring the coast. However, if breathtaking views are more important to you than quaint shops and restaurants, then overnight instead 16 miles south of Mendocino in **Elk**, a tiny old lumber town hugging the bluffs along one of the most spectacularly beautiful stretches of the sensational Mendocino coastline. Elk has several places to stay that are described in detail in the inn section of this guide—each has its own personality, each has a magnificent ocean view. Note: If you choose to overnight in Elk instead of the town of Mendocino, when Highway 128 merges with Highway 1, go south to Elk instead of north to Mendocino.

Staying in this area, you could most successfully be entertained by doing absolutely nothing other than soaking in the natural rugged beauty of the coast. However, there are some sightseeing possibilities. Just north of the town of Mendocino you come to **Fort Bragg**. This is a sprawling town that, when compared to the quaintness of Mendocino, has little to offer architecturally except for an extremely colorful fishing harbor. At 18220 N. Highway One you find the 47 acres of the **Mendocino Coast Botanical Gardens**. The mild rainy winters and cool summers provide ideal growing conditions for the collections in the gardens which are sheltered by a native pine forest. The gardens include a fern-covered canyon, coastal bluffs, a rocky inter-tidal habitat, and wheelchair-accessible trails that connect everything together. There are lots of places to picnic including the sheltered Cliff House with its spectacular views of the ocean. Two electric carts are available for those with special needs. (707) 964-4352.

The most popular attraction in Fort Bragg is the **Skunk Railroad** which runs between Fort Bragg and Willits. During the summer months you can either take the all-day trip which makes the complete round trip to **Willits**, or choose a half-day trip leaving in the morning or the afternoon. The train follows the old logging route through the redwood forests. Frankly, you will have already seen lovelier glens of redwood trees than those you will view on the ride, but the outing is fun, especially if you are traveling with children. The train station is in the center of town just after you pass over the rail tracks. Call ahead for reservations. (707) 964-6371.

Leaving the Mendocino area, continue to follow the coast north and enjoy a treasury of memorable views: sometimes the bluffs drop into the sea, other times sand dunes almost hide the ocean and at one point the beach sweeps right up to the road. At Rockport Highway 1 turns inland and twists and turns its way through forests and over the coastal range on 20 miles of narrow winding road. Arriving at **Leggett** (just before the junction with Highway 101), look for a sign to your right indicating a small privately owned redwood park where you can drive through a hole in a redwood tree.

From Leggett continue north along Highway 101 signposted for Eureka. However, rather than rushing all the way up Highway 101, follow the old highway, called **The Avenue Of The Giants**, that weaves through the **Humboldt Redwoods State Park**. This is a 33-mile-long drive, but we suggest you select the most beautiful section by skipping the first part and joining the Avenue of the Giants at Myers Flat. As you exit at Myers Flat, the two-lane road passes a few stores and then glides into a spectacular glen of redwoods. A lovely section of the forest is at **Williams Grove**. Stop at the nearby park headquarters and obtain a map which directs you off the Avenue of the Giants to **Rockefeller Forest**, the oldest glen of redwoods left in the world—some date back over 2,000 years. The trees are labeled and a well-marked footpath guides you through the forest to the Big Tree, an astounding giant measuring 17 feet in diameter and soaring endlessly into the sky, and to the Flat Iron Tree (another biggie with a somewhat flattened-out trunk) located nearby in an especially serene grove of trees.

About ten minutes after rejoining Highway 101, exit to **Scotia**. Established in 1869, the entire town—homes, shops, school, hotel—is owned by the largest lumber company in the world. The picturesque little redwood homes are dominated by the **Pacific Lumber Company**. You will find the small shopping center worth visiting just for the sake of seeing the redwood building constructed from pillars made from whole tree trunks. Drive to the museum—an all-redwood building resembling a Grecian temple with redwood-tree (bark and all) pillars instead of marble. The museum displays photos, artifacts, and machinery used in the logging camps. It is here you obtain your redwood shingle giving directions for the self-guided mill tour. Pass in hand, you follow the "yellow brick road," a well-marked trail, highlighted with yellow arrows, which guides you throughout the factory. Your first stop is at the hydraulic de-barker where you watch through windows the bark stripped from the logs by high-pressure water which sweeps back and forth over each log like a broom. Bits of bark and sprays of water cover the windows while the entire building rumbles as the giant logs are stripped naked. The next stop is the saw mill where logs are pulled back and forth beneath a giant-sized rotary saw which slices them into large boards. Walking along the overhead ramp, you watch the entire process from the first touch of the saw until the various-sized boards are neatly wrapped and bound tightly with straps. The Pacific Lumber Company mill is closed on weekends and holidays. Passes are given out for tours Monday through Friday, 8:00–1:30 pm. It is best to check times in advance of your arrival by calling (707) 764-2222.

Ferndale

Returning to Highway 101, about a 10-mile drive brings you to the Ferndale exit. Founded in 1852, **Ferndale** is the westernmost town (more of a village than a town) in the continental United States. Its downtown with its gaily painted Victorian buildings has changed very little since the 1890s. **Main Street** is a gem, lined with delightful little galleries and stores—a favorite being the irresistible candy shop where you view, through the window, hand-dipping of delectable chocolates. Many visitors enjoy the **Repertory Theater** on Main Street where some excellent plays are produced. (707) 786-5483. Epitomizing the colorful character of the town is **The Gingerbread Mansion** and the historic bed and breakfast, **The Shaw House**. Stop at Ferndale's **Museum** to learn more about her past as you tour Victorian rooms and see displays of old dairy and smithying equipment. Open Tuesday through Saturday 11–4 pm and Sunday 1–4 pm. Shaw and 3rd Street. (707) 786-4466.

Centerville Beach is 5 miles west of Ferndale on Centerville Road (turn right on Ocean Avenue at the end of Ferndale). Here you have 9 miles of beaches backed by dairy farms to the north and steep cliffs to the south. Watch for harbor seals in the breakers and tundra swans which congregate in the Eel River bottoms north of Centerville Road from mid-November to February.

Leaving Ferndale, retrace your way to Highway 101 and continue north for the 10-mile drive to **Eureka**. The area surrounding the 101 is full of fast-food chains, gas stations, and commercial establishments, but a small portion of this large town, the **Old Town**, is worth a visit (G and D between 1st and 3rd). On the northwestern edge of this restored project lies the ornate **Carson Mansion** (2nd and M), the most photographed ornate Victorian mansion in northern California. Just a short stroll from the Carson Mansion lie the **Carter House Victorians**, a complex of three Victorian buildings offering accommodation and dining.

About 20 miles beyond Eureka exit the 101 for the coastal hamlet of **Trinidad**. Although the houses are now mostly of modern architecture, Trinidad Bay has an interesting history. It was discovered by the Portuguese in 1595, claimed by the Spaniards in 1775, flourished in the 1850s Gold Rush as a supply port for the miners, and was later kept on the map by logging. Now Trinidad is a sleepy little cluster of homes nestled on the bluffs overlooking a sheltered cove where an untouristy wharf stretches out into the bay. Next to the wharf is the **Seascape Restaurant** where you can dine on fish straight from the little fishing boats. Stroll the mile-long path along the headlands enjoying the views and in winter the crashing rollers.

Return almost to the 101 and turn left on Patrick's Point Drive as it winds through conifers often just out of view of the rocky coastline to **Patrick's Point State Park**. (707) 677-3570. The price of admission affords you the opportunity to stroll beside the crashing waves at Agate Beach (you may well find an agate) or enjoy the rocky vistas from the coastal trail which brings you to Wedding Rock and Patrick's Point. Also within the park is a re-created Yurok village which recalls the days when the Yurok Indians camped in this area.

From here, Highway 101 leaves the coast where the waves pound the shore and ventures inland past quiet lagoons (Big Lagoon, Stone Lagoon, and Freshwater Lagoon). At the end of Freshwater Lagoon you enter **Redwood National Park** and turn left for the **Redwood Information Center** set at the edge of the beach (1 mile south of Orick). Enjoy the exhibits, equip yourself with maps, and set off into the park which contains some of the world's tallest trees.

Passing through **Orick**, it seems that there are more small stores advertising every imaginable item made from redwood than there are houses. So if you've always craved taking an 8-foot redwood Indian home to Aunt Tilda, this is a perfect opportunity to stop and buy one.

Turn right onto Bald Hill Road and climb steeply into the trees to **Lady Bird Johnson Grove** where you follow a 1-mile walk which loops through the stillness of a coastal redwood forest with the trees towering high above you and the forest floor carpeted with ferns.

Return to the 101 north and continue for 1½ miles, turning left on Davison Road where a large herd of elk roam the pastures that lead to **Gold Bluffs Beach** (4 miles) where traces of gold were found during the Gold Rush and on to **Fern Canyon** (8 miles from 101) where you proceed along a steep narrow canyon walled with ferns and follow a short looping trail which criss crosses the creek.

Returning to the 101 as it continues north, cross the Klamath River and pass through the fishing resort of **Klamath** to reach **Crescent City**, the last town in California before the Oregon border. Much of the town's waterfront was destroyed in 1964 by a tidal wave resulting from an earthquake in Alaska. While this itinerary should officially end in Crescent City (since this book is about California), we just couldn't resist taking you across the border to sample some of the awesome beauty of Oregon. If you are traveling in the summer when you are more likely to see the sun, strongly consider this extension.

A few miles after leaving Crescent City, you cross the border into Oregon—there is nothing much to mark the transition into a new state. The first town of any size you come to is **Brookings**. Don't take the time to stop now for sightseeing, just continue north on the 101. As the highway snakes close to the coast, you glimpse views to your left of fantastic deserted beaches. You will see many signs designating roads with access to state beaches. If you have time, choose one of these roads for a quick, up-close view of the sea. However, our recommendation is to just sneak a peak of the beaches for the moment and return later as this itinerary details in order to fully enjoy them when given the luxury of a little more time. This stretch of coast offers some of the most majestic scenery in all of Oregon (for that matter, in the entire world). Continue on to your destination, **Gold Beach**, and get settled in your hotel.

Gold Beach is a small town positioned at the mouth of the **Rogue River**. During the Gold Rush era, gold was discovered in the sandy beach. A flood in 1861 washed the last vestiges of gold into the sea, but the name "Gold Beach" remained. After the gold was depleted, Peter Hume opened a salmon cannery, which became one of the largest on the coast and dominated the economy for many years. The "gold" today comes from tourism, and indeed there is a wealth of activities here for those who relish the joys of the out-of-doors. The steelhead and salmon fishing are superb and attract many fishing enthusiasts to the area. Also a great draw is the memorable adventure we describe further on—a jet-boat ride up the Rogue River.

We suggest two places to stay in Gold Beach, the **Tu Tu' Tun Lodge** (pronounced "too–toot'–tun") or the **Inn at Nesika Beach**. Neither is located right in town. Tu Tu' Tun Lodge is a deluxe small fishing retreat snuggled on the banks of the Rogue River, about 7 miles inland from the coast. The Inn at Nesika Beach is a bed and breakfast overlooking the sea, about 6 miles north of town. If you want to stay at the Tu Tu' Tun Lodge, plan well in advance—the secret of this outstanding small inn has spread and space is always at a premium.

Using Gold Beach as your home base, plan to spend at least three nights here. If you are continuing up the coast to Washington, or looping back via Highway 5 to California, then "day 3" could be enjoyed as you continue onwards.

Day 1: Rogue River Jet-Boat Excursion

An absolute must is to take a trip by jet boat up the Rogue River. These excursions were originally strictly utilitarian—because the roads extended only a short distance inland, in olden days the boats were used for the delivery of mail. The round trip to the tiny hamlet of **Agness** used to take four days—by jet boat, you will arrive in just a few hours. **Rogue River Mail Boats**, a company that began the mail service in 1895, is still in operation and there are also several other companies offering jet-boat trips. The price and the excursions offered are almost identical, but because of the wider selection of departure times, we suggest **Jerry's Rogue Jet Trips**. You can call and make a reservation in advance and charge it to your credit card, (800) 451-3645. There are three choices for tours: a 64-mile round trip to Agness (six hours including a two-hour lunch or dinner break in Agness, $30 adult/$12 child), an 80-mile round trip to the lower rapids (six hours including a two-hour lunch break in Agness, $45 adult/$20 child), and a 104-mile round trip that travels far into the wilderness up a series of rapids (eight hours including lunch or dinner break, $75 adult/$35 child). By all means take the 104-mile excursion. After coming all this way, you certainly will want to experience this adventure to the fullest. The trips run from May through October with the greatest choices of departure times from July to Labor Day. Because the weather is more likely to be accommodating, we recommend planning your holiday during the summer season.

For the 104-mile excursion, there are two departures, the first at 8:30 am and the second at 12 noon. If you are staying at the Inn at Nesika Beach, choose the noon departure (available only from July to Labor Day). This allows you ample time for a leisurely breakfast before driving to the pier.

Jerry's Rogue Jet Trips depart from a well-marked dock located on the south side of the bridge that crosses the Rogue. If you are staying at the Tu Tu' Tun Lodge, you can take the early departure because the boat can pick you up at the dock in front of the hotel. You will need to advise the person who takes your reservation that you want to be picked up at the lodge and he or she will discuss with you what time to be ready. You will miss the first bit of the journey, but the convenience of just climbing on board in front of your hotel is worth the loss of time on the boat. Also advise the receptionist at the Tu Tu' Tun Lodge of your boat reservation so that he or she can reconfirm it for you. For those joining the boat in Gold Beach, Jerry's has a reception office by the dock where you can borrow a windbreaker for the journey. The first portion of the trip takes place in the estuary where it is often very chilly, with fog and cold winds, but there are blankets on board which you can wrap around you to counter the elements. As you head inland, the weather warms up considerably—sometimes it can even be very hot. Best advice is to take layers of clothing that can be peeled off as needed.

All of the guides are extremely experienced, eager to share their in-depth knowledge of the wilderness area, and, as an added bonus, the escorts are friendly and lots of fun. If you luck out, you might have Tim as your boatman. He and his adorable golden retriever, Puppy, make marvelous escorts. When not sitting in someone's lap, Puppy bounds from one side of the boat to the other, serious about his self-imposed responsibility to spot wildlife. Tim, on the other hand, is so full of funny stories that your sides will hurt from laughing.

If you have children, they will love this trip. Disneyland pales in the reality of this awesome ride. The boats first meander up the wide estuary where fishermen abound then the river narrows into a ribbon of deep green. When you reach Agness, you change to a smaller boat to more easily navigate the narrow gorges and many rapids.

Amazingly, the jet boats can navigate in about 8 inches of water, which makes this adventure up the Rogue so unforgettable. During your journey, the boat climbs 350 feet. From Agness on, you go through some narrow gorges and encounter a series of rapids, many around hairpin curves, which at first glance look impossible to navigate. However, with what seems like lightning speed, the boats successfully climb the shallow rocky rapids and when the going gets quiet, the guides spin the boats in a circle, splashing water on the laughing children on board.

The turn-around point for the trip is at Paradise Lodge where guests get off to enjoy a simple, hearty meal. There is no access except by boat, so this is a rustic retreat. If you so desire, you can arrange in advance when you book the excursion to spend the night here and return on the boat the next day. The guestrooms are small and plainly furnished, but appropriate for a lodge so far from civilization.

Your journey downstream is just as much fun. Along the way you will spot a profusion of birds, probably river otter, perhaps some deer, and, if you are lucky, even a bear.

Day 2: Exploring the Beaches South of Gold Beach

Because your time was too short to enjoy the rugged coastal area en route to Gold Beach, you should allow a day to retrace your steps and explore this astounding area at your leisure. Although the entire coast of Oregon is beautiful, most agree that this particular area between the California border and Gold Beach is especially outstanding—there seems to be a special splendor to these beaches because they are so untouched and so serene. Frequently you can have miles of beach to call your own. This particular section of the coast, sometimes called the Banana Belt, is also supposed to have the warmest weather and the most sun, but don't take the tourist board too seriously—the days are usually chilly, often foggy, and there are over 90 inches of rain a year, so dress appropriately. But in sun or fog, there is almost a mystical aura to walking these deserted, driftwood-strewn beaches with gigantic rocks thrusting from the sea just off shore.

Practically the entire Oregon coast seems to be a necklace of state parks but it is impossible to visit all the beaches. First make a stop at **Cape Sebastian**, just 6 miles south of Gold Beach. This park includes 1,104 acres of woodlands and open areas, with the highlight being a headland 700 feet above the sea offering a splendid vista of the coast both north and south. About 15 miles south of Gold Beach is the **Samuel H.**

Boardman State Park, a glorious 10-mile stretch of coastline which includes the Arch Rock Point, Natural Bridges Cove, House Rock, and Rainbow Rock.

The beaches are definitely the highlight here, but for those who love flowers, visit the area just south of Brookings where more than 75% of all the Easter lilies in the United States are grown. The season is from late June to early September. You can visit **Flora Pacifica**, 15447 Ocean Drive, Harbor, OR, tel: (541) 469-9741, to enjoy their garden and browse through their gift shop.

Another tidbit of information that fascinated us, was that during **World War II** the only bombing raid made by the Japanese occurred just east of Brookings near Mount Emily. The chamber of commerce can provide you with a tape and a self-guided tour that leads from the Botanical Gardens to the bomb site. We had never heard before that any bombs were dropped in the mainland United States during this war.

Day 3: Gold Beach North to Bandon

Day 3 could conveniently be made as a round-trip excursion from Gold Beach. The other option is to include the following sightseeing as you move on to your next destination. Whichever option you choose, be sure to save time to enjoy the coast north of Gold Beach. As you drive up Highway 101, you soon come to **Port Orford**, the first place settled in Oregon and the most western town in the continental USA. About 4 miles north of Port Orford, take the road signposted to **Cape Blanco State Park**. The road weaves 5 miles west to the coast where the remarkably photogenic **Cape Blanco Lighthouse** comes into view, perched above the sea. Dating back to 1870, this 300,000-candle-power beacon (which can be seen 21 miles out to sea) is Oregon's oldest still-functioning lighthouse. In the same park, in a small meadow above the winding Sixes River, is the **Hughes House**, a beautifully restored, wooden Victorian built by Jane and Patrick Hughes—pioneer dairy farmers who settled in this remote area in 1898. Both the lighthouse and Hughes House are open for tours from April to November, Thursday through Monday, 10 am to 4 pm.

Your next target is **Bandon**, a small town founded by Irish immigrants in the middle of the 19th century. Before swifter means of transportation, Bandon was a stop for the coastal steamers on the popular San Francisco to Seattle run. You must visit the **Bandon Beach State Park**, a glorious stretch of beach highlighted by soaring rock formations with such whimsical names as Elephant Rock and Garden of the Gods. There is an amazingly well-laid-out path on the headlands with signs along the way describing various sights and telling you about the wildlife. During high season, docents are frequently there to further enlighten you about the wonders of nature at your fingertips. As an added attraction, the beaches are especially popular since the ardent beachcomber can sometimes find semi-precious stones such as agates and jasper. In addition, Bandon has a tiny "Old Town," which although not exceptionally quaint is fun to visit. If driftwood interests you, stop at the **Bandon Driftwood Museum**, located in an old general store on 1st and Baltimore streets. (541) 347-3719.

Cranberries were introduced to Bandon in the late 1800s by settlers from Cape Cod. Today you see great cranberry bogs, both north and south of town. Dairy farming was also popular in pioneer days, and cheese is still an important commodity. Stop at the **Bandon Cheese Company** (on the left side of the highway as you leave town) to see how cheddar cheese is produced. (541) 347-2456.

This itinerary ends in Bandon. From here, you might be returning to your hub, Gold Beach. However, if you are continuing north on the 101 to Washington, do not miss the incredible **Oregon Dunes National Recreation Area**, which stretches for 40 miles from Reedsport to Florence. This is the most gigantic area of sand dunes in the world—the average height is 250 feet and sometimes the dunes extend 2½ miles inland. If you visit the sand dunes, stop first at the Oregon Dunes Recreation Area headquarters in Reedsport to see a movie on how the sand dunes are formed.

A highly recommended option for continuing this itinerary is to make a loop back to San Francisco, stopping en route in the charming town of **Ashland**. To do this, from Bandon take the 42 west to Highway 5 and head south to Ashland. In Ashland there is a rich selection of bed and breakfasts where you can settle for a few days to enjoy the excellent **Shakespeare Festival** (in addition to Shakespearean plays in the lovely outdoor Elizabethan theater, there are other more modern productions being performed simultaneously). The Shakespeare Festival runs from mid-June to early October. To reserve seats in advance, call (541) 482-4331. From Ashland, it is about a six-hour drive back to San Francisco.

Places to Stay

ALBION RIVER INN

Map: 1c

The location of the Albion River Inn is splendid, right on the bluff overlooking the handsome bay formed by the mouth of the River Albion as it flows into the ocean. Although this is a newly built inn, the architecture creates the ambiance of a New England village: softly hued clusters of cottages perch on the cliffs surrounded by a meadow where long grass waves in the wind. Gardens filled with brightly colored flowers line the walkways along the bluff and the quiet is broken only by the deep-throated call of the foghorn. Each of the bedrooms offers a sweeping view of the inlet where the fishing boats bob about in the ever-changing tides. All of the rooms are spacious, romantic, and very private and all have wood-burning fireplaces. The decor is most attractive and although not antique, reflects the hand of a professional decorator. The acclaimed Albion River Inn Restaurant is adjacent to the inn with picture windows overlooking the sea—it is a good idea to request dinner reservations in advance. A hearty breakfast is served including fresh fruits, juices, homemade breads, fritatas, French toast, and other specialties of the house. Coffee makers are set up in each room so guests can enjoy hot drinks whenever they want. *Directions*: From San Francisco drive north on Highway 101 to Cloverdale, west on Highway 128 to Highway 1, and north 3 miles to Albion. The Albion River Inn is on the northwest side of the Albion bridge.

ALBION RIVER INN
Innkeepers: Flurry Healy & Peter Wells
3790 N. Highway One
P.O. Box 100, Albion, CA 95410
Tel: (707) 937-1919 or (800) 479-7944
Fax: (707) 937-2604, E-mail: ari@mcn.org
20 Rooms, Double: $170–$260
Open all year, Credit cards: all major
Children accepted, No smoking, Wheelchair friendly
www.karenbrown.com/california/albionriverinn.html

AMADOR CITY — IMPERIAL HOTEL — Map: 4b

Amador City with its quaint old-west style houses was a bustle of activity during the Gold Rush days. Now it's a peaceful place (except for the logging trucks which rumble through town periodically), with its old wooden stores full of antique and craft shops and the Imperial Hotel, looking as though it belongs in a cowboy movie. There is immediate charm as soon as you walk into this renovated western hotel where you wouldn't be surprised to see prospectors leaning at the bar. Beyond the bar lies a spacious, high-ceilinged dining room, its red-brick walls hung with fanciful Victorian art. Dining is casual and the menu is short: usually three appetizers, seven entrees, five or six desserts. Upstairs, the six bedrooms are a delight—nothing fancy or frilly, but each well thought-out and accompanied by a small, sparkling bathroom with tub or shower and heated towel bar. Room 6, decorated warmly in tans and navy, is a real winner with an elaborate art-deco bed. The whimsical hand-painted headboard in room 5 is echoed in the paintings of clothes on the closet in room 3. Rooms 1 and 2 share the large balcony at the front of the hotel. There are two sets of adjoining rooms. Guests help themselves to early-morning coffee and tea before going in for breakfast. *Directions:* Amador City straddles Highway 49, 6 miles north of Jackson. The Imperial Hotel is on your right at the bend in the main street.

IMPERIAL HOTEL
Innkeepers: Bruce Sherrill & Dale Martin
14202 Highway 49, P.O. Box 195
Amador City, CA 95601
Tel: (800) 242-5594, Fax: (209) 267-9249
6 Rooms, Double: $75–$105
Open all year
Credit cards: all major
Children accepted, No Smoking
www.karenbrown.com/california/imperialhotel.html

APTOS BAYVIEW HOTEL Map: 5a

It was wonderful to find that the grand Bayview Hotel, built in 1878, has been attractively refurbished and once again offers comfortable and reasonable accommodation in the seaside village of Aptos. This handsome white Victorian's first floor is now leased and accommodates an attractive restaurant which can offer guests the convenience of dining or the luxury of room service. A lovely wood-banistered stairway winds up to the second and third floors and the 11 guestrooms of the hotel. The rooms are all attractive in their individual decor and vary in size which is reflected in the price: the Cascade room with its full-size bed tucked into a cubby of sunny yellow and rose colors, small yet inviting, is priced at $90; the Loma Prieta room, with both a full-size and a queen-size bed under high ceilings, dressed in colonial blue-and-white stripes, is very appealing and costs $125; rooms on the third floor such as the Seacliff with its king-size bed, large Roman tub, gas fireplace, and side windows are priced at $150. All the guestrooms have private baths and direct-dial phones. Television sets are included in some rooms and available by request in the others. The Bayview Hotel came under new ownership in 1998, but Gwen is still there to greet you with the same friendly smile and warm, attentive service. *Directions:* Located 10 miles south of Santa Cruz. Take the Seacliff Beach exit off Highway 1 east into town.

BAYVIEW HOTEL
Owners: Dan Floyd & Suzie Lankes
Innkeeper: Gwen Burkard
8041 Soquel Drive
Aptos, CA 95003
Tel: (831) 688-8654, Fax: (831) 688-5128
11 Rooms, Double: $90–$160
Open all year, Credit cards: all major
Children accepted, No smoking
www.karenbrown.com/california/bayviewhotel.html

APTOS   MANGELS HOUSE   Map: 5a

Aptos, two hours south of San Francisco, is best known as a beach resort. Most tourists never realize that tucked into the coastal hills are beautiful redwood glens and adjacent to a 10,000-acre forest of redwoods, creeks, and trails is Mangels House, an elegant, large, redwood home, built in the 1880s, painted white and wrapped in a two-tiered verandah. Once the holiday home of the wealthy Mangels family, whose fortune was in sugar beets, Mangels House belongs now to Jacqueline and Ron Fisher. You enter into a large living room dominated by a tall stone fireplace surrounded by two comfortable floral-patterned sofas and an easy chair. To the left is a formal dining room where a full breakfast is served each morning. The six delightful bedrooms at the top of a lovely staircase vary considerably in size, and each is individual in decor and pretty and fresh in its furnishings. One of the nicest aspects of Mangels House is that it is nestled in a woodland of 10,000 acres of creeks and hiking trails, yet is only a five-minute drive to the beach. *Directions:* From Santa Cruz, drive 6 miles south on Highway 1, taking the Seacliff Beach-Aptos exit over the freeway (away from the bay). Turn right at the traffic light to Soquel Drive. Just before the Aptos Station Shopping Center turn left onto Aptos Creek Road (also the entrance to the state park). The house is a half mile farther on your right.

MANGELS HOUSE
Owners: Jacqueline & Ron Fisher
Innkeeper: Jacqueline Fisher
570 Aptos Creek Road, Aptos, CA 95003
Mailing address:
P.O. Box 302, Aptos, CA 95001
Tel: (831) 688-7982
6 Rooms, Double: $120–$160
Closed four days at Christmas
Credit cards: all major
Children accepted over 10, No smoking
www.karenbrown.com/california/mangelshouse.html

Places to Stay

APTOS SEASCAPE RESORT–MONTEREY BAY Map: 5a

We don't often include resorts in our book, but the stunning location of the Seascape Resort prompted us to make an exception. This sprawling complex of seven buildings rests on the bluffs overlooking the Monterey Bay—you can't get much closer without being on the beach. On a stretch of residential street, the resort is quiet and low key. The beach is a short walk down a private paved path (or take the golf-cart shuttle if you prefer), and there are three pools with outdoor Jacuzzis. Guests can choose from studios, one-bedroom suites, or two-bedroom villas. Each suite is handsomely furnished in light colors and offers a private balcony with ocean view, fireplace, full kitchen, and television. Families are easily accommodated in the larger villas (averaging 1200 square feet). Children are quite welcome here: in fact, there is a "kids' club" during the summer months featuring planned activities for children between six and twelve years old. Sanderlings Restaurant, set on two levels of the main building and offering spectacular vistas, is named after the scurrying shorebirds on the beach. The resort makes a good home base for visiting the Monterey Bay Aquarium, taking children to the Santa Cruz Beach Boardwalk, and golfing on nearby courses. *Directions*: About 9 miles south of Santa Cruz, take the Larkin Valley Road exit off Highway 1 and go west on San Andreas Road. Turn right on Seascape Boulevard.

SEASCAPE RESORT–MONTEREY BAY
General Manager: Jim Maggio
One Seascape Resort Drive
Aptos, CA 95003
Tel: (800) 929-7727, Fax: (831) 685-0615
285 Suites & Villas, Double: $200–$390
Open all year
Credit cards: all major
Children accepted, No smoking

BALLARD — THE BALLARD INN — Map: 6c

The lovely Ballard Inn is located in the Santa Ynez Valley, a lush region of rolling hills planted with vineyards or sectioned off with white picket fences. Set just off the road, the Ballard was built as an inn, but carries the appearance of a gracious sprawling residence. White picket fences enclose its narrow front garden and a wide porch winds round it. The dining room, serving bountiful breakfasts (with two or three hot selections) and gourmet dinners (Wednesday through Sunday evenings), is located just off the entry to the right. To the left, another cozy room invites you to linger over a buffet of afternoon hors d'oeuvres, or venture on into the sitting room where large deep sofas steal you away for lazy conversations in front of an open fireplace. Guestrooms are located upstairs or in a neighboring wing just off the graveled driveway. Rooms are comfortable and attractively decorated, each with a small, functional private bathroom. Although, at first, rooms overlooking the front garden seem preferable to those overlooking the parking, select a room at the back for quiet as locals do head off to work and early-morning traffic breaks the silence of the country morning. A final note: If you like horses, ask about the neighboring miniature horse farm. We visited in spring when every mother was matched with a miniature foal—adorable. *Directions:* Take Route 246 off Highway 101 in the direction of Solvang. Travel north on Alamo Pintado Road and then east on Baseline Road.

THE BALLARD INN
Owners: Steve Hyslop & Larry Stone
Innkeeper: Kelly Robinson
2436 Baseline Avenue
Ballard, CA 93463
Tel: (805) 688-7770, Fax: (805) 688-9560
E-mail: innkeeper@ballardinn.com
15 Rooms, Double: $170–$250
Closed at Christmas, Credit cards: all major
Children accepted, No smoking, Wheelchair friendly
www.karenbrown.com/california/theballardinn.html

Places to Stay

BIG SUR — DEETJEN'S BIG SUR INN — Map: 5d

Deetjen's Big Sur Inn, established in the 1930s by "Grandpa" Deetjen from Norway, is a complex of weathered, wood-sided buildings, trimmed in white and topped by green roofs, tucked just off Highway 1 on a narrow road winding back beside a mountain stream into a redwood grove. Deetjen's is very rustic in decor and comfort; however, it exemplifies all that is Big Sur—the attitude, the lifestyle, a desire to enjoy a setting of beauty and nature, uncluttered by possessions. The first building in the complex houses the four intimate rooms that comprise the restaurant. Each candlelit room is set under low-beamed ceilings, warmed by a seemingly ever-burning fireplace and decorated with a wonderful collection of old chairs, benches, and tables dressed with linens. Accommodation is offered in buildings with individual names and characters. Old hand-hewn doors (without locks or keys) open to a medley of varying room configurations, all warmed by fireplaces, wood-burning stoves, or electric heaters. The doorway of Château Fiasco, like a tree house with vaulted ceilings and a private deck, is framed by a tree limb and accessed by climbing a rambling stairway. Downstairs in the same building the Franklin Room is cozy with dark-paneled walls and a fire-stove. If you have accommodation in a complex of four attached buildings, you will be lulled to sleep by the sound of the rushing stream below. *Directions*: Located on Highway 1 to the south side of Big Sur.

DEETJEN'S BIG SUR INN
Innkeeper: Laura Moran
Highway 1, Big Sur, CA 93920
Tel: (831) 667-2377
20 Rooms, 15 with private bathrooms
Double: $90–$180
Open all year, Credit cards: MC, VS
Children accepted over 12, No smoking
www.karenbrown.com/california/deetjensbigsurinn.html

BIG SUR   VENTANA   Map: 5d

Ventana, surrounded by 240 acres of meadows and forests, is nestled in Big Sur, a gorgeous stretch of coast where the hills plunge down to meet the crashing sea. In contrast to the coastline, there is nothing rugged about Ventana. It pretends to be somewhat rustic, but in reality, behind the weathered wooden façade of the cottages lies a most sophisticated, deluxe resort where guests are pampered and provided with every luxury. The Ventana has grown in stages, so each cluster of natural-wood buildings has its own patina of age. The exteriors are not outstanding, but, inside, each guestroom is spacious and decorator perfect. The decor varies (depending upon which section you are in) but each guestroom has the same country ambiance with natural-wood paneling, luxurious fabrics, and wicker chairs. Most rooms have a large terrace with a latticed wood screen—some have private hot tubs. All have a pretty view either of the hills and forest or to the sea on the far horizon. There are three lounges: one where wine and cheese are served in the afternoon and two where breakfast (a scrumptious buffet of home-baked pastries and fruit) is set out each morning. Guests can either take a tray to their room, or eat on one of the tables in the lounge or outside on the terrace. There are two 75-foot swimming pools with adjacent hot tubs (some areas are designated as clothing optional), a fitness center, and a gourmet restaurant. *Directions:* Thirty miles south of Carmel on the east side of Highway 1.

VENTANA
Director: Sal Abaunza
Highway 1, Big Sur, CA 93920
Tel: (800) 628-6500, Fax: (831) 667-2419
59 Rooms, Double: $215–$475 Suite: $375–$575
Open all year, Credit cards: all major
Children accepted over 15
No Smoking, Wheelchair friendly
www.karenbrown.com/california/ventana.html

CALISTOGA   CHÂTEAU DE VIE   Map: 2b

As you turn up the gravel drive to the Château de Vie, you'll glimpse this intimate bed and breakfast tucked away behind a white lattice fence in lush gardens of beautiful roses, exotic flowers, and mature fruit trees. The gray structure, built in 1981, resembles a French country château. Felipe Barragan and Peter Weatherman, the owners, bought the house, which was a bed and breakfast at the time, and have renovated and redecorated it. The decor is elegant, and the use of dark, rich wall colors adds an air of masculinity. The comfortable living room is done in attractive tones of olive and taupe, with linen window coverings and French doors leading to a deck with umbrella-covered tables and a small outdoor refrigerator for guests' use. After enjoying the coffee or tea that arrives outside your door in the morning, mosey down to the handsome dining room with forest-green walls and a large window seat or to the back deck for a gourmet breakfast of fresh-baked scones, breads and muffins, sausage, and vegetable quiche. The three guestrooms are on the snug side, but Felipe and Peter's appealing use of bold colors and textures has resulted in tastefully decorated rooms with queen-sized beds and windows offering garden views. All three rooms have private baths, though one is down the hall. Felipe and Peter plan to expand this charming bed and breakfast to five rooms in 1999. *Directions*: After Calistoga, Highway 29 becomes Highway 128. Take Highway 128 north. When you reach Tubbs Lane, go ¼ mile farther—Château de Vie is on your right.

CHÂTEAU DE VIE
Innkeepers: Felipe Barragan & Peter Weatherman
3250 Highway 128
Calistoga, CA 94515
Tel: (707) 942-6446, Fax: (707) 942-6456
E-mail: chateaudv@aol.com
3 Rooms, Double: $160–$185
Open all year
Credit cards: all major
Children innapropriate, No smoking

CALISTOGA — CHRISTOPHER'S INN   Map: 2b

Within strolling distance from the old-fashioned town of Calistoga with its quaint shops and cute restaurants is the prettily elegant Christopher's Inn which displays the remarkable talents of Christopher Layton, a San Francisco architect and landscape designer. Eight nondescript small homes have been transformed into one exceptionally charming inn. Decorated in simple country décor two new two-bedroom cottages have been added in a rear cottage in 1998. Suitable for families and groups, each has two queen beds and a trundle bed in the sitting room. The guestrooms in the original inn range from pocket size to comfortable and are decorated in a cozy English-country style with Laura Ashley linens, window and wall coverings. The recently completed nine suites are much larger and have a French-country feel. Each room has either a porch or private garden patio, and several offer the romance of a fireplace and Jacuzzi tub. Each morning a basket is delivered to your room with a bounty of delicious treats: fresh coffee, juice, croissants or Danish, fresh fruit with yogurt, or warm baked cobbler. Details such as the carefully tended landscape, fresh flowers, and antiques make this an appealing place to stay. *Directions*: Coming north on Highway 29, the inn is 500 yards past the John Deer tractor sales barn, on the right side of the road, before the blinking light at the intersection of Foothill Boulevard and Lincoln.

CHRISTOPHER'S INN
Innkeepers: Adele & Christopher Layton
1010 Foothill Boulevard
Calistoga, CA 94515
Tel: (707) 942-5755, Fax: (707) 942-6895
22 Rooms, Double: $140–$330
Open all year
Credit cards: all major
Children accepted, No smoking, Wheelchair friendly
www.karenbrown.com/california/christophersinn.html

CALISTOGA — COTTAGE GROVE INN — Map: 2b

In the 1970s Monica Bootcheck, Tom Stimpert, and Bob Beck shared a three-apartment houseboat in Sausalito. Their friendship endured and 20 years later, along with their spouses, they pooled their talents of architecture, contracting, interior design, and marketing and built the Cottage Grove Inn. The inn is a complex of 16 individual cottages tucked into a beautiful grove of century-old Siberian Elm trees. Although of new construction, the property reflects the nostalgic charm of yesteryear. From the outside, each of the sweet, doll-house-like cottages has a similar appearance—a clapboard exterior painted a warm dove gray, accented by deep-coral-colored shutters and crisp white trim. A romantic porch stretches across the front of each cottage with two white wicker rockers just begging you to relax with a good book. Inside, each cottage has its own personality, with a decor reflecting its own theme. Whatever the theme, each guestroom is tastefully decorated using fine fabrics, lovely linens, and high-quality furnishings. Another bonus: each has a wood-burning fireplace and an enormous bathroom featuring a wonderful, deep Jacuzzi tub big enough for two (and fluffy bathrobes). *Directions:* From Highway 29, turn east on Lincoln. Just before the road curves left as it leaves town, you will see the inn on your left.

COTTAGE GROVE INN
Innkeeper: Valerie Beck
1711 Lincoln Avenue
Calistoga, CA 94515
Tel: (707) 942-8400 or (800) 799-2284
Fax: (707) 942-2653
16 Cottages, Double: $195-$245
Open all year, Credit cards: all major
Children accepted over 12
No Smoking, Wheelchair friendly

CALISTOGA   MEADOWLARK COUNTRY INN   Map: 2b

Located at the northernmost end of the Napa Valley, Meadowlark Country Inn is buffered from noise by a long drive and 20 acres of grounds that contain a pasture grazed by magnificent sport horses and woodland walks winding beneath oak trees. The two-story home, originally built in 1886, is decorated with English antiques and comfortable contemporary furniture. Inside, light-wood floors contrast beautifully with country-pine antiques and handsome fabrics. The atmosphere of sophisticated elegance and the hospitality reflect Kurt Stevens' European background—he sets guests at ease and wants them to enjoy his inn as if it were their home in the country. The spacious living room with large French windows, country-French dining room, and large verandah are all for guests' use. Three lovely new guestrooms in a separate building are decorated in earth tones and have four-poster beds and private patios. There are four more basic guestrooms in the main house. Surrounded by a flagstone deck are a large clothes-optional swimming pool, hot tub, and sauna. Meadowlark's guest register reflects numerous repeat visitors. One guest, who had confused the inn with the super-deluxe Meadowood Resort, claims it was the "best mistake she ever made!" *Directions*: Take Foothill Boulevard north from Calistoga to Petrified Forest Road. The road is posted with signs to San Francisco and Santa Rosa. Meadowlark is on the left just a few hundred yards off Foothill Boulevard.

MEADOWLARK COUNTRY INN
Innkeeper: Kurt Stevens
601 Petrified Forest Road
Calistoga, CA 94515
Tel: (800) 942-5651, Fax: (707) 942-5023
7 Rooms, Double: $185–$195
Open all year
Credit cards: all major
Children accepted over 12, No smoking

Places to Stay

CALISTOGA — SCARLETT'S COUNTRY INN — Map: 2b

Although located on the Silverado Trail, one of the two main arteries through the Napa Valley, Scarlett's Country Inn, tucked in a pocket canyon, is blissfully hidden from the road. The inn consists of two buildings: the original turn-of-the century farmhouse with two suites, and behind it, a newer ranch house with dining room, kitchen, and one guestroom. Ask to stay in the original farmhouse which is charming, like a doll house with just two suites, each with its private entrance. The Gamay Suite has a bathroom on the first floor and upstairs a small parlor plus a bedroom tucked under the eaves. The Camellia Suite on the first floor is a real prize, with a living room with sofa bed, wood-burning fireplace, and a wet bar, plus a separate bedroom. Each room has a microwave and mini refrigerator. In the rear garden, is a beautiful swimming pool, tranquilly set amongst the trees. In addition there is an aviary with colorful finches and two plump hens (Blondie and Blackie). Although small, Scarlett's Country Inn offers many niceties often lacking in much fanciers hotels: daily fresh flowers in each of the rooms, turn-down service at night, and complimentary wine upon check-in. *Directions:* Located about mid-way between Calistoga and Saint Helena on the Silverado Trail. Watch carefully for the address number (3918) indicating a small lane leading east from the main road to the inn.

SCARLETT'S COUNTRY INN
Owner: Scarlett Dwyer
Innkeeper: Derek Dwyer
3918 Silverado Trail, North
Calistoga, CA 94515
Tel: (707) 942-6669, Fax: (707) 942-6669
E-mail: scarletts@aol.com
3 Rooms, Double: $115–$175
Open all year, Credit cards: none accepted
Children accepted, No smoking
www.karenbrown.com/california/scarlettscountryinn.html

Places to Stay

CALISTOGA   ZINFANDEL HOUSE   Map: 2b

For a homey, bed-and-breakfast atmosphere, Zinfandel House is just the place. From the moment you're greeted cheerily over the front deck railing of this brown, wood-sided, contemporary home by innkeepers Bette and George, a sense of warm hospitality pervades your stay. A wonderful view overlooking vineyards and mountains awaits from atop the deck, as the inn is perched high on the west side of the valley. Two of the bedrooms are cozily decorated and share a bath, though one of these is available with private bath on request. The largest room, with its own bath, shares the view with a reading room and comfortable living room. All three have goose-down pillows, comforters, and handmade quilts. The Starkes, long-time residents of the Napa Valley, offer their knowledge of the valley's food and wine. George is a wine columnist for local newspapers and is well known on the Napa Valley wine scene. They will gladly make dinner reservations at the many very good restaurants nearby. Their guest book is a delightful collection of comments and memories. *Directions:* Four miles north of Saint Helena on Highway 29, watch for Larkmead Lane on the right. About 200 yards past Larkmead Lane, slow down and look for a group of mailboxes: opposite these, you turn left up Summit Road, bear left around some old farm buildings, go slowly up three tenths of a mile from the highway to the inn's marked driveway on the left.

ZINFANDEL HOUSE
Innkeepers: Bette & George Starke
1253 Summit Drive
Calistoga, CA 94515
Tel: (707) 942-0733, Fax: (707) 942-4618
E-mail: zinhouse@pon.net
3 Rooms, 2 with private bathrooms
Double: $110–$135
Open all year, Credit cards: MC, VS
Inappropriate for children, No smoking
www.karenbrown.com/california/zinfandelhouse.html

Places to Stay

CAMBRIA   BLUE WHALE INN   Map: 6a

As an alternative to the bed and breakfasts near Cambria's shops and galleries, the Blue Whale Inn offers guests more privacy and the opportunity to stroll for miles along Moonstone Beach. The front room and parlor enjoy views across the road to the beach and expansive ocean through six large picture windows. It is here that guests are served a delicious breakfast, and wine, cheese, and cookies are set out in the afternoon. Stretching out behind the main building are the newly constructed guestrooms, each opening at an angle onto a border of front garden that buffers the rooms from the parallel parking. Country in their decor, the rooms are attractive in their light-pine furnishings, chintz and floral fabrics, and canopy beds. Each of the spacious ocean-view mini suites has a television, a telephone, a refrigerator, and a tiled modern bathroom. The innkeepers extend a warm welcome and offer gracious service. Motels and hotels line the beach frontage and without a doubt the Blue Whale Inn is the best of the bunch. *Directions:* Turn west off Highway 1 north at the exit sign for Moonstone Beach. Follow Moonstone Beach Drive past the hotels which line this coastal frontage to the Blue Whale Inn.

BLUE WHALE INN
Owners: Jan Crowther & Kate McGill
Innkeepers: Karleen & Bob Hathcock
6736 Moonstone Beach Drive
Cambria, CA 93428
Tel & Fax: (805) 927-4647
6 Rooms, Double: $155–$220
Open all year
Credit cards: MC, VS
Children accepted over 12, No smoking
www.karenbrown.com/california/bluewhaleinn.html

CAMBRIA   THE SQUIBB HOUSE   Map: 6a

This pretty little Victorian, freshly painted in a warm butter-cream and dressed with green trim, sits at the heart of the original downtown area of Cambria. A gate in the picket fence opens to a brick walkway leading through the garden to the small porch and entry of this lovely inn. Inside, the decor is refreshing, clean, light, and attractive, with whitewashed walls and the warm patina of natural pine floors. Named for the couple who inhabited the home for much of its century-plus history, the inn has photos and memorabilia of their lives proudly displayed throughout its rooms. The house has five simple and extremely tasteful guestrooms, all intimate in size, with modern and functional bathrooms. Downstairs at the back of the inn overlooking a wooded garden, the Garden Room, formerly the kitchen, enjoys its own private entrance and porch. At the front of the inn, the Parlor Room, once used as a school classroom, is now a pretty bedroom with a bay window and bird's-eye-maple furnishings. Upstairs, the Village Room, the Gothic Room, and Louise's Room are all attractive and enjoy the character added by the pitches and angles of the roof-line. *Directions:* From Highway 1 turn east on Burton Drive; at the stop sign turn left (still Burton) and wind down the hill, cross the bridge, and the house is on the left.

THE SQUIBB HOUSE
Owner: Bruce Black
Innkeeper: Martha Gibson
4063 Burton Drive
Cambria, CA 93428
Tel: (805) 927-9600, Fax: (805) 927-9606
5 Rooms, Double: $95–$140
Open all year, Credit cards: MC, VS
Inappropriate for children, No smoking
www.karenbrown.com/california/squibbhouse.html

Places to Stay

CAPITOLA — THE INN AT DEPOT HILL

Map: 5a

The Inn at Depot Hill, just two blocks up the hill from the beach and picturesque village of Capitola-by-the-Sea, dates back to 1901 when it was built as a Southern Pacific railroad station. Limited in terms of the size of the property, the grounds are minimal. Inside, the inn's imaginative decor reflects the theme of first-class train travel at the turn of-the century: the bedrooms are handsomely decorated and named after different parts of the world—as if a guest were taking a railway journey and stopping at different destinations. Suzie (whose grandfather was an architect for the Southern Pacific Railroad) has added many of her own caring touches such as real linen sheets, lacy pillowcases, and sumptuous feather beds. There is a wealth of other amenities: writing desks, tasteful cupboarded televisions and VCRs, fireplaces, bathrobes, hairdryers, luxurious marble bathrooms, some Jacuzzi tubs on private outdoor patios, and even mini-televisions in all of the bathrooms. An elegant breakfast is served each morning either in the dining room, the romantic walled garden, or your room. Complimentary early-evening wine and hors d'oeuvres and late-evening desserts and port are served from the dining-room buffet. Suzie and Dan are not always present as innkeepers, but oversee a managed staff. *Directions:* South on Highway 1 from Santa Cruz. Take the Park Avenue exit, turn right and go 1 mile. Turn left onto Monterey, then immediately left into the inn's driveway.

THE INN AT DEPOT HILL
Owners: Suzie Lankes & Dan Floyd
250 Monterey Avenue
Capitola, CA 95010
Tel: (831) 462-3376, (800) 572-2632
Fax: (831) 462-3697
E-mail: lodging@innatdepothill.com
12 Rooms, Double: $190–$250
Open all year, Credit cards: all major
Children accepted, No smoking, Wheelchair friendly
www.karenbrown.com/california/innatdepothill.html

CARMEL — MISSION RANCH — Map: 5c

The Mission Ranch, which in days long past was a working farm, was bought and renovated with great sensitively to its heritage by Clint Eastwood. The inn is located on 22 acres, just a pleasant walk from the center of Carmel, yet a world away in tranquillity (in fact, sheep still graze in the meadow that stretches out to the sea in front of the hotel). The ranch offers a wide range of accommodations in terms of setting, views, and price. The least expensive guestrooms are found in the old barn, while more deluxe rooms are located in small meadow-front cottages. The latter have fireplaces and private porches with old-fashioned rocking chairs that beckon you to watch the sun set over the sea. There are also six bedrooms in the charming old farmhouse which has an ornate Victorian-style living room with heavy oak furniture and grand piano. Whichever room you choose, you cannot help being captivated by the peaceful beauty of the property and its well-maintained gardens. For exercise, there are six tennis courts and a workout room, plus, of course, a lovely beach within a 15-minute walk. A Continental buffet breakfast including fruits, cereals, juices, and pastries is served in the clubhouse next to the tennis courts. The restaurant, open for dinner, has an attractive terrace where guests can dine outside on warm evenings. *Directions:* From Highway 1 turn west onto Rio Road, then left at the Mission (Lausuen Road), and wind round the Mission to the ranch.

MISSION RANCH
Owner: Clint Eastwood
Innkeeper: John Purcell
26270 Dolores
Carmel, CA 93923
Tel: (831) 624-6436, Fax: (831) 626-4163
31 Rooms, Double: $85–$225
Open all year, Credit cards: all major
Children accepted, No smoking, Wheelchair friendly

CARMEL   SAN ANTONIO HOUSE   Map: 5c

Just a block or two off Ocean Avenue, the principal shopping district of Carmel, and just a block or two up from the beautiful blue waters and white sand of its glorious beach is the charming San Antonio House. Set back from the road, San Antonio House is nestled amongst its own little garden areas with ivy-covered walls and a lush front lawn shaded by trees—walk under a lovely trellis to another, almost secret garden at the back. The San Antonio House has the feel of a cottage set in the Cotswolds. Each of the four guestrooms enjoys its own private entrance and fireplace. Although not spacious, the rooms are cozy and intimate, a delightful retreat on a foggy coastside day. The Patio room opens onto the front garden with its own private stone patio secluded behind a border of colorful flowers; The Dollhouse is reached by a little stairway, is decorated with lace, tapestry, cuddly bears, and a dollhouse and has a cozy little day-bed tucked under the eaves in a separate alcove; Treetops, the most spacious room, located above the carriage house, is secluded and overlooks the gardens; and the delightful Garden Room is country-cozy—its sitting area in front of its fireplace is an inviting spot to linger away an afternoon. A bountiful Continental breakfast is served on a tray to be enjoyed in the privacy of your room or in the garden. *Directions:* Take Ocean Avenue west off Highway 1, then turn south on San Antonio. San Antonio House is in the first block on the east side.

SAN ANTONIO HOUSE
Owners: Dianna & Larry Wells
Innkeeper: Brenda Bell
San Antonio between Ocean & 7th
P.O. Box 3683, Carmel, CA 93921
Tel: (831) 624-4334, Fax: (831) 624-6643
4 Rooms, Double: $130–$195
Open all year, Credit cards: MC, VS
Children accepted over 12, No smoking
www.karenbrown.com/california/sanantoniohouse.html

Places to Stay

CARMEL　　　SEA VIEW INN　　　Map: 5c

With the ocean three blocks away, Sea View Inn is within easy walking distance of the much-photographed Carmel beach and it is possible to catch the tiniest glimpse of the ocean through the trees from the third floor of the inn. This large Victorian house looks as though it were once a large home, when in fact it has always been an inn. Cream-colored board-and-batten wainscoting accented by a plate rail displaying antiques and interesting bric-a-brac sets the welcoming mood for the living room and adjacent parlor—both rooms are warmed by cozy fireplaces. Games, books, and magazines add a comfortable, lived-in feel. The largest bedrooms are found on the second floor. Room 6 has a new, elegant decor with an Oriental rug, Ralph Lauren prints, and white shutters at the window. The adjacent room 7 has stark white walls and window blinds with a dramatic Oriental-style four-poster bed draped with blue-and-white Chinese-motif fabric. The four tiny bedrooms tucked under the steeply slanting attic ceilings on the third floor provide the snuggest of accommodation. Each is lavishly decorated in a mellow English-floral print gathered into canopies and covering huge bed pillows. *Directions:* Take the Ocean Avenue exit from Highway 1 to Camino Real where you turn left—Sea View Inn is just after 11th Street on the left-hand side.

SEA VIEW INN
Owners: Diane & Marshall Hydorn
Innkeeper: Margo Thomas
Camino Real between 11th & 12th Streets
P.O. Box 4138, Carmel, CA 93921
Tel: (831) 624-8778, Fax: (831) 625-5901
8 Rooms, 6 with private bathrooms
Double: $85–$140
Open all year, Credit cards: all major
Children accepted over 12, No smoking
www.karenbrown.com/california/seaviewinn.html

Places to Stay

CARMEL — VAGABOND'S HOUSE INN

Map: 5c

Carmel's quaint gingerbread architecture, profusion of colorful flowers, and tall, shady trees are all happily combined at the Vagabond's House Inn. Set around a flagstone courtyard shaded by a giant oak tree and surrounded by fuchsias, azaleas, camellias, and rhododendrons, the inn is made up of a group of attached story-book English cottages, brick and half-timbered, topped by a thick shake roof, making this one of Carmel's most appealing-looking inns. Most of the guestrooms open directly onto the courtyard with its fountain and profusion of flowers including colorful fuchsias cascading from hanging boxes set in the oak tree. Many of the bedrooms have been refurbished and are very inviting, with pretty coordinating fabrics on the comforters, cushions, and window coverings. There are at least two antique clocks in every bedroom, and many have their own fireplace (be sure to request a room with a wood-burning as opposed to gas fireplace) and cozy sitting nook. In the morning you phone reception to let them know when you would like a breakfast tray brought to your room. When you check in, be sure not to miss the antique toy collection in the lounge. *Directions:* Take the Ocean Avenue exit from Highway 1, turn right on Dolores Street, and go a few blocks to 4th Street. The Vagabond's House Inn is on the corner of 4th Street and Dolores.

VAGABOND'S HOUSE INN
Owner: Dennis Le Vett
Innkeeper: Sally Goss
Dolores & 4th Street
P.O. Box 2747, Carmel, CA 93921
Tel: (831) 624-7738 or (800) 262-1262
Fax: (831) 626-1243
11 Rooms, Double: $85–$165
Open all year, Credit cards: all major
Children accepted over 13, No smoking
www.karenbrown.com/california/vagabonds.html

CARMEL HIGHLANDS   TICKLE PINK INN   Map: 5c

We tend not to recommend hotels versus inns, and yet every once in a while we happen on one, be it large or small, where the service is exceptional and welcoming and we find we want to share it with our readers. The Tickle Pink Inn is a lovely, romantic retreat and the fact that it is family owned and operated is evident in the quality and caring of the service. Set high on the hillside above the well-known Highlands Inn, the Tickle Pink is a two-story pink motel-like building which hugs the hillside and looks out through the greenery of cypress trees to the distant rugged ocean. Rooms are attractively decorated with light-pine furnishings in warm colors of beiges, creams, and pinks. Most guestrooms have their own private deck and handsome stone fireplace; all enjoy a TV with VCR (movies are available for rent), terry robes, and coffee service. Included in the room rate is a lovely afternoon buffet of wine and an assortment of cheeses and fruit, and an appealing Continental breakfast served either in your room or on the patio off the lounge. Ocean views vary depending on the location within the inn, but the staff is extremely helpful in describing the differences in accommodation and patient in assisting you with a selection over the phone. *Directions:* The Tickle Pink is located 4 miles south of Rio Road in Carmel just off Highway 1. Highland Drive is marked by a sign for both the Highlands Inn and the Tickle Pink.

TICKLE PINK INN
Owners: The Gurries Family
Innkeeper: Mark Watson
155 Highland Drive
Carmel Highlands, CA 93923
Tel: (831) 624-1244, Fax: (831) 626-9516
E-mail: mark@ticklepink.com
34 Rooms, Double: $189–$329
Open all year, Credit cards: all major
Children accepted, Smoking
Wheelchair friendly

Places to Stay

CARMEL VALLEY — STONEPINE   Map: 5d

Threading into the hills east of Carmel is the beautiful Carmel Valley where, unlike Carmel, which tends to be foggy, almost every day is blessed with sunshine. Here, tucked into its own 330-acre oasis, is Stonepine, built by the Crockers, an early-California dynasty of great wealth. Anticipation of the very special treat awaiting builds as impressive, wrought-iron gates open magically, allowing you to enter. The road crosses a small bridge then winds through the trees, ending in the courtyard of a beautiful home, Italian in feel with a muted-pink façade accented with red-tile roof, shuttered windows, and fancy grille-work. Inside, a quiet elegance emanates from every niche and corner. No expense is spared in the splendid furnishings which give no hint that this is a commercial operation. You definitely feel like a guest in a private mansion as you roam from library to sitting room to dining room, each decorated to perfection. The dining room, handsomely lined in mellow antique paneling, is set exquisitely for dinner each night with fine crystal and china. Upstairs are eight beautiful guestrooms, plus there are four bedrooms in the paddock house and two in the Briar Rose Cottage. Although there is a swimming pool and a tennis court, Stonepine was built as a ranch, and horses are the main attraction. Stonepine is very expensive and exclusive. *Directions:* Signposted on the right after leaving Carmel Valley Village going east on G16.

STONEPINE
Owner: Gordon Hentschel
150 E. Carmel Valley Road
Carmel Valley, CA 93924
Tel: (831) 659-2245, Fax: (831) 659-5160
14 Rooms, Double: $295–$2,500
Open all year, Credit cards: all major
Children accepted over 12, No smoking

CATALINA ISLAND–Avalon — INN ON MT. ADA — Map: 7c

Staying at the Inn on Mt. Ada is like stepping into a fairy tale—suddenly you are "king of the mountain." This is not too far from reality, since the inn is the beautiful Wrigley family mansion (chewing gum, you know), their vacation "cottage" built high on the hill overlooking Avalon harbor. If you arrive by ferry at Catalina Island, you cannot miss the house: the mansion appears like a white wedding cake to your left above the harbor. The inn is expensive, but money seems almost immaterial, because, once through the door, you have bought a dream. You are truly like a pampered guest in a millionaire's home, with hardly a hint of commercialism (until you pay the bill) to put a damper on the illusion. The lounges and dining room have been redecorated with soft, pretty colors and traditional furniture and fabrics appropriate to the era when the house was built. Upstairs are six individually decorated bedrooms, the grandest having a fireplace, sitting area, and a terrace with breathtaking views of the harbor. Rates include all the extras such as complimentary use of your own golf cart, a full scrumptious breakfast, a deli-style lunch, and traditional country-inn dinner. Coffee, tea, soft drinks, fruit juice, and freshly baked cookies are always available in the den and sun porch. *Directions*: Boats from Long Beach, San Pedro, and Newport Beach. Helicopters from Long Beach and San Pedro.

INN ON MT. ADA
Innkeepers: Marlene McAdam & Susie Griffin
P.O. Box 2560
398 Wrigley Road
Avalon, Catalina, CA 90704
Tel: (310) 510-2030, Fax: (310) 510-2237
6 Rooms, Double: $350–$630*
*Includes all meals
Closed Christmas
Credit cards: MC, VS
Children accepted over 14, No smoking

Places to Stay

COLOMA COUNTRY INN

Map: 4b

The Coloma Country Inn, a handsome early-American farmhouse, was built in 1852, four years after gold was discovered at Sutter's Mill which is located just down the street. Today Coloma is a sleepy little village where the scant remains of the heady Gold Rush days are separated by wide green lawns sloping up from the American River which give it the air of being a well-kept park. The Coloma Country Inn sits in the middle of the park, its wrap-around porch inviting guests to relax and sip a glass of wine while soaking in the beauty of the surrounding tranquil countryside. Inside, the decor is perfectly lovely, simple, very appealing American country style, though some rooms do have some Victorian pieces. Each bed is accented by a lovely antique quilt from Cindi's large collection. Some rooms feature a balcony or brick patio with a rose garden. An 1898 carriage house features two suites, each with its own flowering courtyard and kitchenette. Behind the inn is an attractive pond with a little boat moored at the dock. The surrounding Gold Country is a great attraction to visitors to these parts, but, if you are looking for alternative means of transportation, Alan, a commercial hot-air-balloon pilot, can arrange to take you aloft. If you are game for more excitement, he can arrange one-or two-day raft trips on the nearby river. *Directions:* Take Highway 50 from Sacramento to Placerville, then exit on Highway 49 heading north for the 8-mile drive to Coloma.

COLOMA COUNTRY INN
Innkeepers: Cindi & Alan Ehrgott
345 High Street
P.O. Box 502, Coloma, CA 95613
Tel: (530) 622-6919, Fax: (530) 622-1795
7 Rooms, 5 with private bathrooms
Double: $95–$145
Open all year, Credit cards: none accepted
Children accepted over 6, No smoking
www.karenbrown.com/california/colomacountryinn.html

Places to Stay

COLUMBIA — CITY HOTEL   Map: 4b

Columbia is a state-preserved town whose shops and stores have been re-created to show life in the heyday of the California Gold Rush. On Main Street is the exquisitely restored City Hotel. Prior to 1874 the building was a gold assay office, the state company headquarters, an opera house, and a newspaper office. Now it is owned by the state of California and partially staffed by students from Columbia College's hotel management program (consequently the staff, dressed in their period costumes, are exceedingly young and wonderfully friendly). The excellent restaurant and the conviviality of the adjacent What Cheer bar provide an especially pleasant way to spend an evening. The high-ceilinged bedrooms have Victorian or early-American furniture. The very nicest rooms open directly onto the parlor, rooms 1 and 2 having the added attraction of balconies overlooking Main Street. All the bedrooms have private en-suite toilets and washbasins. It is not a problem to have showers down the hallway when slippers, robes, and little wicker baskets to carry soap, shampoo, and towels are provided. A bountiful Continental breakfast is served on the buffet in the dining room. *Directions:* From Sonora take Highway 49 north for the 4-mile drive to Columbia.

CITY HOTEL
Owner: Columbia City Hotel Corporation
Manager: Tom Bender
Main Street
Columbia State Historic Park, CA 95310
Tel: (209) 532-1470 or (800) 532-1479
Fax: (209) 532-7027
E-mail: info@vcityhotel.com
10 Rooms with half baths, showers down the hall
Double: $85–$105
Open all year, Credit cards: all major
Children accepted, No smoking
www.karenbrown.com/california/cityhotel.html

Places to Stay

| COLUMBIA | FALLON HOTEL | Map: 4b |

The Fallon Hotel is owned and operated in the same way as the nearby City Hotel in this gem of a Gold-Rush town. The hotel opened in 1986 after receiving a $4,000,000 refurbishment from the state of California. The bedrooms are perfect reflections of the opulent 1880s, with patterned ceilings, colorful, ornate wallpaper, and grand antique furniture. Front rooms have shaded balconies. All have en-suite pull-chain toilets and ornate washbasins. Like the nearby City Hotel, showers are down the hall and slippers, bathrobes, and baskets of toiletries are handily provided. One downstairs room has wider doors for wheelchair access. A simple buffet-style Continental breakfast is served in the adjoining ice-cream parlor. In the Fallon Hotel building is the Fallon Theater, offering a year-round schedule of contemporary dramas, musicals, and melodramas. When making reservations at either the City or Fallon hotels, ask about their excellent value-for-money theater and dinner packages. *Directions:* From the San Francisco area take Highway 580 for 60 miles, then Highway 120 east to Sonora and Highway 49 north from Sonora for the 4-mile drive to Columbia which is off the main highway.

FALLON HOTEL
Owner: Columbia City Hotel Corporation
Manager: Tom Bender
Washington Street
Columbia State Historic Park, CA 95310
Tel: (209) 532-1470, Fax: (209) 532-7027
E-mail: info@cityhotel.com
14 Rooms with half baths, showers down the hall
Double: $50–$105
Closed Monday-Wednesday during the Winter
Credit cards: all major
Children accepted, No smoking, Wheelchair friendly
www.karenbrown.com/california/fallonhotel.html

CROMBERG   TWENTY MILE HOUSE   Map: 4b

Barbara Gage's lovely old two-story home with its weathered brick exterior, a restored former stage stop, sits just a garden's distance from the Middle Fork of the Feather River. You enter into the coolness of the house into the front room with a lovely old trestle table banked by two wonderful old benches set before a large open fireplace. Stools are drawn up to a counter in front of the open country kitchen. The two guestrooms on the first floor are off the large (what was once the front) porch of the home, set with wicker furniture, and both have private bathrooms. The Parlor Room is for the romantic—a warm paneled library room with a fireplace and double Victorian brass bed, while the larger Trading Post Room has a western theme and one single and two double beds. Cross the bridge and follow a forested footpath to the charming white one-bedroom cottage with its inviting porch, dear little kitchen, lovely small central sitting area with wood-burning pot-bellied stove, and small back bedroom with private bath. The inn is set on 250 acres and Barbara proudly claims her 1-mile (2-mile if you count both sides of the river!) frontage on the Feather River which she also makes available to non-resident fishing enthusiasts. *Directions*: From Cromberg on Highway 89 take the Old Cromberg Road and follow it as it winds past the wonderful old cemetery to the bottom of the hill and Twenty Mile House.

TWENTY MILE HOUSE
Innkeeper: Barbara Gage
Old Cromberg Road
P.O. Box 30001, Cromberg, CA 96103
Tel: (530) 836-0375, Fax: (530) 836-2128
2 Rooms, 1 Cottage, Double: $110
Open all year, Credit cards: none
Children by prior arrangement, No smoking
www.karenbrown.com/california/twentymilehouse.html

Places to Stay

| DANA POINT | BLUE LANTERN INN | Map: 7a |

The Blue Lantern Inn, perched on a bluff offering unparalleled views of the fascinating harbor of Dana Point and the blue Pacific, is an outstanding inn on southern California's Riviera. The new construction is designed in a Cape Code style—a most appealing building whose many gables, towers, and jutting roof lines create a whimsical look. The façade is painted a soft gray made even prettier by its crisp white trim. Inside, the color scheme reflects the sea with the use of hues of periwinkle blue, soft lavender, and sea-foam green. Each of the 29 guestrooms is individually decorated—some with light-pine, some with wicker, others with dark-mahogany furniture. The traditional-style furnishings are mostly reproductions and are of excellent quality. Each room has a gas log fireplace and spacious bathroom with Jacuzzi tub. Many of the rooms capture magnificent views of the sea. Breakfast is served each morning in the lounge, a cheerful room where sunlight streams through the wall of windows. Off the reception area is the library where tea is served in the afternoon. Other amenities include a conference room and a well-equipped exercise room. The Blue Lantern is more of a sophisticated small hotel than a cozy bed and breakfast, but the management is superb and the warmth of welcome cannot be surpassed. *Directions:* From the Pacific Coast Highway 1, turn west on Street of the Blue Lantern and go one block.

BLUE LANTERN INN
Innkeeper: Lin McMahon
34343 Street of the Blue Lantern
Dana Point, CA 92629
Tel: (949) 661-1304 or (800) 950-1236
Fax: (949) 496-1483
29 Rooms, Double: $140–$500
Open all year, Credit cards: all major
Children accepted, No smoking, Wheelchair friendly
www.karenbrown.com/california/bluelanterninn.html

DRAKESBAD   DRAKESBAD GUEST RANCH   Map: 1b

Deep within Lassen National Park lies Drakesbad Guest Ranch, set in an idyllic high mountain valley. A broad sweep of grassy meadow cut by a tumbling river gives way to towering pines rising to rocky peaks. There's no electricity at Drakesbad—the warm glow of a kerosene lamp lights your cozy paneled bedroom. Furnishings are simple: polished pine-log chairs and beds topped by quilts, simple country curtains, and a pine dresser and bedside table. Our favorite rooms are in the little cabins that nestle at the very edge of the meadow with their smart modern bathrooms and sliding doors which open to a tiny deck where you can sit and watch the deer grazing at twilight. Other cabins nestle in the pines. Rooms upstairs in the main lodge have half baths. Evenings are for books, games, and conviviality by the fireplace in the lodge, conversation around the campfire, or star-gazing from the soothing warmth of the swimming pool which is fed by the natural warmth of a hot spring. Days are for walks, horseback riding, and swimming. A bell is rung to announce meals which are served in the rustic pine dining room whose tables are topped with flowery mats and napkins. It's a family place full of people who came as children returning year after year with children and grandchildren—some who remember when guests slept in tents on the meadow. *Directions:* Turn left at the fire station in Chester and follow Warner Valley Road to the ranch. The last 4 miles are dirt road.

DRAKESBAD GUEST RANCH
Innkeepers: Billie & Ed Fiebiger
End of Warner Valley Road
Lassen National Park, Chester, CA 96020
Winter tel: (530) 529-9820, Fax: (530) 529-4511
Summer tel: ask AT&T operator for Drakesbad toll station #2 via 530 area code
19 Rooms, Double: $220–$250 (includes all meals)
Open second Fri. in June to second Sun. in October
Credit cards: MC, VS
Children accepted, No smoking, Wheelchair friendly

Places to Stay

DULZURA BROOKSIDE FARM B & B INN Map: 7d

Tucked seemingly miles away deep in the countryside, Brookside Farm is actually only a 35-minute drive from the outskirts of San Diego. Sally and Edd Guishard have done a remarkable job of converting an ordinary complex of farm buildings into an inviting inn. The location and mood set the theme of many of the rooms: the Bird's Nest tucked under the eaves has lovely bird stenciling on the walls, while Captain Small's room has a red-and-blue quilt and blue-checked chairs. Four rooms, Peter Rabbit's House, Room with a View, Jennie's Room, and La Casita, are housed within the walls of the old the barn. The original well house is now the Hunter's Cabin and has a rustic decor, wood-burning stove, and planked floors and overlooks the creek through a wall of paned windows and screened porch. Edd is responsible for the inn's stained glass windows as well as being a wonderful chef. On weekends he prepares an inviting four-course dinner, inviting guests to share in the preparation (he owned several restaurants in the San Diego area before moving here). On weekday nights, a complimentary supper is served to guests. The setting of the inn is lovely: play badminton on the lawn, laze away the hours on the patio, or relax in the spa under the grape arbor. *Directions*: From San Diego take Highway 94 east to Dulzura, go 1½ miles past the café, then right on Marron Valley Road.

BROOKSIDE FARM B & B INN
Owners/Innkeepers: Sally & Edd Guishard
Manager: Guillermo Campa
1373 Marron Valley Road
Dulzura, CA 91917
Tel: (619) 468-3043, Fax: (619) 468-3228
11 Rooms, Double: $80–$115
Open all year, Credit cards: all major
Children accepted over 12
No smoking, Wheelchair friendly
www.karenbrown.com/california/brooksidefarm.html

ELK COVE INN

The Elk Cove Inn, on the south edge of town as the road winds down the hill, is the town's grandest homes and enjoys a million-dollar view of cove and towering weathered by the crashing sea. Its new owner, Elaine Bryant, a charming hostess, takes great pride in extending a warm welcome and lavishing southern hospitality and attention on her guests. In the main house, the gathering room is set with breakfast tables in front of two walls of windows looking out on the spectacular coastline—a wonderful, memorable spot for a morning repast. Another intimate spot to settle is the cozy oceanfront bar where you can enjoy beer, wine, and cocktails. The bedrooms' decor is feminine with silk- and fresh-flower arrangements, patterned comforters, throw pillows and lace. In the main house, three rooms are found on the first floor. The smallest, off the back hallway, has a bed dressed in blue gingham and a small bathroom. Upstairs there are three rooms, all with private bath, and an intimate sitting area with television, VCR, microwave, and stocked refrigerator. The four bedrooms in the two separate cottages enjoy full ocean views through large picture windows. Five new each enjoy a large living room with a spectacular view and deck, a large bath equipped with Jacuzzi, and a spacious bedroom. *Directions*: Elk is 15 miles south of Mendocino, or 6½ miles south of the junction of Highway 128 on Highway 1.

ELK COVE INN
Innkeeper: Elaine Bryant
6300 South Highway 1, P.O. Box 367, Elk, CA 95432
Tel: (707) 877-3321 or (800) 275-2967
Fax: (707) 877-1808
E-mail: elkcove@mcn.org
14 Rooms, Double: $108–$298
Open all year, Credit cards: all major
Children accepted over 12
No smoking, Wheelchair friendly
www.karenbrown.com/california/elkcoveinn.html

GRIFFIN HOUSE

Maps: 1c & 2a

The Griffin House, a pretty little clapboard house painted gray with white trim and with a white picket fence, dates back to the late 1800s when it served as the local doctor's office and pharmacy. Later, five cottages were added behind the office to house some of the lumber men coming to the growing town of Elk. The present owner, Leslie Lawson, has opened an Irish pub in the main house and renovated the cottages for guests. The pub offers evening meals and good cheer (hours vary). The garden cottages are pleasant, but truly outstanding are the doll-house-like cottages on the edge of the bluff. In fact, these four separate little houses offer the most sensational views anywhere on the California coast. Each of these cottages, named after one of the early settlers of Elk, has a wood-burning stove, a sitting area, a wall of window overlooking the coast, and a private redwood deck with chairs and table. These tiny cottages are very simple in decor, nothing contrived or quaintly cute, just providing old-fashioned, basic comfort. But these cottages offer a vista so breathtaking that you will be back again and again. Leslie, the gracious, easy-going, warm-hearted owner, is a natural at innkeeping—which she finds a breeze by comparison to her previous job as Dean of Students at the UC Santa Barbara where she "mothered" 18,000 students. *Directions:* Off the west side of the Highway 1, at the center of Elk.

GRIFFIN HOUSE
Innkeeper: Leslie Griffin-Lawson
Manager: Terry Smith
5910 South Highway 1
P.O. Box 190, Elk, CA 95432
Tel: (707) 877-3422, Fax: (707) 877-1853
E-mail: griffin@mcn.org
4 Rooms & 4 Cottages, Double: $95–$225
Open all year, Credit cards: all major
Pub open most nights, Children over 3 accepted
No smoking, Wheelchair friendly
www.karenbrown.com/california/griffinhouse.html

ELK   THE HARBOR HOUSE INN   Maps: 1c & 2a

The Harbor House has a fantastic location—on one of the prettiest bluffs along the Mendocino coast. There is even a little path, with benches along the way, winding down the cliff to a secluded private beach. The home was built in 1916 as a guest house for the Goodyear Redwood Lumber Company, so it is no wonder that everything inside and outside is built of redwood. The inn is appealing, reflecting the ambiance of a beautiful, elegant country lodge. You enter into a charming redwood-paneled living room dominated by a large fireplace, also made of redwood. An Oriental carpet, comfortable sofas, beamed ceiling, soft lighting, and a piano tucked in the corner add to the inviting warmth. Doors lead from the lounge to the verandah-like dining room, stretching the length of the building, with picture windows looking out to the sea. A broad wooden staircase leads upstairs to comfortably furnished, homey bedrooms. Other guestrooms are in adjacent cottages. Most of the bedrooms have sea views, and all but one have wood-burning fireplaces. Included in the room rate are both a fixed-menu dinner and breakfast—and the food is good with home-baked breads, freshly ground coffee, garden vegetables, and, of course, wonderful seafood. *Directions:* Take Highway 101 north from San Francisco to Cloverdale, then Highway 128 west to the ocean and Highway 1 south for 5 miles to Elk.

THE HARBOR HOUSE INN
Innkeepers: Elle & Sam Haynes
5600 South Highway 1
P.O. Box 369, Elk, CA 95432
Tel: (800) 720-7474
E-mail: harborhs@mcn.org
10 Rooms, Double: $185–$300*
*Includes breakfast & dinner
Open all year, Credit cards: all major
Children accepted over 12, No smoking
www.karenbrown.com/california/harborhouseinn.html

ELK *7 day cancellation* SANDPIPER HOUSE INN   Maps: 1c & 2a

The Sandpiper House Inn is superbly positioned on a bluff overlooking the most beautiful section of the Mendocino coast. The front of the gray shingled house, enclosed with a white picket fence, is most inviting. But just wait: it is not until you come inside and look out the windows to the ocean that you realize what a prize you have discovered. Behind the house, a beautifully tended green lawn embraced by an English garden stretches out to the edge of the bluff below which the waves crash against awesome rock formations. Benches are strategically placed to capture the glory. A path leads down the steep incline with a half-way resting point before continuing on down to the private beach. Because of the setting the house would be a winner if it were just a shell within, but, happily, the interior does justice to the setting. The decor is unpretentiously lovely with an elegant homelike ambiance and excellent taste. Four of the bedrooms capture the sensational view and as I saw each, one it became my favorite. Choose Evergreen for complete privacy, a luxurious bathroom with a tub for two, and fireplace; Headland for its garden patio and view capturing sitting area; Clifton for its bay window with chairs placed to capture the view; and Weston for its fireplace and breathtaking panoramic view of rocky headland and vast expanse of seascape through windows at the foot of the bed. The owners are as warm and gracious as their home they share with guests. *Directions:* Located on Highway 1 at the north end of the village.

SANDPIPER HOUSE INN
Innkeepers: Claire & Richard Melrose
5520 South Highway 1
P.O. Box 149, Elk, CA 95432
Tel: (707) 877-3587 or (800) 894-9016
E-mail: eclaire@mcn.org
5 Rooms, Double: $130–$220
Open all year, Credit cards: all major
Children accepted over 12, No smoking
www.karenbrown.com/california/sandpiperhouseinn.html

146   *Places to Stay*

EUREKA   CARTER HOUSE VICTORIANS   Map: 1a

Carter House Victorians are a group of three buildings: the majestic Carter House, the adorable Bell Cottage next-door, and the adjacent Hotel Carter. The inns are the dream of Mark Carter who grew up in Eureka and, after restoring several Victorian homes, chose to build his own (the Carter House), using the original plans for a Victorian house designed by the architect who built the Carson Mansion, a Victorian showplace in Eureka. All of their bedrooms are generously appointed with antique furniture, original artwork, and cozy flannel robes to make guests really feel "at home." While the Carter House offers the most delightful antique-filled rooms, if you are in the mood for something more sensuous, opt for a suite. The suites at the Hotel Carter offer large whirlpool tubs with marina views (in the bedroom), fireplaces, king beds, large showers with two heads, entertainment centers, and well-stocked refrigerators (not complimentary). The Hotel Carter's lobby and dining room are the center for socializing—guests enjoy hors d'oeuvres and wine in the early evening, a nightcap of homemade cookies and tea before bed, outstanding dinners, and bountiful breakfasts. The ebullient Mark Carter sets the friendly welcoming tone for this delightful inn. *Directions:* Take Highway 101 north to Eureka. The highway turns into 5th Street. From 5th Street, turn left on L Street and go two blocks.

CARTER HOUSE VICTORIANS
Innkeepers: Christi & Mark Carter
301 L Street, Eureka, CA 95501
Tel: (707) 444-8062 or (800) 404-1390
Fax: (707) 444-8067
E-mail: carter52@carterhouse.com
31 Rooms, Double: $152–$225, Suite: to $500
Open all year, Credit cards: all major
Children accepted, No smoking, Wheelchair friendly
www.karenbrown.com/california/carterhousevictorians.html

Places to Stay

EUREKA — THE CORNELIUS DALY INN — Map: 1a

Brothers Cornelius and John Daly came from Ireland to Eureka and in 1895 founded a successful chain of northern California clothing shops. When their business flourished, the brothers returned to Ireland in search of wives, married sisters Annie and Eileen, and returned to Eureka to build them impressive homes next door to each another. Now Annie and Con's home is a delightful bed and breakfast run with warm enthusiasm by Sue and Gene Clinesmith who fell in love with their house while visiting their son at Humboldt State University. Sue and Gene have lavished time and attention on their lovely home and the result is that it is an extremely comfortable place for guests to stay. Enjoy wine and cheese in the parlor, watch a movie in the den, or relax in the wicker parlor or on the back patio overlooking the garden. Upstairs, I particularly enjoyed the Garden View and Victorian Rose suites with their spacious bedrooms, sitting rooms (in what were once sleeping porches), and modern bathrooms. A short walk takes you through Eureka's more commercial district to its handsome historic old town (between D and G and 1st and 3rd streets) with its attractive shops and restaurants occupying restored buildings. *Directions*: From San Francisco take Highway 101 275 miles north to Eureka. The highway turns into 5th Street. From 5th Street turn right into H Street: The Daly Inn is on your left.

THE CORNELIUS DALY INN
Innkeepers: Sue & Gene Clinesmith
1125 H Street, Eureka, CA 95501
Tel: (707) 445-3638 or (800) 321-9656
Fax: (707) 444-3636
E-mail: dalyinn@humboldt1.com
5 Rooms, 3 with private bathrooms
Double: $85–$150
Open all year, Credit cards: all major
Children accepted over 12, No smoking
www.karenbrown.com/california/thedalyinn.html

FERNDALE — THE GINGERBREAD MANSION

Map: 1a

Ferndale is a jewel—a wonderfully preserved Victorian town 5 miles from the northern California coast. Happily, the town's most beautiful Victorian, a fantasy of ornate turrets and gables, is an inn, The Gingerbread Mansion. Walking through the parlors and breakfast room is like taking a step back into Victorian times. While the bedrooms continue the Victorian theme, I feel certain that the prude Victorians would be quite aghast at several of Ken Torbert's more sensuous rooms. If money is no object, request the Empire Suite, an open-plan bedroom and bathroom combination where you can soak in a claw-foot tub in front of one of the fireplaces (there are two), relish the complexity of operating a shower with eight heads, and sleep in a king-size bed where towering Ionic columns (pillars) soar to the rafters. Alternatively, request your room by whether you want a tub in the room (Lilac), his-and-her tubs in the room (Gingerbread), fireplaces (five rooms), or a sleeping loft for a child (Hideaway). I particularly enjoyed the Garden Room with its fireplace, old-style bathroom, and French windows opening onto a private balcony overlooking the clipped hedges and colorful flowerbeds of the garden. Guests often combine their stay with a play performed by the Ferndale Repertory Company. *Directions:* Ferndale is approximately 250 miles north of San Francisco. From Highway 101 traveling north, take the Fernbridge/Ferndale exit, following signs to Ferndale. When you reach Main Street, turn left at the Bank of America and go one block.

THE GINGERBREAD MANSION
Innkeeper: Ken Torbert
400 Berding Street, Ferndale, CA 95536
Tel: (707) 786-4000 or (800) 952-4136, Fax: (707) 786-438
E-mail: kenn@humboldt1.com
11 Rooms, Double: $140–$180 Suite: $170–$350
Open all year, Credit cards: all major
Children accepted over 9, No smoking
www.karenbrown.com/california/thegingerbreadmansion.html

FERNDALE   THE SHAW HOUSE   Map: 1a

The quaint Victorian town of Ferndale lies almost midway between San Francisco and Ashland, making it an ideal stop for those traveling between these two lovely spots. Situated on Main Street on a 1-acre parcel which isolates it from the road, the Shaw House was built in 1854 by Seth Shaw, one of the founders of Ferndale. Now it is the home of Norma and Ken Bessingpas who do an excellent job of welcoming guests to their bed and breakfast and making certain that they have all the necessary information to enjoy this lovely area. A memento of the house's historic importance is the gilded overmantle in the parlor to which Norma has added a garland festooned with fairylights and next to it placed a tailor's dummy wearing a Victorian bridal gown. The adjacent library is a restful place to relax. Up the main staircase you find four guestrooms ranging from a snug bedroom with a bathroom down the hall to the spacious Honeymoon room with its domed ceiling and large bathroom with claw-foot tub and shower. I also very much enjoyed the privacy offered by the three ground-floor rooms which have their own entrances and patios. Main Street has changed very little since the 1890s and offers galleries, antique shops, restaurants (guests usually dine at Curleys Grill), and an excellent bookstore. *Directions*: Coming from San Francisco on Highway 101, take the Fernbridge/Ferndale exit and follow signs to Ferndale. The Shaw House is on the right on Main Street.

THE SHAW HOUSE
Innkeepers: Norma & Ken Bessingpas
703 Main Street
P.O. Box 1125, Ferndale, CA 95536-1125
Tel (800) 557-SHAW, Fax: (707) 786-9958
E-mail: shawhse@humboldt1.com
7 Rooms, Double: $85–$145
Open all year, Credit cards: all major
Children accepted over 10, No smoking
www.karenbrown.com/california/theshawhouse.html

GARBERVILLE   BENBOW INN   Map: 1a

You would think you were in England instead of northern California when you first see the large Tudor-style Benbow Inn. The English theme continues as you step inside the lounge with its large antique fireplace flanked by comfortable sofas, antique chests, paintings, needlepoint, cherry-wood wainscoting, two grandfather clocks, potted green plants, and a splendid Oriental carpet. At tea time complimentary English tea and scones are served along with mulled wine when the days are nippy. The dining room, too, is very English: a beautiful, sunny room with beamed ceiling and dark-oak Windsor chairs. Both the reception hall and the dining room open out to a pretty courtyard overlooking the river. The traditionally decorated bedrooms vary in size—all the way up from small bedrooms located both in the main hotel and in an annex which also opens onto the courtyard. The one disadvantage of the Benbow Inn is its proximity to the freeway, but loyal guests do not seem to mind. A wonderful feature here is the very special Christmas celebration—events including Christmas movies, caroling, and dancing are planned each day, and there is a very festive English Christmas dinner. *Directions:* Drive north on Highway 101. Just south of Garberville, take the Benbow exit. The hotel is on west side of the freeway.

BENBOW INN
Owners/Innkeepers: Teresa & John Porter
445 Lake Benbow Drive
Garberville, CA 95440
Tel: (707) 923-2124, Fax: (707) 923-2122
E-mail: benbow@benbowinn.com
55 Rooms, Double: $89–$295
Closed January 2 to mid-April
Credit cards: MC, VS
Children accepted, No smoking
www.karenbrown.com/california/benbowinn.html

GEORGETOWN — AMERICAN RIVER INN

Map: 4b

Georgetown's unusually wide, tree-lined streets faced by wood-frame buildings give character and charm to this town perched high on a hill 9 miles above the South Fork of the American River. The American River Inn was once a boarding house for gold miners who came to make their fortune, but they certainly did not have today's luxuries of a spa and swimming pool. The main house is a picture-perfect Victorian whose interior beautifully complements the lovely exterior. Inside, the individually decorated bedrooms are furnished with antiques appropriate to the period and the bathrooms have claw-foot tubs and pull-chain toilets. A full breakfast is served in the dining room or on the patio and guests have the use of a comfortable parlor. Across the lawn and past the swimming pool and spa is the Queen Ann House which is perfect for seminars, retreats, or wedding parties. A more recent addition to the complex are the Woodside Mine Suites, very basic non-descript rooms with little charm. Guests with children are usually offered the suites—it is disappointing not to be able to enjoy the character of the old home. The inn is happy to make arrangements for white-water rafting or kayaking, and mountain bicycling is complimentary. We have learned that the inn is for sale, so there may be changes with new ownership. *Directions:* From Sacramento take Highway 50 or 80 to Auburn or Placerville, then Highway 49 to 193 which brings you into Georgetown. The American River Inn is on Main Street at Orleans.

AMERICAN RIVER INN
Innkeepers: Maria & Will Collin
Main at Orleans Street
P.O. Box 43, Georgetown, CA 95634
Tel: (530) 333-4499 or (800) 245-6566
Fax: (530) 333-9253, E-mail: ari@pcweb.net
25 Rooms, 18 with private bathrooms
Double: $85–$115
Open all year, Credit cards: all major
Children accepted over 8, No smoking
Wheelchair friendly

GEYSERVILLE   CAMPBELL RANCH INN   Maps: 1c & 2a

Mary Jane and Jerry Campbell have perfected innkeeping in the decade and a half that they have opened their home to overnight guests. Time has served not to weather but rather enrich their enthusiasm and warmth of welcome. The Campbell Ranch Inn, in the heart of the Sonoma county wine country, is a contemporary home whose appeal lies in its hosts and its absolutely spectacular location. Set on the 35-acre hillside with a backdrop of fir and pine trees, views from the inn stretch out across its lovely garden and swimming pool to the miles and miles of vineyards that carpet the surrounding countryside and rolling hills. It is a beautiful setting, very quiet and very soothing—the perfect escape. If you could survive on a bountiful breakfast and the wonderful homemade pie offered each evening as dessert, you might never choose to venture back down the Campbells' drive. The idyllic setting encourages you to relax, read by the pool, or perhaps muster up energy for a game of tennis. With the exception of one cottage, the guestrooms (all with king-sized beds) are actual bedrooms in the Campbell home. Guestrooms have all recently been refurnished in a traditional décor. The cottage affords more privacy and has a bedroom, sitting area with a fireplace, a vine-covered deck with a hot tub, and a million-dollar view. The cottage is just adjacent to the room where Jerry keeps his model trains. *Directions:* On Highway 101, 80 miles north of San Francisco, take the Canyon Road exit at Geyserville and travel west 1-6/10 miles.

CAMPBELL RANCH INN
Innkeepers: Mary Jane & Jerry Campbell
1475 Canyon Road, Geyserville, CA 95441
Tel: (707) 857-3476 or (800) 959-3878
Fax: (707) 857-3239
5 Rooms, Double: $125–$165, Cottage: $225
Open all year, Credit cards: all major
Children accepted over 7, No smoking
www.karenbrown.com/california/campbellranchinn.html

Places to Stay

| GLEN ELLEN | BELTANE RANCH | Map: 2d |

It is hard not to notice Beltane Ranch, a pale-yellow board-and-batten house encircled on both stories by broad verandahs, set on the hillside off the Valley of the Moon Road. Rosemary, the owner, will probably be in the cozy country kitchen when you arrive, but if away from home, she will write you a welcoming note on the chalkboard hung by the back door. The house has no internal staircase, so each room has a private entrance off the verandah—which was probably a very handy thing when this was the weekend retreat of a San Francisco madam. Incidentally, this also explains the southern architecture of the house as "madam" hailed from Louisiana. The bedrooms, decorated in family antiques, have a very comfortable ambiance. Chairs and hammocks are placed on the verandah outside each room and offer a wonderful spot to settle and enjoy peaceful countryside views beyond Rosemary's well-tended garden. A small yellow cottage behind the main house has a private entrance and French doors leading to a patio. The décor is tasteful and simple. Beltane has been in the family for 60 years and produces a well known Chardonnay as well as other varieties of wines. For the energetic, there are a tennis court and walking trails. Beltane Ranch remains a personal favorite. *Directions:* From Sonoma take Highway 12 towards Santa Rosa: Beltane Ranch is on your right shortly after passing the turnoff to Glen Ellen.

BELTANE RANCH
Owner: Rosemary Wood
Innkeeper: Anne Soulier
11775 Highway 12 (Sonoma Highway)
P.O. Box 395, Glen Ellen, CA 95442
Tel: (707) 996-6501
6 Rooms, Double: $130–$240
Open all year, Credit cards: none accepted
Children accepted over 6, No smoking
www.karenbrown.com/california/beltaneranch.html

GLEN ELLEN   GAIGE HOUSE INN   Map: 2d

On the main road that weaves through the quaint town of Glen Ellen, the Gaige House is an elegant inn whose owners, Greg and Ken, are making their own statement as to decor with contemporary, Indonesian, and Japanese details. Since acquiring the inn just a few years ago, they have made major upgrades and added four guestrooms. They take great pride in their new home, and it shows from the bountiful gourmet breakfasts to the hand-ironed quality linens. There is a sense of perfection, and everything is fresh and handsome, airy and light. Each of the thirteen bedrooms has its own personality, but all exude a similar ambiance with a predominant use of Calvin Klein fabrics. The Gaige Suite is a spacious, sunny room with large windows on three sides and a wrap-around deck overlooking the garden. Dominating the room is a four-poster bed with a lace-canopy trim and a bathroom (with Jacuzzi tub) as large as bedrooms in some hotels. Two brand new suites are housed in a building next to the pool. Though both are sophisticated, the Creekside Suite is outstanding with its interesting contemporary design and a private deck overlooking the creek. An added bonus—a large pool and spa are set in the lawn in the rear garden. *Directions:* Driving north on 12 from Sonoma, turn left on Arnold Drive which is signposted to Glen Ellen. The inn is on the right, just before you arrive in town.

GAIGE HOUSE INN
Owners: Greg Nemrow & Ken Burnet, Jr.
Innkeeper: Susan Burnet
13540 Arnold Drive
Glen Ellen, CA 95442
Tel: (707) 935-0237 or (800) 935-0237
Fax: (707) 935-6411
E-mail: gaige@sprynet.com
13 Rooms, Double: $170–$325
Open all year, Credit cards: all major
Children accepted over 12, No smoking
www.karenbrown.com/california/gaigehouseinn.html

Places to Stay

GOLD BEACH, Oregon — INN AT NESIKA BEACH

Map: 1a

The Inn at Nesika Beach, painted a soft blue-gray, was built along the appealing lines of a handsome large New England home. There is a wrap-around porch, many gables, and a steeply pitched roof accented by chimneys. The setting also could be Cape Code, but instead of overlooking the Atlantic, the Inn at Nesika Beach is perched on a romantic wind-blown bluff overlooking the blue Pacific. The setting is superb. Below it (and accessible by a nearby footpath) is a deserted sweep of beach that stretches for miles, while just off shore giant rock formations catch the impact of crashing waves. Whereas many bed and breakfasts started out first as a family home, the Inn at Nesika Beach was purpose-built to take guests, so all the rooms have a private bathroom and are especially commodious. If you stay here, be sure to splurge—request one of the two guestrooms facing the back, overlooking the sea. Except for the decor, these two especially large bedrooms are carbon copies of each other, with gas fireplaces, oversized feather beds, and spacious bathrooms with Jacuzzi tubs big enough for two. But what makes these rooms truly memorable is that each has a large balcony overlooking the sea. *Directions*: Driving north on Highway 101, go over the Rogue River bridge and continue for 5½ miles, then turn left at the blinking yellow light. Go for almost a mile and the inn is on your left.

INN AT NESIKA BEACH
Innkeeper: Ann Arsenault
33026 Nesika Road
Gold Beach, OR 97444
Tel: (541) 247-6434
4 Rooms, Double: $100–$130
Open all year, Credit cards: none accepted
Inappropriate for children, No smoking
www.karenbrown.com/california/innatnesikabeach.html

| GOLD BEACH, Oregon | TU TU' TUN LODGE | Map: 1a |

Tu Tu' Tun (pronounced "too–toot'–tun") is a delightful small fishing lodge hugging the banks of the Rogue River, 7 miles from the coast. Although it is appealing at first glance, when you go inside you realize how truly special Tu Tu' Tun Lodge is and why its rooms are booked solid all season (often months ahead). The heart of the inn includes a spacious lounge with a massive stone fireplace and a wall of windows facing the river, an intimate bar, cozy library, and a nationally acclaimed gourmet dining room. A separate two-story wing, joined by a walkway to the lounge-dining area, houses the guestrooms. All have tall windows overlooking the river, and decks or patios with dramatic views. Many of the bedrooms have fireplaces and some even have outdoor soaking tubs. Throughout the lodge, the furnishings are of fine quality and the tasteful decor, exuding a rustic yet sophisticated simplicity. Stretching across the entire side of the lodge, facing the intensely green water of the Rogue, is a large deck—a favorite place for guests to relax with a good book during the day or to gather around the "camp fire" in the evening. Terraced below the deck is a swimming pool, and below that the lawn sweeps down to the banks of the river where there is a small boat pier from which guests leave each morning for fishing excursions or jet-boat trips up the Rogue. *Directions*: From Gold Beach, drive north over the bridge and immediately turn right on the North Rogue. Continue for about 6 miles, following signs for the inn.

TU TU' TUN LODGE
Innkeepers: Laurie & Dirk Van Zante
96550 North Bank Rogue, Gold Beach, OR 97444
Tel: (541) 247-6664 or (800) 864-6357
Fax: (541) 247-0672
E-mail: tututun@harborside.com
20 Rooms, Double: $185–$210, breakfast & dinner
Double: $85 to $125, offseason, breakfast only
Open May to Nov., full service; Nov. to May, B&B only
Credit cards: MC, VS, Children accepted, No Smoking
www.karenbrown.com/california/tututunlodge.html

Places to Stay

GRASS VALLEY — MURPHY'S INN

Map: 4b

Grass Valley has continued to prosper since the heady Gold Rush days when Cornish miners arrived from England seeking their fortunes in gold. Although the town cannot compete for charm with nearby Nevada City, it certainly has a first-class hostelry in Murphy's Inn—this small inn, its broad verandah decorated with topiary ivy baskets, was once the mansion of North Star Mine owner Edward Colman. It has been lovingly restored and refurbished. Bedrooms in the main house range from Theodosia's Suite with its king-size bed sitting before the fireplace, to a cozy, small upstairs bedroom. One room just off the kitchen has a delightful gas stove and sunny skylights. The entire inn is furnished in Victorian finery. The Donation Day House, just across the street, has two suites, one with a full kitchen, which could accommodate guests with children. Ted and Nancy encourage guests to make themselves at home and stock the refrigerators with juices, sodas, and goodies and supply the "best chocolate chip cookies west of the Mississippi." *Directions:* From the San Francisco area take Highway 80 to 49 north to Grass Valley, exit on Colfax, then go left on South Auburn and left on Neal.

MURPHY'S INN
Owners: Nancy & Ted Daus
Innkeeper: Linda Jones
318 Neal Street
Grass Valley, CA 95945
Tel: (530) 275-6873 or (800) 895-2488
Fax: (530) 273-5157
8 Rooms with private bathrooms
Double: $100–$155
Open all year, Credit cards: all major
Children accepted, No smoking
www.karenbrown.com/california/murphysinn.html

GROVELAND   THE GROVELAND HOTEL   Map: 4d

Groveland is a quaint Gold Rush town just half an hour from the west entrance to Yosemite. Highway 120 becomes Groveland's one main street as it transects the charming town. It is a great place to break the drive and stop for either breakfast or lunch at the corner PJ's Café and for those who choose to overnight and just take a day trip into the park, the Groveland Hotel offers very comfortable and attractive accommodation. Fronting Main Street, the Groveland Hotel is actually two buildings dating from 1849 and 1914 joined by a wrap-around verandah. One building dates from the Gold Rush and the other was built as a boarding house to accommodate the executives from San Francisco here to oversee the building of the massive Hetch Hetchy water project. No two rooms are alike and yet each is pleasing in its decor, decorated with a blend of antiques and attractive fabrics. Although opening onto the street, some of the main floor and front upstairs rooms enjoy lovely bay windows and there are two rooms, one with a queen the other twin beds, which each have only one window and therefore no views, but they are a great value for their price. A Continental breakfast is included in the room rate, and the restaurant also offers dinner. *Directions:* Groveland is a two hours from Sacramento along the historic stretch of Highway 120.

THE GROVELAND HOTEL
Innkeepers: Peggy & Grover Mosley
18767 Main Street
P.O. Box 481, Groveland, CA 95321
Tel: (209) 962-4000 or (800) 273-3314
Fax: (209) 962-6674
E-mail: peggy@groveland.com
17 Rooms, Double: $115–$195
Open all year, Credit cards: all major
Children accepted, No smoking
www.karenbrown.com/california/groveland.html

GUALALA — NORTH COAST COUNTRY INN

Maps: 1c & 2a

With a backdrop of towering redwood and pine trees, the weathered, wood-sided cottages of the North Coast Country Inn step up the hillside just off the eastside of Highway 1. Although it does not have ocean views, the inn's wooded setting is lovely and the accommodation is some of the best in the area. Nancy and Loren Flanagan use the original old farmhouse, once part of a local sheep ranch, as their private residence and patterned the neighboring cottages after its rustic and appealing design. Each spacious guestroom cottage is attractive in its individual and country decor, enjoys its own private entrance off a porch or surrounding deck, and is equipped with dining and kitchenette areas, a wood-burning fireplace, and private bathroom. Although it was hard to select a favorite, I loved the space of the Aquitaine Room with its handsome four-poster bed, beamed ceiling, and large windows. A maze of brick walkways weaves through an immaculately cared for garden of green lawn and fruit trees, while a wooded path winds up the hillside to a secluded hot tub set into a two-level redwood deck, magical at night under the beauty of dramatic stars whose intensity is not diminished by city lights. In 1998 two rooms were added on the hillside above the garage. Price includes a wonderful full breakfast served in the new common room. *Directions:* Located at Highway 1 and Fish Rock Road, 4 miles north of Gualala and ¼ mile north of Anchor Bay.

NORTH COAST COUNTRY INN
Innkeepers: Nancy & Loren Flanagan
34591 South Highway One
Gualala, CA 95445
Tel: (707) 884-4537 or (800) 959-4537
6 Rooms, Double: $150–$195
Credit cards: all major
Inappropriate for children, No smoking
www.karenbrown.com/california/northcoastinn.html

GUALALA — OLD MILANO HOTEL Maps: 1c & 2a

The Old Milano Hotel has been welcoming guests since the first day the doors opened in 1905. Although built upon a bluff overlooking the ocean in what appears to be quite an isolated location, at the turn of the century the hotel was a center of activity, serving overnight stagecoach guests, lumber barons, and travelers on their way up the coast by train. Today, the old hotel has been restored to reflect its original Victorian elegance and two lovely new cottages are currently being built on the beautiful acreage. In the original hotel, none of the six guestrooms upstairs has a private bath, but all are decorated with Victorian antiques and although pocket-sized and a bit worn, most enjoy some spectacular ocean views. Just off the living room on the first floor is the largest guestroom in the old hotel, another room is tucked into a cottage in the rear garden and still another is housed in an old-fashioned train caboose set amongst the trees. Each new cottage has two guestrooms with ocean views, private baths, and gas fireplaces. In the main house, the large dining room and wine parlor, with a massive stone fireplace, are especially attractive. Gourmet dinners are offered nightly. Although it has many attributes, the hotel's most outstanding feature is its perfect location on a lawn which sweeps down to a bluff overlooking the ocean. *Directions*: The Old Milano Hotel is on the Coastal Highway just north of Gualala.

OLD MILANO HOTEL
Innkeeper: Leslie Linscheid
38300 Highway 1
Gualala, CA 95445
Tel: (707) 884-3256, Fax: (707) 884-4249
E-mail: lll@mcn.org
13 Rooms, 7 with private bathrooms
Double: $80–$210
Open all year, Credit cards: MC, VS
Inappropriate for children, No smoking, Wheelchair friendly

GUERNEVILLE APPLEWOOD, INN & RESTAURANT Maps: 1c & 2a

Until it was converted to a inn, Applewood was a private residence. The present owners, Jim Caron and Darryl Notter, have transformed it into a well-tended, European-style inn—not trendy, just quietly elegant. The atmosphere is that of a country lodge, with a large stone fireplace opening on two sides, warming both the living room and a cheerful glassed-in dining room. Just off the living room is another dining room with an enormous crystal chandelier hanging above a central table surrounded by individual small tables. In addition to breakfast, with a reservation, Applewood offers their guests and the community dinner featuring fresh Sonoma County produce, much of it grown in the hotel's own gardens. Dining-room windows look over a wooded area. Guestrooms are found in the main house or in Piccola Casa, a new building that fronts the inn's lovely new courtyard entry. The immaculate bedrooms are all individual in their decor, although each has a TV, direct-dial phone, and comfortable queen bed decked with down comforter and pillows. The seven suites have Jacuzzi tubs or showers for two. Prices reflect the room's size and location, and whether or not it has a fireplace. The furnishings are elegant, slightly formal, but still showing the homey touch of the owners. *Directions:* On Highway 116, half a mile south of the bridge as you leave Guerneville.

APPLEWOOD, INN & RESTAURANT
Innkeepers: Jim Caron & Darryl Notter
13555 Highway 116 (Pocket Canyon Area)
Guerneville, CA 95446
Tel: (707) 869-9093 or (800) 555-8509
Fax: (707) 869-9170
E-mail: stay@applewoodinn.com
16 Rooms, Double: $125–$185, Suite:$200–$250
Open all year, Credit cards: all major
Inappropriate for children
No smoking, Wheelchair friendly
www.karenbrown.com/california/applewoodinn.html

HALF MOON BAY BEACH HOUSE Map: 3c

Beach House, situated on the coast 3½ miles from the town of Half Moon Bay, overlooks the bay and Princeton Harbor. Welcoming guests since 1997, the Beach House has 54 lofts, each with a patio or balcony, most boasting spectacular vistas of the entire 7-mile stretch of crescent-shaped coastline aptly named Half Moon Bay. Although the hotel fronts a highway, double-paned windows on the street-facing rooms block the noise, and inside, the highway is quickly forgotten. Each loft is a tastefully decorated two-tiered suite (separate living room and bedroom areas) with a king-size bed and sleeper sofa. Designed with the guest's comfort in mind, every loft enjoys a wood-burning fireplace, wet bar, refrigerator, CD/stereo system, robes, and bathroom with double sinks and deep tub. If you are traveling with children, ask about their "family accommodation"—two neighboring lofts that share a common main door. Those on a budget might opt for a non-view room. For extra space and comfort, the 800-square-foot Half Moon Suite has two decks, vaulted ceilings, and a sitting area in the bedroom (there is an additional charge for this suite). Guests may enjoy the Continental breakfast buffet of croissants, muffins, scones, and fruit either on the outdoor patio or in their rooms. With its breathtaking views of the ocean combined with the comforts of a quality hotel, Beach House is sure to please. *Directions*: From San Francisco take Highway 1 south (about 25 miles). Beach House is on the right just after the harbor.

BEACH HOUSE
Manager: David Smith
4100 North Cabrillo Highway
P.O. Box 129, Half Moon Bay, CA 94019-0129
Tel: (800) 315-9366, Fax: (650) 712-0693
E-mail: view@beach-house.com
54 Rooms, Double: $190–$265
Open all year, Credit cards: all major
Children accepted, No smoking
Wheelchair friendly

HALF MOON BAY–Miramar Beach CYPRESS INN   Map: 3c

For those who love to be lulled to sleep by the rhythmic sound of crashing waves, the Cypress Inn might be just your cup of tea. It is positioned directly across the road from the 5-mile-long sandy stretch of Miramar Beach. The Cypress Inn is a contemporary building with a weathered-wood façade with turquoise trim. Giving credence to the inn's name, a windswept cypress tree towers by the entrance. Inside, a native folk-art theme prevails. As you enter, there is a snug sitting area to your left with wicker chairs and sofa grouped around a fireplace. Small rather than spacious, all of the guestrooms have terracotta floors and are very similar in decor except that each has its own color scheme (most painted in bright colors). Each of the rooms has a gas-log fireplace, built-in bed with reading lamps, cactus plants, wicker chairs, a writing desk, and doors opening onto private balconies—each overlooking the ocean. The adjacent Beach House offers four more quietly decorated king-bedded rooms, three of which have filtered ocean views. We particularly enjoyed Dunes Beach, decorated in soft-pink shell motif on the fabric, with its bed facing ocean-view windows. Owners Suzie and Dan are not on-site innkeepers, but oversee a managed staff. *Directions:* Take Highway 1 south from San Francisco. Turn right on Medio Avenue (1½ miles beyond the stop light at Pillar Point harbor). Cypress Inn is at the end of the street.

CYPRESS INN
Owners: Suzie Lankes & Dan Floyd
407 Mirada Road, Miramar Beach
Half Moon Bay, CA 94019
Tel: (650) 726-6002, Fax: (650) 712-0380
E-mail: lodging@cypressinn.com
12 Rooms, Double: $165–$275
Open all year, Credit cards: all major
Children accepted, No smoking
Wheelchair friendly
www.karenbrown.com/california/cypressinn.html

HEALDSBURG BELLE DE JOUR INN Maps: 1c & 2a

The Belle de Jour Inn, a complex of farm cottages built in 1873, has a wonderful country, hillside setting. It is approached by a long drive shaded by pine trees and bordered by lush lawn. The impeccably maintained complex has five cottages with guestrooms plus a single-story farmhouse which is the home of Brenda and Tom. They run their small inn with a professional eye to detail and a genuine warmth of welcome that keeps guests coming back year after year. Once the grain and tack room, the Caretaker's Suite has a pine four-poster, king-size canopy bed topped with Battenberg lace and French doors opening onto a trellised deck. The Terrace Room is charming, with a fireplace and a whirlpool tub for two, overlooking terrace and valley. The Morning Hill Room is cozy with a fireplace and a shuttered window seat. The Atelier, with sitting room, is large and lovely. The carriage house accommodates a magnificent deluxe, second-floor country suite with vaulted ceilings, plank wood floors, old-world antique pine furniture, fireplace, and a whirlpool tub for two in its own stained-glass alcove—very romantic. All rooms have gas fireplaces, refrigerators, CD players, robes, and hairdryers. A full country breakfast is served in the owners' breakfast room. For a memorable wine-tasting experience, Tom will take you in his 1925 vintage auto along the backroads of the wine country. *Directions:* Traveling north on Highway 101, exit at Dry Creek Road, go east to Healdsburg Avenue. Turn left at the lights and go north for 1 mile. The entrance is directly across from the Simi Winery.

BELLE DE JOUR INN
Innkeepers: Brenda & Tom Hearn
16276 Healdsburg Avenue
Healdsburg, CA 95448
Tel: (707) 431-9777, Fax: (707) 431-7412
5 Rooms, Double: $150–$300
Closed Christmas, Credit cards: all major
Inappropriate for children, No smoking
www.karenbrown.com/california/belledejourinn.html

Places to Stay

HEALDSBURG HAYDON STREET INN Maps: 1c & 2a

Haydon Street Inn is set in a very quiet neighborhood of Healdsburg four blocks from the main plaza of this especially nice town. Like the town, the inn is most attractive: a lovely, soft-blue Victorian with a crisp, white trim, fronted by a white picket fence heavily laden with pink roses. Cody, the Bertapelles' dog, greets guests at the door. The main house has a lovely country living room, sitting room, and dining area for guests' use. The six bedrooms, one downstairs and five upstairs, are decorated with homey, comfortable furnishings. The Turret Room, though on the small side, has a fireplace and lovely claw-foot soaking tub. At the rear of the lovely garden is a Victorian-style cottage with two large guestrooms occupying the upper floor. Each cottage room has a private entrance and beautiful pine floors. As an added touch of luxury, the bathrooms in the cottage have double whirlpool bathtubs. The Bertapelles prepare a full country breakfast and serve it on Luneville French or Spode china in the dining room. After a day of wine-tasting, guests can enjoy a leisurely afternoon under the umbrellas on the lawn of this charming bed and breakfast. *Directions*: Traveling north on Highway 101, take the Central Healdsburg exit. Travel straight ahead to the light at Matheson, turn right and right again at Fitch, then continue on to Haydon, where you make a left turn.

HAYDON STREET INN
Innkeepers: Pat & Dick Bertapelle
321 Haydon Street
Healdsburg, CA 94558
Tel: (707) 433-5228 or (800) 528-3703
Fax: (707) 433-6637
8 Rooms, Double: $95–$175
Closed Christmas
Credit cards: MC, VS
Children accepted, No smoking

HEALDSBURG — THE HONOR MANSION — Map: 1c & 2a

The Honor Mansion, a soft-beige Victorian with white trim and a maroon door, sits behind a white picket fence on a residential street. In one corner of the immaculate yard you'll notice a bench under a gazebo covered with tiny white flowers. The first floor houses the gathering areas—a parlor and dining room, tastefully decorated with rich colors and traditional furnishings. From the deck just off the parlor guests can enjoy the gentle sound of water falling into the Koi pond. Although the bed and breakfast now has just six rooms, the Fowlers plan to enlarge to ten rooms by year's end. The guestrooms are found on the second floor and are well appointed with everything from robes to bath salts to garment steamers to lap desks, while the feather beds, down comforters, and fine linens will make you want to just melt into bed. Guests have the use of a small refrigerator upstairs, and a back staircase leads to a lap pool. For more privacy there is a spacious cottage next to the house, which has a private entrance and all the comforts you could desire. An ample gourmet breakfast is served in the dining room at 9 o'clock, and you can even start with a cappuccino or café latte. If you prefer to stay at a bed and breakfast but don't want to sacrifice any of the amenities of a hotel, The Honor Mansion might be just your cup of tea. *Directions:* Traveling north on Highway 101, exit at Dry Creek Road and turn right. At the first stoplight, Grove Street, turn right. The Honor Mansion is on your right.

THE HONOR MANSION
Innkeepers: Cathi & Steve Fowler
14891 Grove Street
Healdsburg, CA 95448
Tel: (800) 554-4667, Fax: (707) 431-7173
6 Rooms, Double: $130–$250
Open all year
Credit cards: MC, VS
Children welcome in some rooms, No smoking

Places to Stay

HEALDSBURG INN ON THE PLAZA Maps: 1c & 2a

Healdsburg's main square is a green park bordered by shops and restaurants. If you want to stay in this charming town, the Inn on the Plaza overlooking the main square is a great choice. Entrance to the Inn is through double doors into a freshly painted, high-ceilinged reception area that doubles as an art gallery and gift shop. A dramatic, long flight of stairs winds up to a central lounge where a jigsaw puzzle is left for each successive guest to work on a bit. Off the lounge are ten bedrooms decorated in a very Victorian style, a few of which overlook the old plaza through bay windows. Most have fireplaces and some have tubs for two. An enclosed rooftop room has white marble tables and chairs and lots of greenery. The carriage house behind the main building is quite large and has a full kitchen, fireplace, and deck off the bedroom. There are two breakfast servings: cereal, toast, jam, and hot beverages are available for early risers and later, around 9 am, a hot egg dish plus fresh fruit platter, hot muffins, and juice are served. Complimentary wine and fresh buttered popcorn are set out at 5:30 pm and on weekends party trays are added. On Saturdays and Sundays there is a spectacular morning brunch with champagne, choice of hot entrees, salads, and dessert. The Inn on the Plaza is a very friendly, welcoming hotel and Genny or her competent staff are always there to greet you. *Directions*: The inn is on the south side of Healdsburg's main square.

INN ON THE PLAZA
Innkeepers: Genny Jenkins & LeRay Steck
110 Matheson, Healdsburg, CA 95448
Tel: (707) 433-6991 or (800) 431-8663
Fax: (707) 433-9513
11 Rooms, Double: $185–$285
Open all year, Credit cards: MC, VS
Children accepted over 5
No smoking, Wheelchair friendly
www.karenbrown.com/california/innontheplaza.html

IDYLLWILD — THE CEDAR STREET INN — Map: 7b

We greatly appreciate the letters we often receive from readers sharing a particular favorite inn along with the unwritten implication that they are astounded that we could have missed such a gem. In the case of The Cedar Street Inn, I received a letter from the owner herself! My only defense is that I simply missed the inn, tucked just off North Circle Drive on a small quiet street of the same name. Within walking distance of the cute shops and restaurants at the heart of Idyllwild, The Cedar Street Inn offers quiet accommodation in cottagey rooms which open onto a central patio. The guestrooms, some of which are housed in private cabins, are individual in decor and offer their own special appointments and appeal. To name just a few of the rooms: the Victorian Suite enjoys a large Roman tub and fireplace; the Attic is accessed by its own private spiral staircase to an outside deck and boasts a bathroom which overlooks the treetops; the Captain's Quarters is decorated in a nautical decor and is warmed by a river-rock fireplace; the Carriage House is a tri-level suite with fireplace and a bathroom equipped with both tub and shower. Patty and Gary Tompkins are your gracious innkeepers, intent on making your stay at The Cedar Street Inn a special and memorable one. *Directions*: Turn off Route 243, turn east on North Circle Drive, and then turn right on Cedar Street.

THE CEDAR STREET INN
Innkeepers: Patty & Gary Tompkins
25880 Cedar Street
P.O. Box 627, Idyllwild, CA 92549
Tel: (909) 659-4789, Fax: (909) 659-3540
E-mail: cedarstreet@idyllwild.com
8 Rooms & 3 Cabins, Double: $75–$145
Open all year, Credit cards: all major
Children accepted in cabins, No smoking
Conference & wedding room
www.karenbrown.com/california/cedarstreetinn.html

Places to Stay

IDYLLWILD   FERN VALLEY INN   Map: 7b

Idyllwild is a mile-high village of some 3,000 residents, and with its magnificent hiking trails affords a wonderful weekend getaway from the metropolitan areas of southern California. The Fern Valley Inn is a rustic country inn of 11 charming cabins nestled in the pines. On a recent visit to the inn I was fortunate to be able to get to know the owners who are enthusiastic about their role as innkeepers and have ambitious plans to refurbish and redecorate. In transition, Colleen was experimenting with new quilts and knickknacks for the various rooms at the time of my visit, but she stated that she still plans to maintain a theme for each room to be reflected in the decor. Themes vary from a southwestern motif to The School Room with its old school prints, a drawing slate, and printed rules for teachers. Rooms are supplied with coffee, teas, and homemade banana nut bread as breakfast fare. Each cottage is equipped with a refrigerator, coffeemaker, television, and fireplace or log stove. Colleen and Mike McCann personally tend to the inn and care for their guests. The grounds are immaculately kept—swept pathways wind amongst the cottages, leading to the heated pool, rose garden, and parlor. The parlor with its porch is a welcoming place for guests to congregate and enjoy a glass of sherry or a challenging game of chess. *Directions:* Take Highway 10 west from Los Angeles to Banning and Highway 243 to Idyllwild. Turn left on North Circle, right on South Circle, left on Fern Valley Road.

FERN VALLEY INN
Innkeepers: Colleen & Mike McCann
25240 Fern Valley Road
P.O. Box 116, Idyllwild, CA 92549
Tel: (909) 659-2205, Fax: (909) 659-2630
E-mail: fernvalleyinn@idyllwild.com
11 Rooms, Double: $65–$105
Open all year, Credit cards: all major
Children accepted over 12, No smoking
www.karenbrown.com/california/fernvalleyinn.html

| IGO | BRIGADOON CASTLE | Map: 1b |

Brigadoon Castle is spectacular. Tucked away on a private oasis of 86 acres and bounded by national forest, it is a magnificent property and a wonderfully romantic hideaway. The turreted entrance to the castle is through a handsome arched wooden door framed by ivy and wisteria. Inside, although impressive with its vaulted archways, dramatic stair, lofty ceilings, wide passageways, and regal decor, the ambiance is also welcoming and intimate. The two-tiered living room is magnificent with sofas set before its brick fireplace which rises to the loft library, a lovely room looking out through towering windows to the surrounding greenery. Outside the living room a brick terrace stretches to the edge of the woods and a path beckons on up to the hot tub. Five bedchambers are found in the main castle, each more beautiful than the next, from feminine Korysa's Garden Room with its hand-painted whitewashed sleigh bed and armoire and delicate decor to the two-level Tyler's Tree Top Room in the turret with its mural-covered walls and ceiling. The gatekeeper's house, The Cottage, has its own living room, fireplace, full kitchen, loft bedroom, deck with hot tub, and a gorgeous setting next to the rushing creek. This is hostess Geri MacCallum's adventure of a lifetime, and she invites you to come to Brigadoon and let the magic stir your heart! *Directions*: A bit complicated! For a general orientation, Igo is located 15 miles south west of Redding. Call for directions.

BRIGADOON CASTLE
Innkeeper: Geri E. MacCallum
9036 Zogg Mine Road
P.O. Box 324, Igo, CA 96047
Tel: (530) 396-2785 or (888) 343-2836
Fax: (530) 396-2784, E-mail: brgadoon@c-3one.net
5 Rooms, Double: $150–$285
Open all year, Credit cards: all major
Children accepted by prior arrangement
No smoking
www.karenbrown.com/california/brigadooncastle.html

Places to Stay

INVERNESS — BLACKTHORNE INN

Maps: 1c, 2c, & 3a

The Blackthorne Inn is the whimsical creation of Susan and Bill Wigert. They have built a Hansel and Gretel house tucked among the treetops, loaded with peaked roofs, dormer windows, funny little turrets, bay windows, and an octagonal tower. You wind up through the trees to the main entry level which is wrapped by an enormous wooden deck, emphasizing the tree-house look. The living room is dominated by a floor-to-ceiling stone fireplace. Skylights, a stained-glass window, a Chinese carpet, wood-paneled walls, baskets of flowers, and walls of windows looking out into the trees make the room most appealing. The guestrooms, located on various levels, are not decorated in any particular period or style, and because of the wooded setting vary in outlook and available sunlight. The favorite choice of many is the Eagle's Nest, located in the octagonal tower, where walls of glass give the impression one is sleeping under the stars—camping at its best. (Note: It is a bit rustic as the bathroom is outside, in the dressing room opposite the hot tub.) Each of the other guestrooms has its own personality, whether it be with stained-glass windows, a private entrance, a separate sitting room, or a bay window looking out into the trees. *Directions:* Take Sir Francis Drake Boulevard off Highway 1 to Olema. Turn right, go 2 miles, then left toward Inverness, go 1 mile, then left on Vallejo Avenue (at the Knave of Hearts Bakery).

BLACKTHORNE INN
Innkeepers: Susan & Bill Wigert
266 Vallejo Avenue
P.O. Box 712, Inverness, CA 94937
Tel: (415) 663-8621, Fax: (415) 663-8635
E-mail: susan@blackthorneinn.com
5 Rooms, Double: $175–$250
Open all year, Credit cards: MC, VS
Children by prior arrangement, No smoking
www.karenbrown.com/california/blackthorneinn.html

INVERNESS — MANKA'S INVERNESS LODGE Maps: 1c, 2c, & 3a

Built as a hunting lodge by the Empire Club in 1917, this dark-shingled building highlighted with a white trim porch hung with greenery is a wonderful escape in the woods just up from the bay. Under the artistically brilliant direction of its owner, Manka's now offers intimate accommodation and a restaurant (open Thursday through Monday) whose menu is in keeping with the theme of a hunting lodge—much of the food is grilled over an open fire. Four guestrooms are found up a narrow flight of stairs above the restaurant. They occupy the four corners of the lodge and open onto a hallway hung with antlers and old paintings which creaks round the stairwell. Two of the rooms enjoy an expanse of deck looking out through the trees to the bay. Four rooms are located in a rambling annex at the back of the wooded property. Two cabins just below the lodge and two a short drive away, both nestled on the edge of the water enjoying its own acreage and private beach, offer the guest even more privacy and rustic seclusion. We love the wonderful four-poster beds made from rough-hewn Oregon fir, enhanced by warm flannel checks and plaids, and draped with heavy throw blankets. Manka's charm is its appealing, comfortable, rustic ambiance—a homey hideaway inviting you to nestle in with a good book and romantic company. Note: Breakfast is offered from a tempting menu at tables set in the lobby in front of the fire and is additional to the cost of the room. *Directions:* Manka's is at Argyle and Callendar Street.

MANKA'S INVERNESS LODGE
Owner: Margaret Grade
Innkeeper: Linda Rose
30 Callendar Way
P.O. Box 1110, Inverness, CA 94937
Tel: (415) 669-1034, Fax: (415) 669-1598
8 Rooms, 1 Suite, 3 Cabins, Double: $145–$365
Open all year, Credit cards: MC, VS
Children accepted, No smoking
www.karenbrown.com/california/mankasinvernesslodge.html

Places to Stay

INVERNESS   SANDY COVE INN   Maps: 1c, 2c, & 3a

Sandy Cove Inn offers guests a spectacular setting of wilderness, beauty, and quiet. Its grounds boast a riding arena and stable, an expanse of well-tended garden, and, unbelievably, its own private stretch of sand beach on Tomales Bay. Without venturing beyond the fenced compound one can picnic, swim, beachcomb, tidepool, kayak, or birdwatch. In addition to a parklike setting, the inn offers very private guest accommodation in cottages of weathered wood smartly trimmed in white, each with its own entrance. One feels ultimately pampered with every need anticipated: you are provided not only with the expected amenities, but with imaginative extras such as binoculars, first-aid kits, flashlights, backpacks, hats, walking sticks, insect repellent, beach maps, and slippers at the front door—an attention to detail I have seen nowhere else. A bountiful breakfast including a hot entree is delivered to your room. The handsome guestrooms are individual in decor and offerings. The North Suite has its own fire stove, a pine bed, a decor of rich cranberry with a nautical theme, and a deck overlooking the dressage arena, stables and Inverness Ridge; the South Suite, dressed with a subtle equestrian theme, enjoys a wood stove and a small sitting area overlooking the arena; and the West Suite has its own porch, a gas fireplace, and a decor of rich blues and burgundies. *Directions:* Travel Sir Francis Drake Boulevard north through Inverness. Just before the road veers inland towards Point Reyes beaches, watch for the gated entry to the inn on the right.

SANDY COVE INN
Innkeepers: Kathy & Gerry Coles
12990 Sir Francis Drake Blvd
P.O. Box 869, Inverness, CA 94937
Tel: (415) 669-2683 or (800) 759-2683
Fax: (415) 669-7511
E-mail: innkeeper@sandycoveinn.com
3 Rooms, Double: $185–$250
Open all year, Credit cards: all major
Children accepted over 13, No smoking indoors or outdoors
www.karenbrown.com/california/sandycoveinn.html

Places to Stay

INVERNESS — TEN INVERNESS WAY

Maps: 1c, 2c, & 3a

Ten Inverness Way is an attractive-looking inn—a cozy, redwood-shingled building originally built in 1904 as a family home. A flagstone path leads from the road up a slope, through the carefree, cheerful English garden to the front door. Inside, a staircase takes you to the second level and opens to the living room which has an informal ambiance with a large stone fireplace and is decorated in blue and white with comfortable furniture slip covered in denim and striped fabric. The room is inviting and homey. Guests relax and make themselves at home here—playing games or snuggling up in a window seat with a good book. Teri and Scott, the new owners of the inn, have converted what once was the breakfast room into a cozy library full of good books, and now small tables are set for breakfast along the windows of the living room. Simply decorated, the four small bedrooms are fresh and immaculately clean, with handmade quilts on the beds adding a special touch. A ground-level suite has a kitchen, French doors leading to its own garden, and a handpainted mural surrounding the bed. Guests can reserve a hot tub in the back garden for a private soak. In the morning Teri and Scott serve a delicious full breakfast, and they are happy to pack a picnic lunch for your exploration of Point Reyes National Seashore. *Directions*: Drive into Inverness on the main road, Sir Francis Drake Boulevard, and watch for the sign pointing to your left to Ten Inverness Way.

TEN INVERNESS WAY
Innkeepers: Teri & Scott Mowery
Ten Inverness Way
P.O. Box 63, Inverness, CA 94937
Tel: (415) 669-1648, Fax: (415) 669-7403
E-mail: inn@teninvernessway.com
5 Rooms, Double: $145–$180
Open all year, Credit cards: MC, VS
Children accepted in suite
www.karenbrown.com/california/teninvernessway.html

JAMESTOWN   JAMESTOWN HOTEL   Map: 4d

Jamestown, with its high wooden sidewalks and wooden storefronts with broad balconies hanging to the street, wears an air of yesteryear—you expect to see old-time cowboys emerging from the saloon and a stagecoach rumbling down its Main Street. It seems that every Gold Rush town had a hotel similar to this one, but today few can boast of a city hotel that has received the careful restoration that the Jamestown Hotel has. The outside looks much as it did in its heyday, a simple brick false-front building whose second-story balcony forms a roof above the sidewalk. The lobby, cocktail lounge (where drinks are available in a cozy fireside setting in the evening and breakfast is served in the morning), and dining room occupy the ground floor. The restaurant abounds with the same old-world ambiance as the rest of the hotel and prides itself on serving excellent food. On summer days meals are served on the patio. The bedrooms are quaintly Victorian, neat as new pins. Some are two smaller rooms made into a sitting room and bedroom combination. All have attractive, spotless bathrooms and are named for famous western personalities, being decorated with that person in mind, for example, Lola Montez, Lotta Crabtree, Jenny Lind, and Lily Langtry. *Directions:* From the San Francisco area take Highway 580 for 60 miles, then Highway 120 east to Jamestown which is just before Sonora.

JAMESTOWN HOTEL
Innkeepers: Janet & Lee Hammond
18153 Main Street
P.O. Box 539, Jamestown, CA 95327
Tel: (209) 984-3902 or (800) 205-4901
Fax: (209) 984-4149
E-mail: reserve@jamestownhotel.com
11 Rooms, Double: $70–$135
Open all year, Credit cards: all major
Children accepted, No smoking
www.karenbrown.com/california/jamestownhotel.html

Places to Stay

JAMESTOWN — THE NATIONAL HOTEL Map: 4d

Built in 1859 and proudly claiming to be one of California's ten oldest hotels, the National Hotel is located on the main street of Jamestown, considered the gateway to the Gold Country. The first floor accommodates a wonderful restaurant where an extravagant breakfast buffet and morning newspaper is set out for resident guests and where lunch, dinner, and a Sunday champagne brunch is available to residents and non-residents. You can also opt to enjoy lunch or dinner at tables set on a side terrace under the shade of a vine-covered trellis. The handsome old redwood bar in the Gold Rush Saloon offers refreshment, possible entertainment, and local gossip. A steep stairway just off the entry leads to the 9 guestrooms on the second floor. Wonderful old brass and iron beds decked with handmade patchwork quilts, handsome trunks, lovely old armoires, antique washbasins, and lace curtains at the windows dominate the decor which is pleasing and reminiscent of the Gold Rush era—but with modern comforts. All guestrooms enjoy private bathrooms and the hotel has a wonderful "soaking room" which accommodates oversized claw-foot bathtub—available to all guests who are decadently supplied with bathrobe and slippers. The guestrooms are comfortable, air conditioned, and are all accessed off the one central hallway. The two front rooms overlook the front balcony and the action of main street. *Directions*: Jamestown's Main Street intersects both Highways 108 and 49 on the east and west end of town.

THE NATIONAL HOTEL
Innkeepers: Pamela & Stephen Willey
77 Main Street
P.O. Box 502, Jamestown, CA 95327
Tel: (209) 984-3446, Fax: (209) 984-5620
E-mail: info@national-hotel.com
9 Rooms, Double: $80–$100
Open all year, Credit cards: all major
Children accepted over 9, Smoking
www.karenbrown.com/california/nationalhotel.html

Places to Stay

JULIAN THE JULIAN WHITE HOUSE Map: 7d

Located in a residential area south of the old Gold Rush town of Julian, is a miniature southern mansion, painted white with four stately columns accenting the front of the house. The style especially appealed to Alan whose family, many years ago, used to own a plantation, while the tranquil setting appealed to Mary. Inside, the home is simple, but very pleasant. The living room opens onto a sunlit dining room with a wall of windows looking out to a sloping forest of trees. Guests gather in the dining room for a lavish, homemade breakfast served elegantly on family china and silver. Downstairs there is one bedroom wallpapered in muted shades of tan and dusty pink with a handsome Louis XVI antique bed. This is the French Quarter Room where feather masks and Mardi Gras memorabilia set the New Orleans theme. Upstairs, two bedrooms are nicely decorated in pastel blues and pinks, while the Honeymoon Suite has recently been redecorated in burgundy and tapestry. Also recently redecorated, the East Room is described by Mary as "subdued Victorian," decorated in blues and whites to complement the colors in the bath. Gas fireplaces are also new, romantic additions to both the Honeymoon Suite and East Room. *Directions:* From Julian head south on Highway 78. Turn left on Pine Hills Road, then right at the second street which is Blue Jay Drive. (Total driving distance from Julian is about 4 miles.)

THE JULIAN WHITE HOUSE
Innkeepers: Mary & Alan Marvin
3014 Blue Jay Drive
P.O. Box 824, Julian, CA 92036
Tel & fax: (760) 765-1764 or (800) 948-4687
E-mail: stay@julian-whitehouse-bnb.com
4 Rooms, Double: $90–$165
Open all year, Credit cards: MC, VS
Children accepted over 12, No smoking
www.karenbrown.com/california/julianwhitehouse.html

JULIAN ORCHARD HILL COUNTRY INN Map: 7d

Just a block off main street on a Julian hillside sits a lovely property, open for just a few years, that already boasts a very loyal clientele. It is not surprising when you see the accommodation: guestrooms are lovely, with handsome country furnishings complemented by beautiful wallpapers and coordinating fabrics. The Yellow Bellflower, for example, is decorated in tones of soft blues and yellow, with a beautiful blue arch or faience hung over the bed, materials of a subtle pinstripe and blue check, and a multi-colored quilt draped at the foot of the bed. There is nothing country-cute in the decor—rather, rooms are spacious and subtle in their elegance. Cottage guestrooms all enjoy private entrances, tucked in a garden setting, along a wandering path and central courtyard. All rooms are equipped with TV, VCR (complimentary video library), all but one have a fireplace, and half have whirlpool tubs. Bathrooms are spacious, modern, and wonderfully appointed. At the top of the property, the handsome lodge offers more standard rooms in terms of size and price, a lovely large public room with high vaulted ceilings and river-stone fireplace, a dining room, and an upstairs common area with sofa, lounge chairs, and a TV. Room prices include a full breakfast and evening hors d'oeuvres. In the intimacy of the lovely dining room a delicious menu is offered three evenings per week. *Directions*: Washington Street crosses Main Street at the north end of town.

ORCHARD HILL COUNTRY INN
Innkeepers: Pat & Darrell Straube
2502 Washington Street
P.O. Box 425, Julian, CA 92036-0425
Tel: (760) 765-1700 or (800) 716-7242
Fax: (760) 765-0290, E-mail: information@orchardhill.com
22 Rooms, Double: $155–$265
Closed Christmas, Easter and one week in January
Credit cards: all major
Children accepted over 12, No smoking, Wheelchair friendly
www.karenbrown.com/california/orchardhillcountryinn.html

Places to Stay

LAGUNA BEACH — EILER'S INN — Map: 7a

Eiler's Inn, although on a busy highway, has been carefully designed so that the guestrooms do not face the traffic, but front onto a central courtyard where the only sound is that of the gurgling fountain. This inner brick-paved patio, filled with colorfully blooming plants and potted greenery, is the heart of the inn where guests gather in the evening for wine and cheeses and again in the morning for a wonderful buffet breakfast. If the weather is chilly, guests congregate around the blazing fire in the front lounge. Henk and Annette Wirtz, from Germany, were the previous owners of the inn but, sadly, Henk Wirtz recently passed away, so the tradition of welcome and camaraderie is now being continued by his son, Nico, and the resident managers. There is a true European ambiance and a mood of warmth and informal friendliness at Eiler's Inn. The bedrooms all differ in decor and were recently refurbished, with the majority receiving new carpets and new spreads to deck the beds. The rooms are pleasant, but on the cozy side in terms of size and beachside casual in their appointments, many with rattan and wicker predominating. However, guests seem happy with both the hotel and its proximity to the beach, just a two-minute walk down the hill. *Directions*: On the coastal Highway 1, just south of the town center between Cleo and St Anne streets. (There is limited parking.)

EILER'S INN
Owner: Nico Wirtz
Innkeepers: Cynthia & Norman Wright
741 South Coast Highway
Laguna Beach, CA 92651
Tel: (949) 494-3004, Fax: (949) 497-2215
12 Rooms, Double: $85–$195
Open all year, Credit cards: all major
Inappropriate for children, No smoking
www.karenbrown.com/california/eilersinn.html

Places to Stay

LA JOLLA — THE LA JOLLA BED & BREAKFAST INN — Map: 7c

From the street The La Jolla Bed & Breakfast Inn is a nondescript building with a pale-peach stucco wash, but behind its façade is a surprising oasis of comfort. The inn is located two blocks from the heart of La Jolla's elegant shopping district as well as its lovely beach and directly across the street from public tennis courts. Management describes the decor as "elegant cottage style": beautiful furnishings, lovely fabrics, handsome prints, and a few antiques have been carefully selected to suit the mood of each room. Guestrooms vary dramatically in size and have been refurbished and redecorated. Ten rooms are located in the historic house and five in the annex. On sunny days pass through the arched doorway and laze in the back yard at tables set on a brick patio bordered by grass and flowers. Breakfast is served in the dining area, on the patio, or in your bedroom. Not owner managed, a young staff oversees your welcome. *Directions:* From San Diego take Route 5 and exit right on La Jolla Village Drive. Turn left on Torrey Pines Road and proceed 2½ miles to Prospect Place. Turn right, drive nine blocks, then turn left on Draper Avenue.

THE LA JOLLA BED & BREAKFAST INN
Innkeeper: Ron Shanks
7753 Draper Avenue
La Jolla, CA 92037
Tel: (619) 456-2066 or (800) 582-2466
Fax: (619) 456-1510
15 Rooms with private bathrooms
Double: $110–$250
Open all year, Credit cards: all major
Children accepted over 12
No smoking, Wheelchair friendly

LA JOLLA — LA VALENCIA HOTEL — Map: 7c

Doing justice to La Jolla is the romantic La Valencia Hotel: subtle-pink adobe-like walls, thick Spanish-tiled roof, and a characterful tower domed with blue-and-gold mosaics set the stage for this special hotel. There is a captivating, old-world charm from the moment you stroll under the colonnade, alongside the palm-shaded garden restaurant, and through the front door. The hotel dates back to the 1920s: thankfully the essence and dream of the original hotel have been faithfully preserved—and even bettered. The reception parlor opens onto a dramatic long parlor whose soft-buff-colored walls, wrought-iron chandeliers, subdued lighting, blue-and-yellow tiled planter, luscious displays of fresh flowers, and painted ceiling are dramatized at the end of the room by a wall of glass framing the sea. All of the guestrooms are individually decorated in a traditional style of furnishings and fabrics. The most expensive rooms are those with a view of the ocean, but even the less expensive rooms (such as those next to the garden) are lovely. One of my favorites, room 813 overlooking the front street, is especially spacious and has the added bonus of a kitchenette. On one of the lower terraces there is a lovely pool enhanced by perfectly tended gardens and nearby a "secret gate" allows guests to stroll from the hotel grounds down the road to La Jolla's beautiful little coves. *Directions:* Exit Highway 5 north at Ardath Road (5 south at La Jolla Village), travel to Torrey Pines Road and right on Prospect Street.

LA VALENCIA HOTEL
Director: Michael J. Ullman
1132 Prospect Street
La Jolla, CA 92037
Tel: (619) 454-0771 or (800) 451-0772
Fax: (619) 456-3921, E-mail: valencia@adnc.com
100 Rooms, Double: $225–$900*
*Breakfast not included
Open all year, Credit cards: all major
Children accepted, Smoking, Wheelchair friendly

Places to Stay

LA JOLLA—San Diego   SCRIPPS INN   Map: 7c

The Scripps Inn enjoys an absolutely magnificent setting just steps away from the white sand of La Jolla's gorgeous cove and beach and expanse of sparkling blue water. One can walk or bike for miles along the pedestrian trail that contours along the bluff and it is also just a few short blocks up the hill to the heart of the village with its elegant shops and delightful restaurants. The location alone of this attractive two- and three-story tan building, trimmed in dark green, and colored with bougainvillea would warrant inclusion, but I was pleased to find the rooms also very attractive. Two wings of rooms wrap around the central car park and upstairs guestrooms are accessed off a covered walkway. Recently redecorated, the rooms are fresh and pretty, light and airy in their décor whose mix of tans, creams and beiges selected for the fabrics compliment beautifully the light woods of the country style furnishings. In terms of ocean view, all the rooms have some view while a few are exceptional. Room 6, a on the first floor, and rooms 11 and 12 on the second floor all enjoy king beds, fireplace and sweeping views looking up and down the coast. On the third floor with a separate sitting area, Suite 7 has two queen beds, a kitchen and living room and spectacular views and on the second floor, Suite 14 is exceptional with a king bed and four large bay windows through which one has unobstructed views of La Jolla Cove. A continental breakfast is set out in the cozy office niche and one can either opt to sit at the few tables set on the terrace or take it back to the privacy of your guestroom. Directions: The Scripps Inn is on the corner of Coast Boulevard and Cuvier Street just off of La Jolla Boulevard.

SCRIPPS INN
Resident Manager: Pamela L. Millan
555 Coast Boulevard, South, La Jolla, California 92037
Tel: (619) 454-3391, Fax: (619) 456-0389
E-mail: plmlajolla@aol.com
14 Rooms, Double: $145–$300, Breakfast: included
Open: all year, Credit cards: all major
Children accepted in first floor rooms, No smoking

Places to Stay

LAKE ARROWHEAD — EAGLE'S LANDING

Although Eagle's Landing is a bed and breakfast, it is run so professionally that guests have the feeling that they are in a miniature hotel. There are four guestrooms with private bath and, although each varies in decor, they all maintain a comfy-homey ambiance and are all meticulously kept—everything "neat as a pin." One of the bedrooms, the Lake View Suite, is enormous, with its own fireplace and a spacious private deck with a view of the lake. However, my favorite room is the cozy Woods Room, tucked amongst the trees with its own little terrace and entrance. The living room has a large fireplace in the corner and a splendid long wooden trestle table, big enough for all the guests to gather and share their day's adventures. Just off the dining room is a cozy nook where guests can enjoy breakfast. Speaking of breakfast, Dorothy prides herself on treating her guests to a special brunch on Sunday mornings, a hearty start for exploring the lake which is located a short walk from Eagle's Landing. Since this is a private lake, public access is available only in the town of Arrowhead (about a five-minute drive away). *Directions:* Turn north from Highway 18 following signs for Blue Jay. Before you reach the lake, the road splits. Turn left on North Bay and watch for Cedarwood on your left—Eagle's Landing is on the corner of North Bay and Cedarwood.

EAGLE'S LANDING
Innkeepers: Dorothy & Jack Stone
27406 Cedarwood
Lake Arrowhead, CA 92352
Mailing address:
P.O. Box 1510, Blue Jay, CA 92317
Tel (800) 835-5085, Tel & Fax: (909) 336-2642
4 Rooms, Double: $95–$195
Open all year, Credit cards: all major
Children accepted over 12, No smoking
www.karenbrown.com/california/eagleslanding.html

LAKE ARROWHEAD   SADDLEBACK INN   Map: 7b

The Saddleback Inn is tucked into its own wooded oasis just a short stroll from Lake Arrowhead Village. Although the inn dates back almost 70 years when it was built in the style of an English tavern by two sisters from the Midwest, there is nothing "dated" about this small inn. Its present owners have completely renovated every nook and cranny, creating a slick, very sophisticated hotel. Luckily, they have kept the old-world look with the use of a few antiques plus many reproductions in the decor. The reception area is located in the main lodge which exudes a Victorian mood in its cozy bar and dining room. The original staircase leads off the lobby to ten guestrooms, some quite small but all attractive. Scattered throughout the 3½ acres are small cottages connected by pathways which house the remaining guestrooms. All of the rooms are decorated with Laura Ashley fabrics and wallpapers, and most have a Jacuzzi tub in the bathroom—a wonderful respite after a day of hiking or sightseeing. The Saddleback Inn appears more "slick" than "homey," but behind its commercial façade is the warmth of the manager, Liza Colton, who creates the ambiance of a small inn. This hotel is an especially suitable choice when traveling with children, as a pretty beach is within walking distance. *Directions:* From Highway 173 take the Lake Arrowhead turnoff. Drive 2 miles and the hotel is on the left at the entrance to Lake Arrowhead Village.

SADDLEBACK INN
Innkeepers: Kurt & Bonnie Campbell
300 S. State Highway 173
P.O. Box 1890
Lake Arrowhead, CA 92352
Tel: (909) 336-3571, Fax: (909) 337-4277
10 Rooms, 24 Cottages, Double: $140–$230*
*Breakfast not included
Open all year, Credit cards: all major
Children accepted, Smoking, Wheelchair friendly

RIVER   GLENDEVEN   Map: 1c

Glendeven is a charming New-England-style farmhouse built in 1867 by Isaiah Stevens for his bride, Rebecca. Today, this beautiful clapboard home, elegant in its simplicity, is owned by Jan (pronounced Yan), who hails from Holland, and his wife Janet who purchased the property in 1977 and created one of the most delightful inns on the Mendocino coast. Over the years they have expanded the inn to include a two-bedroom suite in the adjacent Barn House and four lovely guestrooms in Stevenscroft, a gabled, barn-sided building in the garden (most rooms have wood-burning fireplaces). Both Jan and Janet are very talented designers whose eye for proportion, style, and color are apparent in every detail. After enjoying a country breakfast in their room, guests usually stroll across to the gallery in Barn House, where they find furniture made by Jan and contemporary artwork and fine crafts chosen by Janet, an interior decorator. Across the highway a path leads through parkland to end at cliffs high above the ocean. Glendeven is just above Van Damme State Park with its scenic walking paths. *Directions*: Glendeven is located on the east side of Highway 1, south of Mendocino.

GLENDEVEN
Owners: Janet & Jan deVries
8221 North Highway 1
Little River, CA 95456
Tel: (707) 937-0083 or (800) 822-4536
Fax: (707) 937-6108
9 Rooms, 1 Suite, Double: $98–$240
Open all year, Credit cards: MC, VS
Children accepted in specific rooms
No smoking, Wheelchair friendly
www.karenbrown.com/california/glendeven.html

LIVERMORE — PURPLE ORCHID INN

Map: 3d

Vineyards are beginning to dress the foothills of the Livermore Valley as numerous wineries take residence in the shadow of the windmills. With such giants as Wente, Ivan Tamas, Stony Ridge Thomas Coyne, and Concannon as neighbors, the recently opened Purple Orchid Inn is a convenient and luxurious retreat from which to explore the wineries. A beautiful, sprawling log cabin set against a backdrop of its own olive orchards, the inn is intended to be a destination in its own right. With a background and current career in health care, owner, Karen Hughes, describes the inn as, "a place of wellness, where guests can visit, relax, and make healthy life choices." One could easily settle at the inn simply to enjoy the beautiful pool, play tennis, practice one's swing by making use of the golf cage or the 20 foot-on-center passage naturally created by the olive orchard, or take advantage of the full range of on-site spa services such as massages, special wraps, skin care, and mineral baths. If dining in appeals, the concierge will pick up your menu selection from local restaurants, and with proper notice, the chef will prepare your craving as the breakfast repast. The guestrooms are attractive in their "newness" and bathrooms enjoy nice fixtures and Jacuzzi tubs for two. Gorgeous hand-carved scenes on each guestroom door depict the sentimental theme and hence, the décor for each guestroom. *Directions:* Exit Highway 580 at Vasco Road to the south. At its end turn left on Tesla road and then take a left on Cross Road to the inn.

PURPLE ORCHID INN
Innkeeper: Karen Hughes
4549 Cross Road, Livermore, CA 94550
Tel: (925) 606-8855 or (800) 353-4549
Fax: (925) 606-8880
E-mail: info@purpleorchid.com
8 Rooms, Double: $150–$250
Open all year, Credit cards: MC, VS
Children over 14, No smoking, Wheelchair friendly
www.karenbrown.com/california/purpleorchid.html

Places to Stay

LOS ANGELES   HOTEL BEL-AIR   Map: 6d & 7a

Nestled in the hills of Beverly Hills in a neighborhood of exclusive real estate, the Hotel Bel-Air is exceptional—elegant and sophisticated, but unpretentious and extending a truly warm welcome. An awning-covered walkway leading to the hotel's reception area gives you your first glimpse of the lush 12 acres transected by babbling streams. Furnishings are gorgeous, with handsome antiques and dramatic flower arrangements. The one- or two-story buildings nestling in the greenery are painted in a soft pastel wash with white doors, creating a peaceful and soothing effect. There is an elegant interior dining room and a terrace for dining under the shade of umbrellas and trees. Light meals are also available poolside as is a summertime grill. The setting is quiet, with the sound of fountains and a running stream breaking the natural silence. Most of the beautifully decorated guestrooms enjoy handsome tiled floors warmed by lovely Oriental carpets, and a welcome tea service and a personalized card are left as a welcome to incoming guests. Service is ever present but subtle, with the wishes of guests seemingly anticipated, and nothing is too much of a problem or effort on the part of the staff. In my research I have seen some of the world's finest hotels and the Bel-Air made such an impression, it is one I am determined to return to as others do—on vacation! *Directions*: Take Sunset Boulevard west off Highway 405 and then turn north on Stone Canyon Road for about 1 mile. The hotel is found on the left just past the intersection of Tortuosa Way

HOTEL BEL-AIR
General Manager: Mr. Frank Bowling, V.P.
701 Stone Canyon Road
Los Angeles, CA 90077
Tel: (310) 472-1211 or (800) 648-4097
Fax: (310) 476-5890
92 Rooms, Double: $350–$2,500
Open all year, Credit cards: all major
Children accepted, Smoking, Wheelchair friendly

Places to Stay

LOS ANGELES — LE MONTROSE SUITE HOTEL   Map: 6d & 7a

Elegant in its simplicity, Le Montrose is not an inn, but offers great value and exceptional accommodation in a safe neighborhood on the edge of Beverly Hills just up from the design center. Converted from an apartment complex, Le Montrose has a nondescript concrete square façade which belies the charm of the interior. Guest suites, all with a sunken living room, are described as corporate suites and come with welcome baskets of fruit, twice-daily maid service, color televisions equipped with VCRs, state-of-the-art multi-line phones, private E-mail, faxes, gas fireplaces, great mattresses, excellent lighting, and comfortable sitting areas. The decor in the rooms is handsomely elegant—tones of browns, beiges, golds, and blacks are used in the furnishings against the soft hues of the subtly elegant wallpapers and the classically framed art. The intimate, private library restaurant serves fine cuisine in a quiet ambiance or will provide room service. A small but well-equipped fitness center is available to guests at no charge, lighted tennis courts are found on one level of the rooftop, and on a lower level a lovely large pool looks out to the rooftops of Los Angeles. *Directions*: Located one block east of Beverly Hills. Take a long journey east on Sunset Boulevard off the I-405, turn right on Hammond Street, just past Doheny. Or from I-10 take La Cienega north, turn east on Sunset Boulevard (past Santa Monica Boulevard), then turn left on Hammond.

LE MONTROSE SUITE HOTEL
General Manager: John Douponce
900 Hammond Street
West Hollywood, CA 90069
Tel: (310) 855-1115 or (800) 776-0666
Fax: (310) 657-9192
128 Suites, Double: $175–$475
Open all year, Credit cards: all major
Children accepted, Smoking, Wheelchair friendly
www.karenbrown.com/california/lemontrosehotel.html

Places to Stay

LOS OLIVOS — FESS PARKER'S WINE COUNTRY INN
Map: 6c

On a quiet shaded street of Los Olivos sits a distinguished, subtly elegant hotel, traditional in its ambiance. Beautiful in decor and lavish in its comfort, the inn is most definitely grand yet intimate in its number of guestrooms. With just 21 rooms, but staffed as if it had 50, the hotel gives guests personal and gracious attention. Accommodations are a good value when compared to the tariffs charged in neighboring Santa Barbara. Each of the guestrooms, whether upstairs from the main lobby or in an attractive annex across the street, features a western or classic impressionist artist whose work is beautifully presented and featured throughout the room. Wood moldings, brass fixtures, and French armoires create a romantic turn-of-the-century ambiance. Guestroom amenities include a mini refrigerator, television, fireplace, beds topped with plump down comforters, and, in selected rooms, a Jacuzzi tub. A lovely heated swimming pool and Jacuzzi are a welcome treat for summer travelers. Fess Parker's Wine Country Inn is a full-service hotel with an excellent restaurant with the ambiance of a quiet country lodge. *Directions:* South from San Francisco on Highway 101, take Highway 154 approximately 2 miles to Grand Avenue in Los Olivos.

FESS PARKER'S WINE COUNTRY INN
Director: Dale Swanson
2860 Grand Avenue
P.O. Box 526
Los Olivos, CA 93441
Tel: (805) 688-7788 or (800) 446-2455
Fax: (805) 688-1942
21 Rooms, Double: $225–$340
Open all year, Credit cards: all major
Children accepted, No smoking, Wheelchair friendly

MALIBU CASA MALIBU Map: 7a

The bland roadside exterior with its 50s motel sign is all that is left of the earlier version of this motel. Behind the façade is a simple, attractive entry dressed with fresh flowers opening onto the back central courtyard. The manicured back garden is beautifully landscaped and flows to a tiled patio which extends out to a glass-enclosed bay window alcove set with tables overlooking the ocean. A single-story wing of rooms sits right on the beach. Decorated in a simple, fresh look with wicker furniture, the beachfront rooms open onto a deck whose glass wall topped by a driftwood banister tempts one to climb right over and onto the sand. Other rooms are found in the building that fronts the Pacific Coast Highway, either on the first floor overlooking the lush interior courtyard or on the second floor enjoying views of the courtyard garden and glimpses of blue water. Some rooms are equipped with kitchenettes, some with gas fireplaces, and thoughtful touches such as bathroom amenities, in-room coffee makers, a soda and snack concession just off the courtyard, and colorful beach towels piled high behind the reception desk are indicators of the caring owners. For more than 40 years guests have been charmed by the ocean setting of this roadside motel, but under the ownership of Richard and Joan Page, the motel has taken on a special charm. *Directions*: Located south of town, on the Pacific Coast Highway between Cross Creek and Carbon Canyon Roads.

CASA MALIBU
Innkeepers: Joan & Richard Page
22752 Pacific Coast Highway
Malibu, CA 90265
Tel: (310) 456-2219 or (800) 831-0858
Fax: (310) 456-5418
E-mail: casamalibu@earthlink.net
21 Rooms, Double: $99–$329
Open all year, Credit cards: all major
Children accepted, Smoking

Places to Stay

| MALIBU | MALIBU BEACH INN | Map: 7a |

Newly constructed, the Malibu Beach Inn resembles the type of small hotel you would find on the Mediterranean, washed in a soft peach, detailed with green awnings and door trim, white doors, and tile roof. Guestrooms at the back of the inn open up to magnificent ocean views and the sound of surf. The entrance sits opposite the parking lot and an attractive fountain set amongst a small ring of palm trees. The public area is open and lovely, handsome handpainted tiles are found throughout, a fountain cascades, a fireplace dresses a sitting area, and an arched doorway opens out to a tiled deck set with tables. Standard rooms are a good value—at the heart of Santa Monica, the same ocean view would carry a price tag of $400. All first-floor rooms have two-person Jacuzzis on the outside deck. One suite is found on each floor, enjoying a larger deck, Jacuzzi, and fireplace. Simple, clean decor is similar throughout, with bamboo furniture and motel floral prints, and rooms have every amenity such as fully stocked wet bars. I liked room 318, a "Pier Room," which has a corner view of the beach and pier and a nice corner deck, and, as with all third-floor rooms, enjoys a vaulted beamed ceiling and a gas fireplace. Room 310, a standard third-floor room, is also lovely. Robes are offered in third-floor rooms, suites, and first floor Jacuzzi rooms. *Directions*: South of Malibu on the Pacific Coast Highway with Carbon Canyon Road as the closest cross street.

MALIBU BEACH INN
General Manager: Alan Goldscheider
22878 Pacific Coast Highway
Malibu, CA 90265
Tel: (310) 456-6444, Fax: (310) 456-1499
E-mail: reservations@malibubeachinn.com
47 Rooms, Double: $169–$300
Open all year
Credit cards: all major
Children accepted, Smoking, Wheelchair friendly
www.karenbrown.com/california/malibubeachinn.html

MANCHESTER — VICTORIAN GARDENS — Maps: 1c & 2a

Set on 92 acres of meadow, woodland, and creek, Victorian Gardens, dating back to 1904, is a lovely two-story, four-bedroom classic Victorian. Decoration is respectful of the Victorian period and yet the furnishings are an artistic arrangement of both traditional and contemporary, with Pauline and Luciano's family heirlooms and treasures on display. The kitchen, where breakfast is sometimes served, is definitely the "heart of the home" and Luciano's domain, a wonderful room warmed by a large open fireplace which Luciano also uses for cooking. Dinner, by reservation only and also open to non-guests, is an elegant presentation of seven courses featuring Italian regional dishes, with specially selected wines to complement the fixed menu which changes daily. While Victorian Gardens has four guestrooms (two sharing a hall bath and two with private bath), they rent only three rooms out at a time if the guests are not affiliated. The Master Bedroom enjoys a sweeping view of meadow and the surrounding foothills; the Poppy Bedroom has an intimate reading nook; the Golden Bedroom is an inviting front corner room with a lovely nook enticing you to settle and enjoy glimpses of the distant ocean; and the handsome Northwest Bedroom is blessed with wonderful views and the most lavish bathroom. *Directions*: From San Francisco take 101 north to 128 west until it ends on Highway 1 then turn south. Travel 5 miles to Elk and then 8 miles to Victorian Gardens.

VICTORIAN GARDENS
Innkeepers: Pauline & Luciano Zamboni
14409 South Highway 1, Manchester, CA 95459
Tel: (707) 882-3606, Fax: (707) 882-2467
4 Rooms, 2 with private bathrooms
Double: $125–$185
Open all year, Credit cards: all major
Children accepted over 12, No smoking
www.karenbrown.com/california/victoriangardens.html

McCLOUD — HOGIN HOUSE BED & BREAKFAST Map: 1b

An elevated wooden walkway trimmed by flowers and bordered by lawn leads to the front door and porch of the Hogin House Bed & Breakfast, a dear, soft-yellow clapboard house trimmed in white and green. The passage beyond the small front entry leads through the kitchen adorned heavily with country knickknacks and on into the living room with its informal clustering of chairs and sofas in front of the handsome riverstone fireplace. The four guestrooms are found on the second floor under the eaves. The Front Room is spacious, with two double beds and a private bathroom with shower, The Blue Room has a queen bed decked with a lovely old quilt and a bathroom with shower, and steps down to a little sitting room enclosed by a wall of windows which then steps up to another guestroom, The Hideaway, is cozy with an iron bed (double), which shares a hallway bathroom. Grandma's Room is a cute room which shares The Hideaway's bathroom. Guests breakfast together either in the dining room or at tables set on the porch, enjoying raisin bran cereal, a bounty of fresh fruit, and an assortment of home-baked muffins and breads accompanied by a wonderful variety of homemade jams. *Directions*: From Mount Shasta travel Highway 89 east for 10 miles. Take a left turn on Columbero and continue ¾ mile to Lawndale Court. Turn right and Hogin House is the second house on the left.

HOGIN HOUSE BED & BREAKFAST
Innkeepers: Angie & Richard Toreson
424 Lawndale Court
P.O. Box 550
McCloud, CA 96057
Tel & Fax: (530) 964-2882
4 Rooms, 2 with private bathrooms
Double: $65–$95
Open all year, Credit cards: all major
Children accepted, No smoking

McCLOUD — McCLOUD GUEST HOUSE — Map: 1b

The McCloud Guest House has a wonderful setting—in its own pretty little park, surrounded by green lawn and trees, while in the distance is Mount Shasta, northern California's 14,162-foot giant. The inn is not pretentious, but most attractive in its simplicity. Built entirely of wood, the square building is wrapped with a spacious verandah whose supporting columns reach up to a steeply pitched roof from which little dormer windows peek out into the trees. Built in 1907, the inn was originally the home of J. H. Queal, the president of the McCloud River Lumber Company. After extensive renovations, it reopened as a restaurant on the ground level with five bedrooms upstairs. As you enter the foyer, the massive stone fireplace and wood-paneled walls set the country-lodge feeling. Upstairs, the guests have their own private parlor highlighted with an ornate pool table from the Hearst collection. The original master bedroom is decorated with flowered wallpaper in soft shades of mauve and pink set off by white wicker chairs. Each of the other guestrooms has it's own color scheme. Most have antique white iron beds, but one has a four-poster bed which looks quite handsome against a dark plaid wallpaper. *Directions:* Drive north on Highway 5, then east on Highway 89 for 12 miles to McCloud. Before the village turn left on Colombero Drive.

McCLOUD GUEST HOUSE
Owners: Pat & Dennis Abreu
Innkeepers: Patti & Bill Leigh
606 West Colombero Drive
P.O. Box 1510
McCloud, CA 96057
Tel: (530) 964-3160
5 Rooms, Double: $90–$115
Closed Mondays & Tuesdays, Credit cards: MC, VS
Inappropriate for children, No smoking

McCLOUD — McCLOUD HOTEL — Map: 1b

With great determination, expenditure, and hard work, Lee and Marilyn Ogden renovated a long-abandoned historic building at the heart of the mountain town of McCloud and now the McCloud Hotel with its pretty yellow façade proudly dominates Main Street. Inside, the high beamed ceiling and informal grouping of sofas and chairs set before a large fire give the feeling of a mountain lodge. Although the exterior of the hotel was in relatively good shape and required only cosmetic repairs, guestrooms benefit from the complete renovation and modernization of the interior. At the top of a wide, handsome staircase is an inviting upstairs parlor with a large-screen television and access to the front expanse of porch. Rooms on the first floor facing Main Street are a wonderful value with a nice-size room, washbasin, toilet, and private bathroom. Rooms on the first and second floors at the back of the inn have four-poster beds and an additional but small sitting area. Four suites enjoy big Jacuzzi tubs, three of which are found in the room proper. The decor is similar in theme throughout, with the use of country patterns, old trunks, and washstands to house in-room washbasins. Breakfast and afternoon tea are served at tables set in the lobby and guests staying in the suites have the extra option of having breakfast delivered to the room. *Directions*: From Interstate 5 take the McCloud-Reno Exit and travel east on Highway 89 for 10 miles. Turn left on Colombero Avenue and follow it into town, cross the tracks, and turn right on Main Street.

McCLOUD HOTEL
Innkeepers: Marilyn & Lee Ogden
408 Main Street
P.O. Box 730 , McCloud, CA 96057
Tel: (530) 964-2822 or (800) 964-2823
Fax: (530) 964-2844
17 Rooms, Double: $74–$163
Open all year, Credit cards: all major
Children accepted only in first-floor rooms
No smoking, Wheelchair friendly

MENDOCINO — AGATE COVE INN — Map: 1c

The Agate Cove Inn is a beautiful property on a bluff across the road from the ocean. The heart of the inn is a delightful 1860s blue-trimmed white clapboard farmhouse where you find the reception area and an inviting lounge with comfy sofas and chairs facing a brick fireplace where a cozy fire crackles on chilly days. Windows stretch across the entire west wall of the lounge, giving guests a spectacular view of the coast as they enjoy a scrumptious hot breakfast. Two of the bedrooms are in the main farmhouse, while the others are scattered about the property in cute cottages painted a pretty country blue with white trim. Most of the rooms have a gas fireplace, a deck, and a view of the sea. Even the least expensive rooms, although smaller and simpler, are sweet and pretty. All of the guestrooms are gradually undergoing total renovation. Agate Cove Inn was bought in 1995 by a charming young couple, Betsy and Scott Buckwald, who had previously run a very successful bed and breakfast in bustling southern California. Although Melody helps in management, both Betsy and Scott are very involved with the day-by-day operation of the inn, and their loving care certainly shines forth. The gardens display one of their most dramatic improvements—to look out over the brilliantly colored beds of flowers to the sparkling blue of the sea framed by windswept cypress trees is quite breathtaking. *Directions:* From Highway 1 take Little Lake left (west), then Lansing right (north).

AGATE COVE INN
Owners/Innkeepers: Scott & Betsy Buckwald
Manager: Melody Merriman
11201 North Lansing Street
P.O. Box 1150, Mendocino, CA 95460
Tel: (707) 937-0551 or (800) 527-3111
Fax : (707) 937-0550
10 Rooms, Double: $109–$250
Open all year, Credit cards: all major
Children accepted over 12, No smoking
www.karenbrown.com/california/agatecoveinn.html

Places to Stay

MENDOCINO BLUE HERON INN Map: 1c

The Blue Heron Inn is not the typical Mendocino Victorian, but a simple, New England-style house, painted white with blue trim. A white picket fence encloses the garden to each side, completing the adorable cottage look. The ground floor is a delightful restaurant (The Moosse Café) where daily specials (usually fish fresh from the ocean and pasta dishes) are posted on the board and complemented by a short menu card. Enjoy a Caesar salad for lunch and cioppino for dinner. In the morning a breakfast with croissants or coffeecake and freshly squeezed orange juice is served here. Upstairs, you find three completely delightful bedrooms, each simply furnished with country antiques containing a lovely queen-sized bed made with the most attractive linens. Sunset Room (in cool greens) captures distant ocean views across the rooftops and shares a modern bathroom with the adjacent Bay Room which offers a tempting peek of the ocean from its window. The Blue Heron Room offers equally delightful decor, more space and a pristine en-suite shower room. *Directions:* Follow Highway 1 north into Mendocino. Turn left at Jackson Street, follow Jackson Street to Kasten Street, and turn right.

BLUE HERON INN
Innkeeper: Linda Friedman
390 Kasten Street
Mendocino, CA 95460
Tel: (707) 937-4323, Fax: (707) 937-3611
E-mail: innkeeper@theblueheron.com
3 Rooms, 1 with private bathroom
Double: $85–$100
Closed Jan 3-Feb 11
Credit cards: none accepted
Children accepted over 12, No smoking
www.karenbrown.com/california/blueheroninn.html

MENDOCINO THE HEADLANDS INN Map: 1c

The Headlands Inn is an especially attractive inn located within walking distance of all the pretty shops and fun little restaurants in Mendocino. This New England-style home, dating from 1868, is a three-story, saltbox Victorian with a bay window in front and gables peeking out from the steep roof. A picket fence encloses the front yard which is usually a bloom with flowers in a cheerful English garden. Afternoon tea and cookies are served in the restful upstairs parlor. While all the bedrooms are particularly attractive, with antique furniture, feather beds, and down comforters, I especially enjoyed Strauss with its large bay window and view across the garden to the bay and Wilson with its private verandah with a table and chairs strategically placed to enjoy the distant ocean view. There are wood-burning fireplaces in five of the bedrooms and an old-fashioned wood-burning parlor stove in another. One of the rooms is a little cottage which opens directly onto the street. Whatever room you are in, a bountiful full breakfast is brought to you on a tray decorated with fresh flowers from the garden—breakfast at The Headlands is a special treat. *Directions:* From San Francisco drive north on Highway 101. Just past Cloverdale, turn left on Highway 128 west to Highway 1 and north to Mendocino.

THE HEADLANDS INN
Owner: Gail Erickson
Innkeeper: Larry Maul
Howard & Albion Streets
P.O. Box 132, Mendocino, CA 95460
Tel: (707) 937-4431 or (800) 354-4431
6 Rooms, Double: $110–$195
Open all year, Credit cards:all major
Children accepted over 12, No smoking
www.karenbrown.com/california/theheadlandsinn.html

Places to Stay

MENDOCINO — JOSHUA GRINDLE INN   Map: 1c

The Joshua Grindle Inn, located just a short walk from the center of Mendocino, is surrounded by a 2-acre plot of land. A white picket fence encloses the front yard of this most attractive white clapboard farmhouse which, although architecturally simple, has hints of the Victorian era in the fancy woodwork on the verandah. In the 1879 farmhouse you find the guest lounge, a sedate room with old paintings and portraits on the walls, a fireplace, white lace curtains, a trunk for a coffee table, and an antique pump organ tucked in the corner. The light, airy guestrooms have a New-England country ambiance enhanced by the owner's early-American antiques and some have their own fireplace. Of the five guestrooms in the main building two overlook the town of Mendocino and the distant ocean, and all their bathrooms were recently remodeled with luxurious enhancements such as marble counters, whirlpool, and deep soak tubs. A natural-wood cottage just behind the house contains two additional bedrooms, and very popular, are those tucked romantically into the age-weathered watertower in the rear garden. Especially attractive is Watertower II, a sunny, cozy room on the second floor where the ocean can be glimpsed through the trees. All of the bedrooms are spotlessly maintained, immaculately decorated, have well lighted, comfortably arranged sitting areas, and private bathrooms. *Directions:* Go north on Highway 1 through town, left on Little Lake Road.

JOSHUA GRINDLE INN
Owners: Arlene & Jim Moorehead
Innkeeper: Christine Wagner
44800 Little Lake Road
P.O. Box 647, Mendocino, CA 95460
Tel: (707) 937-4143 or (800) 474-6353
E-mail: stay@joshgrin.com
10 Rooms, Double: $100–$195
Closed at Christmas Credit cards: MC, VS
Children accepted over 12, No smoking
www.karenbrown.com/california/joshuagrindleinn.html

Places to Stay

MENDOCINO

MENDOCINO FARMHOUSE

Map: 1c

Most of our selections for Mendocino feature the coastal splendor, but although not next to the ocean, the Mendocino Farmhouse has its own special qualities. It is located at the end of a narrow lane which weaves through a beautiful redwood glen, crosses a small creek, and then opens into a lovely meadow. There, amidst beds of flowers, next to a pond and surrounded by a white picket fence, you will find an appealing farmhouse with white trim. Inside, the decor is fresh and pretty, with antique accents giving it an eclectic style. The breakfast tables capture the sunshine in a many-windowed niche overlooking the flower garden, or dining outside under redwoods is an option in good weather. A large family kitchen is located off the living room. Upstairs there are three bedrooms, each sparkling clean and with its own bathroom. Our favorite rooms are Cedar and Pine, found in the converted barn surrounded by its own little garden. Each is rustic in its mood with either cedar or bleached-pine paneling, a sitting area, and a large wood-burning fireplace. *Directions:* Just south of Mendocino, turn right off Highway 1 on Comptche-Ukiah Road. Go 1½ miles and turn left on Olson Lane—the Mendocino Farmhouse is at the end of the road.

MENDOCINO FARMHOUSE
Innkeeper: Margie Kamb
Olson Lane
P.O. Box 247, Mendocino, CA 95460
Tel: (707) 937-0241 or (800) 475-1536
E-mail: mkamb@mcn.org
5 Rooms, Double: $85–$135
Open all year, Credit cards: MC, VS
Children accepted over 8, No smoking
www.karenbrown.com/california/mendocinofarmhouse.html

Places to Stay

MENDOCINO — THE STANFORD INN BY THE SEA   Map: 1c

At first glance The Stanford Inn by the Sea appears to be more like a motel than a country inn, but this is definitely untrue. Joan and Jeff Stanford have created a cozy, sophisticated little hotel within an attractive, but not unusual, two-story, natural-wood building. The inn is located at the crest of a grassy meadow where a few llamas graze in a paddock. The building is cleverly constructed so that every room has a view, either from a private deck or patio. Each of the guestrooms, many with four-poster beds, has been transformed into a snug little hideaway, with country antiques, color television (movies can be rented), telephone, posies of flowers, and either a wood-burning fireplace or stove—with plenty of wood to keep you warm on nippy nights. Everything is fresh and pretty and immaculately clean. The entire operation seems extremely professional and yet has a very personal touch. Each room has a complimentary bottle of Mendocino vintage wine. A wonderful bonus is the glass-enclosed sauna and "greenhouse" pool where guests can enjoy a swim even on blustery days. Constantly renovating and making improvements the inn now boasts a vegetarian restaurant and some new suites, and on a reservation basis it offers some appealing poetry, garden, and music seminars and workshops. *Directions:* A quarter of a mile south of the village of Mendocino at the intersection of Highway 1 and Comptche-Ukiah Road.

THE STANFORD INN BY THE SEA
Innkeepers: Joan & Jeff Stanford
Highway 1 and Comptche-Ukiah Road
Mendocino, CA 95460
Tel: (707) 937-5615 or (800) 331-8884
Fax: (707) 937-0305
E-mail: stanford@stanfordinn.com
33 Rooms, Double: $215–$365
Open all year, Credit cards: all major
Children accepted, No smoking, Wheelchair friendly
www.karenbrown.com/california/stanfordinn.html

MENDOCINO — WHITEGATE INN

Map: 1c

If you are looking for a place to stay in the heart of Mendocino that absolutely oozes Victorian charm, the Whitegate Inn is definitely for you. This adorable, white clapboard home, built in 1883, is set off from the sidewalk by a white picket fence and, of course, a *white gate*. Inside, you step into an elegant home of the last century brimming with antiques. To the right of the entry hall there is a nostalgic old-fashioned parlor whose decor perfectly captures the Victorian era, with Oriental carpet, crystal chandelier, dark wood furniture, gilt mirrors, ornate lamps, fancy drapes, knick knacks, bouquets of fresh flowers, and even an upright piano. The parlor opens to a formal dining room where a gourmet breakfast is presented each morning on a beautifully set table using English bone china and sterling silver. The guestrooms also capture the Victorian mood, with patterned carpets, many antique beds, fireplaces, and the clever use of old-fashioned wallpapers. However, except for the fireplaces, feather beds, and fine linens, the bedrooms have jumped into the 20th century with their modern bathrooms, cable television, and queen- or king-sized beds. However, in my opinion, the most outstanding attribute of the Whitegate Inn is its gardens—here you find a terrace with lattice gazebo, lacy wrought-iron tables and chairs, and a cobblestone path that winds through a romantic display of gorgeous flowers. *Directions*: From the 101 take the first street into Mendocino. Turn right on Howard and the inn is in the first block on your right.

WHITEGATE INN
Innkeepers: Carol & George Bechtloff
499 Howard Street, Mendocino, CA 95460
Tel: (707) 937-4892 or (800) 531-7282
Fax : (707) 937-1131
E-mail: staff@whitegateinn.com
6 Rooms, Double: $129-$229
Open all year, Credit cards: all major
Children under 12 accepted in the cottage, No smoking
www.karenbrown.com/california/whitegateinn.html

MONTEREY — OLD MONTEREY INN — Map: 5a

Ann and Gene Swett converted their family home into what continues to be one of the very nicest country inns in California. Their home is a most attractive Tudor-style house shaded by giant oak trees in an acre of wooded gardens full of colorful begonias, fuchsias, rhododendrons, and lush ferns in a quiet Monterey suburb. Everything is beautifully tended, giving the grounds a parklike appearance. The inside of the house is an oasis of gentility and tranquillity where everything is done with the comfort of the guest in mind. Most of the bedrooms in the main house, cottage, and carriage house have fireplaces, and all are beautifully decorated and thoughtfully appointed. The Library stands out as a particularly memorable bedroom with its book-lined walls, cozy fireplace, and private balcony overlooking the garden. A refrigerator is kept stocked with complimentary beverages, and juices and hot beverages are always available. In the evening the Swetts join their guests for wine and cheese in the living room. They are especially gracious hosts, adding great warmth and professionalism to their little inn. Breakfast is served at the long oak table in the dining room or brought to your room on a tray. *Directions:* Traveling south on Highway 1, exit at Soledad/Munras, cross Munras Avenue, go right on Pacific Street: Martin Street is on the left in a little over half a mile.

OLD MONTEREY INN
Owners/Innkeepers: Ann & Gene Swett
500 Martin Street
Monterey, CA 93940
Tel: (831) 375-8284 or (800) 350-2344
Fax: (831) 375-6730
E-mail: omi@oldmontereyinn.com
10 Rooms, Double: $200–$350
Closed at Christmas, Credit cards: MC, VS
Children accepted over 12, No smoking
www.karenbrown.com/california/oldmontereyinn.html

MONTEREY — SPINDRIFT INN — Map: 5a

As an alternative to a bed and breakfast we recommend the Spindrift Inn, a lovely hotel with a great location overlooking the Monterey Bay. Just down the street from the fabulous Monterey Bay Aquarium, its rooms overlook either the bustle of Cannery Row or the serenity of the bay. We stayed in a front room overlooking Cannery Row and were pleasantly surprised to find that the deep-set windows and heavy drapes blocked out the noise of late-night revelers. Guestrooms on the bay side enjoy wonderful water views and corner rooms are spacious and enjoy a lovely window seat. The Spindrift Inn offers 42 bedrooms, each handsomely decorated with rich European fabrics, all with wood-burning fireplaces, beds topped with down comforters and featherbeds, and bathrooms finished in marble and brass. The feeling is European and the amenities are first class. A Continental breakfast of Danish or fresh baked breads and a selection of fruit is served on a silver tray in the room and in the evening a buffet of wine and cheese is offered in the front lobby. Service is cordial. There is almost always someone at the front desk in the lobby to assist with information or reservations, but shifts change regularly. This is a hotel, efficient, attractive, and comfortable, with a premier location. *Directions:* Take the Pacific Grove, Del Monte exit off Highway 1. Follow signs to Cannery Row and the Aquarium. The Spindrift is located right on Cannery Row.

SPINDRIFT INN
Director: Randy Venard
652 Cannery Row, Monterey, CA 93940
Tel: (831) 646-8900 or (800) 841-1879
Fax: (831) 646-5342
42 Rooms, Double: $209–$439
Open all year, Credit cards: all major
Children accepted
Smoking, Wheelchair friendly
www.karenbrown.com/california/spindriftinn.html

| MOSS BEACH | SEAL COVE INN | Map: 3c |

Karen (Brown) Herbert and her husband, Rick, have built their own romantic English-manor-style hideaway, Seal Cove Inn. Located just half an hour's drive south of San Francisco, the inn is bordered by towering, windswept cypress trees and looks out over fields of wild flowers and acres of parkland to the ocean. You enter through a spacious entrance hall into an elegantly comfortable living room with a large fireplace centered between French doors. Adjoining the living room is a dining room, and next to that, a small conference room—all with park and ocean views. Antiques are used throughout: grandfather clocks, cradles filled with flowers, handsome tables, antique beds, armoires, trunks, etc. Each of the large bedrooms has a wood-burning fireplace, comfortable reading chairs, television, VCR, hot towel rack, and a refrigerator stocked with complimentary soft drinks and wine. Best yet, each of the bedrooms has a view of the distant ocean and doors opening either to a private balcony or onto the terrace. From the inn you can walk to a secluded stretch of beach or stroll through the forest along a path that traces the ocean bluffs. Karen has already had the pleasure of welcoming many guests to Seal Cove Inn who are also readers of her travel guides. *Directions:* From San Francisco take Highway 1 south to Moss Beach (about 20 miles). Turn west on Cypress (at the Moss Beach Distillery sign). Seal Cove Inn is one block off the road on the right.

SEAL COVE INN
Innkeepers: Karen & Rick Herbert
221 Cypress Avenue
Moss Beach, CA 94038
Tel: (650) 728-4114, Fax: (650) 728-4116
E-mail: sealcove@coastside.net
10 Rooms, Double: $190–$270
Closed at Christmas, Credit cards: all major
Children accepted in garden-level rooms
No smoking, Wheelchair friendly
www.karenbrown.com/california/sealcoveinn.html

MUIR BEACH — PELICAN INN

Maps: 1c, 2d, & 3a

The Pelican Inn, nestled among pine trees, jasmine, and honeysuckle, is a wonderful re-creation of a cozy English tavern with a few attractive guestrooms tucked upstairs. Wide wood-planked floors, an appealing small bar (with dart board), low-beamed ceilings, a giant fireplace with priest hole (secret hiding place), a cozy little guest lounge, and a dining room with trestle tables complete the first-floor scene. Besides the large indoor dining room, there is also a trellised patio where guests can have snacks or dine (in the evenings the candlelit tables are set with linens). Lunch features such English treats as succulent bangers and mash and fish and chips; dinner includes prime rib, rack of lamb, etc. Upstairs there are seven cozy bedrooms where the English motif is carried out with heavily draped half-tester beds, Oriental carpets, a decanter of sherry, and fresh flowers. Rooms are small but cozy and reminiscent of a wonderful old English inn. The location of the Pelican Inn is fabulous: only a few minutes' drive from the giant redwood grove at Muir Woods and a short walk to the ocean. Note: Reservations are needed six months in advance for weekends. Also know that the pub attracts hundreds of people on weekends and noise from the revelers can persist until the 11pm closing time. *Directions:* From Highway 101 take the Stinson Beach/Highway 1 turnoff. At the Arco station, go left for 5 miles on Highway 1 to Muir Beach. Pelican Inn is on the left.

PELICAN INN
Owners: Ed & Susan Cunningham
Innkeeper: Katrinka McKay
10 Pacific Way
Muir Beach, CA 94965-9729
Tel: (415) 383-6000, Fax: (415) 383-3424
E-mail: innkeeper@pelicaninn.com
7 Rooms, Double: $158–$180
Open all year
Credit cards: MC, VS
Children accepted, No Smoking
www.karenbrown.com/california/pelicaninn.html

Places to Stay

MURPHYS DUNBAR HOUSE, 1880 Map: 4b

As the gold boom passed, Murphys was left to sleep under its locust and elm trees until tourists discovered its beauty and slower pace of life. A few old stone buildings survive, and one houses the Old Timers' Museum filled with pioneer and Gold Rush regalia. The Dunbar House, 1880, is a handsome inn with a wrap-around porch where guests can sit and sip Gold-Country wine or enjoy a refreshing glass of lemonade. Bob and Barbara's pride in their small inn is apparent—they have lavished their time and attention on making it extremely comfortable. Each of the four cozy guestrooms has a fireplace and a small refrigerator with ice and a bottle of wine. The Sequoia room has a queen-size bed and a claw-foot tub set before a wood stove. The Cedar room, just off the downstairs parlor, is a suite offering a luxurious Jacuzzi. Upstairs the Ponderosa room has a king bed, large claw-foot tub, views of the garden and the Sugar Pine room is a two-room suite that enjoys a private balcony shaded by trees. Each room also provides a TV with VCR hidden away in an armoire. Breakfast, served in the dining room by the fire, in the century-old garden, or in the privacy of your room, includes juice spritzer, fresh fruit, muffins, turnovers, an egg dish, and a hot beverage. An appetizer buffet is offered in the afternoon. *Directions:* From San Francisco take Highway 580 to Highway 99 north to Highway 4 east, then drive through Angels Camp towards Arnold. Murphys is 9 miles east of Angels Camp.

DUNBAR HOUSE, 1880
Innkeepers: Barbara & Bob Costa
271 Jones Street
P.O. Box 1375, Murphys, CA 95247
Tel: (209) 728-2897 or (800) 692-6006
Fax: (209) 728-1451
E-mail: innkeeper@dunbarhouse.com
4 Rooms, Double: $125–$190
Open all year, Credit cards: all major
Children accepted over 10, No smoking
www.karenbrown.com/california/dunbarhouse.html

MURPHYS — THE REDBUD INN

Map: 4b

Located just off the main street of Murphy's, the Redbud Inn runs the length of a short side street. The reception, small public sitting area, and side breakfast room, sparsely decorated in reproduction antiques, shout of newness. There are 11 guestrooms in the main house—Mae's Room on the first floor provides wheelchair access while the others are found at the top of a lovely staircase. From the Anniversary Suite, Room 2, which is spacious and elegant with its bay window overlooking a side street, private balcony, enormous spa tub, and romantic king bed draped in French ribbon and silk flowers, to the rooms at the back which benefit from the shade of a mature sycamore tree, the rooms all have lovely modern private baths, are individual in decor, and vary in size and floor plan. Across from the main house, more spacious accommodation is offered in the Garden House, a two-bedroom, two-bath apartment equipped with a full kitchen. Decorated in sunny shades of yellow, the new Wisteria Cottage has a private entrance and porch, fireplace, and spacious bath with two-person Jacuzzi. The Redbud Inn thrives under the unique efforts of a wife, husband, and daughters team of innkeepers—truly a family affair. Breakfast is a scrumptious feast with hot entrees and fresh pastries baked daily. *Directions:* From San Francisco take Highway 580 to Highway 99 north to Highway 4 east, then drive through Angels Camp towards Arnold. Murphys is 9 miles east of Angels Camp.

THE REDBUD INN
Innkeeper: Pamela Hatch
402 Main Street, Murphys, CA 95247
Tel: (209) 728-8533 or (800) 827-8533
Fax: (209) 728-9123, E-mail: innkeeper@redbudinn.com
11 Rooms, 1 Apartment, 1 Cottage Double: $90–$245
Open all year, Credit cards: MC, VS
Children accepted in apartment, cottage, & Ope's Cabin
No smoking, Wheelchair friendly

Places to Stay

NAPA OAK KNOLL INN Maps: 2d & 3b

With 600 acres of vineyards as its backdrop, the Oak Knoll Inn has one of the most idyllic settings in the Napa Valley. You find the entry and prettily decorated front sitting room in the original stone farmhouse. An additional building was later added to each side to house guestrooms, each with a private entrance opening onto a wrap-around deck overlooking the vineyards. Breakfast is a feast served on winter mornings in front of the stone fireplace and on warm mornings outside on the deck where you can often watch the graceful hot-air balloons as they drift silently over the vineyards in the early-morning sunshine. The guestrooms are luxurious in their size, magnified further by the high vaulted ceilings. My favorite, number 6 (a corner room at the end of the house), has an arched window which towers to the height of the ceiling and offers a splendid view of the vineyards. Each bedroom enjoys a king-size bed, a sitting area before a fireplace, and thick stone walls which provide efficient insulation. The bedrooms have been individually redecorated with lovely, richly hued fabrics in a traditional style. The Oak Knoll Inn provides the perfect end to a perfect day of sightseeing. After sampling Napa Valley's many vineyards, you can sit poolside with a glass of wine and enjoy the quiet and beauty of a backdrop of vineyards and the valley's gorgeous hills. *Directions:* Go north on Highway 29 through Napa, then right on Oak Knoll Avenue, which has a left-right-zig-zag across Big Ranch Road.

OAK KNOLL INN
Innkeepers: Barbara Passino & John Kuhlmann
2200 E. Oak Knoll Avenue
Napa, CA 94558
Tel: (707) 255-2200, Fax: (707) 255-2296
4 Rooms, Double: $315–$395
Open all year, Credit cards: MC, VS
Children accepted over 14, No smoking
www.karenbrown.com/california/oakknollinn.html

NAPA — LA RESIDENCE — Maps: 2d & 3b

La Residence is an inn that has grown around The Mansion—a beautiful Gothic-revival home built in the 1870s as a farmhouse to accommodate the large family of Harry Parker, a riverboat pilot from New Orleans. In later years additions more Victorian in style changed the appearance of the home. Nine rooms, housed in the original mansion, are dramatic in their decor which blends well with the grand feeling of the home. Rooms vary from cozy, top-floor rooms tucked under slanted ceilings to spacious and elegant accommodations with fireplaces on the first floor. The 11 rooms in Cabernet Hall, shingled and built in the style of a French barn, are beautifully designed and commodious, each enjoying a private bath, fireplace, and French doors opening onto a patio or balcony. These bedrooms are handsomely decorated with pine antiques imported from France and England and Laura Ashley prints. The gorgeous new suite is smartly done in muted shades of yellow with lovely floral fabric, double French doors, and many amenities. Breakfast is served in the Cabernet Hall's lovely dining room with tables set before a blazing fire. On the lovely grounds are a heated swimming pool and Jacuzzi spa and tall trees that afford plenty of shade. The excellence of the inn reflects the expertise and talents contributed by the partners who share in the management. *Directions:* Take Highway 29 through Napa. Take the first right turn after the Salvador intersection onto a frontage road (no name) which winds back south to the inn.

LA RESIDENCE
Innkeepers: David Jackson & Craig Claussen
4066 Saint Helena Highway
Napa, CA 94558
Tel: (707) 253-0337, Fax: (707) 253-0382
20 Rooms, all with private bathrooms
Double: $185–$300
Open all year, Credit cards: all major
Children accepted, No smoking, Wheelchair friendly
www.karenbrown.com/california/laresidence.html

NEVADA CITY   DEER CREEK INN   Map: 4b

Chuck and Elaine Matroni are always ready to serve, spoil, pamper, and welcome guests to their three-story, soft-blue Victorian home, tiered on a hillside above gardens and lawn cascading down to the babbling Deer Creek. The parlors and dining room are quite formal with their Victorian furnishings and Oriental accents. The country kitchen at the back seems to be the nucleus of the home, where guests gather while observing the innkeepers prepare their gourmet, multi-course breakfast which is served either in the dining room or outside on the verandah. Deer Creek has five guestrooms, each named for the women who have owned the home over the past 136 years. Sheryl's Room is a cheerful front corner room whose iron bed is set on an Oriental carpet. Lela's Room boasts a dramatic four-poster bed and a claw-foot tub framed in an alcove, romantically draped with lace curtains. Winifred's Room features a canopied bed, an in-room claw-foot tub, and a private deck. The antique oak furniture in Ida's Room is lovely against a floral backdrop and the trundle bed accompanying the white and brass day bed comfortably accommodates an additional person. Elaine's Room enjoys a lace-draped bed, a large Roman tub, and a private patio overlooking the grounds and the creek. *Directions*: Exit Highway 20/49 at Broad Street, traveling south across the creek. Turn left on Nevada Street. The inn is located just up the street on the right.

DEER CREEK INN
Innkeepers: Elaine & Chuck Matroni
116 Nevada Street, Nevada City, CA 95959
Tel: (530) 265-0363 or (800) 655-0363
Fax: (530) 265-0980, E-mail: deercreek@gv.net
5 Rooms, Double: $95–$145
Open all year, Credit cards: MC, VS
Children over 13, No smoking
www.karenbrown.com/california/deercreekinn.html

NEVADA CITY   EMMA NEVADA HOUSE   Map: 4b

This lovely Victorian at the top of Broad Street, childhood home of 19th-century opera star Emma Nevada, is very pretty and feminine with a soft-peach façade trimmed in white set behind a white picket fence bounded by roses. Guestrooms open off public areas that are central to the inn. The first guestroom off the entrance, Nightingale's Bower, was formerly the parlor and enjoys a bay window, antique pot-bellied stove, elegant Italian bedding and Jacuzzi tub. Mignon's Boudoir, which has a fireplace, is luxurious in size but quite cozy with its French country decor and Laura Ashley prints. A claw-foot tub in the bathroom is painted blue to cleverly match the decor and a sink is housed in a beautiful antique cabinet. Ruth Ann Riese's favorite is the regal Empress's Chamber with its wealth of light streaming through a wall of windows and bath with Jacuzzi tub. At the top of the stairs are three additional lovely rooms—Mockingbird's Nest overlooking the front garden, Palmer's Loft whose ceilings and walls are still in the handsome bead boarding original to the house, and Emma's Hideaway, a secluded room set under a steeply pitched roof. Public areas are also very attractive, with many windows. A full breakfast may be taken in the formal dining room, on the back deck under the shade of a 140-year-old cherry tree, or in the Sun Room with its interesting tower ceiling. *Directions*: Take the Broad Street exit off Highway 49 and travel up the hill, through the heart of town, when the road splits, continue on Broad Street to the right.

EMMA NEVADA HOUSE
Innkeeper: Ruth Ann Riese
528 E Broad Street, Nevada City, CA 95959
Tel: (530) 265-4415 or (800) 916-3662 (EMMA)
Fax: (530) 265-4416, E-mail: emmanev@oro.net
6 Rooms, Double: $100–$160
Open all year, Credit cards: all major
Children accepted over 10, No smoking
www.karenbrown.com/california/emmanevadahouse.html

Places to Stay

NEVADA CITY — GRANDMERE'S INN — Map:4b

When gold was discovered, Nevada City became an affluent boomtown. It remains prosperous-looking today, its beautifully restored downtown area full of tempting restaurants and inviting shops. Just beyond Broad Street's historic shopping district, enclosed within a mature garden of long rolling lawns, tidy bushes, and flowers, sits Grandmere's Inn, a stately Colonial Revival home built in 1856 for Aaron Sargent, a U.S. Senator, and his suffragette wife, Ellen, whose friend, Susan B. Anthony, often stayed here. Sargent authored the bill that eventually gave women the right to vote. Now Grandmere's is a lovely country inn decorated with flair, and each of the rooms has a very different personality. The Master Suite is a luxurious ground-floor suite with a four-poster bed and a separate parlor and porch. Mama's and Papa's is a spacious upstairs bedroom with a sitting area. Gertie's, a downstairs suite, has a private garden entry and a sofa-sleeper. Decorated in cheery yellow colors, Dawn's Room is inviting, with French doors that lead to a sun porch overlooking the garden. In the morning the aroma of coffee fills the air and at 9 o'clock the sideboard is loaded with unusual goodies for the buffet breakfast. Portions are so bountiful that there is no need to worry about lunch. *Directions*: From the San Francisco area take the I-80 to 49 north 29 miles to Nevada City. Exit at Broad Street and turn left up the main street of town.

GRANDMERE'S INN
Owner: Ruth Ann Riese
Innkeeper: Deborah Gutierrez
449 Broad Street
Nevada City, CA 95959
Tel: (530) 265-4660, Fax: (530) 265-4416
E-mail: grandmere@nevadacityinns.com
7 Rooms, Double: $115–$180
Open all year, Credit cards: all major
Children welcome in Gertie's Room, No smoking

NEWPORT BEACH   DORYMAN'S INN   Map: 7a

It was fun to discover The Doryman's Inn, a sophisticated, elaborately decorated small hotel next to the Newport Beach pier. In fact it sits just across the street, next to the old wooden wharf, where the fishermen still go to sea every day (as they have for 100 years) in their brightly painted dories, returning to sell their catch from the back of the boats. For beach buffs, the sand stretches for miles to the entrance to Balboa harbor. The hotel entry is quite discreet: just a tiny hall where an elevator, takes you up to the reception area—the inn is located above the 21 Ocean Front restaurant, a dining establishment famous for its seafood. When you step off the elevator you are cordially greeted by managed staff and then immersed in the romantic ambiance of the Victorian era with elaborate paneling, reproduction gas lamps, dark wallpaper, and busy floral carpeting. The bedrooms open off the long hallway which is lit with skylights and graced by baskets of hanging ferns. Each of the bedrooms is elaborately decorated with splendid antique beds, fireplaces, and Italian-marble sunken bathtubs. No expense was spared—and it shows. In the morning a light breakfast of fresh pastries, seasonal fruits, yogurts, and assorted cheeses is served buffet-style in the small dining room or out on the patio. *Directions:* Take Highway 5 west to 55 south toward Newport Beach and follow the signs to the Newport pier: the hotel is across the street.

DORYMAN'S INN
Owners: Fi Laing & Michael D. Palitz
2102 West Ocean Front
Newport Beach, CA 92663
Tel & Fax: (949) 675-7300
10 Rooms, Double: $185–$340
Open all year, Credit cards: all major
Children accepted over 5, No smoking

OAKHURST — CHÂTEAU DU SUREAU

Map: 4d

Heavy iron gates swing open magically, allowing you to enter a world far removed from the neon signs that line the main street of Oakhurst, a town just to the south of Yosemite National Park. You enter through the château's heavy doors, cross a cool, flagged limestone foyer, and step down into a stunning living room opening onto a circular tower room where a grand piano sits center stage beneath a whimsically frescoed ceiling. Doors open to reveal a sunny breakfast room and a tiny chapel. A spiraling stone staircase leads up to the individually decorated bedrooms named for herbs and flowers: Saffron has an enormous ebony bed and black-marble fireplace, Lavender is sunny in colors of periwinkle blue and lavender, and Elderberry is cool in blue and white. Each of the splendid bedrooms has a wood-burning fireplace (placed at just the right height to see it from the bed), goose-down duvet, hidden CD player, luxurious bathroom with a deep soaking tub (many large enough for two), the finest toiletries, thick towels, and the softest of robes. In the evening, walk across the garden, by the swimming pool, to the Elderberry House Restaurant where the château's owner, Erna Kubin-Clanin, presents a spectacular fixed-price six-course dinner. *Directions:* From the center of Oakhurst take Highway 41 toward Fresno. As the road climbs the hill, turn right at Victoria Lane and in through the wrought-iron gates.

CHÂTEAU DU SUREAU
Owner/Innkeeper: Erna Kubin-Clanin
48688 Victoria Lane
P.O. Box 577, Oakhurst CA 93644
Tel: (209) 683-6860, Fax: (209) 683-0800
E-mail: chateau@sierratel.com
10 Rooms, Double: $285–$550, Suite: $750-$1400
12% service charge
Closed first two weeks of Jan, Credit cards: all major
Inappropriate for children, No smoking
www.karenbrown.com/california/chateaudusureau.html

OCCIDENTAL — THE INN AT OCCIDENTAL

Maps: 1c & 2c

Occidental is a dear country town nestled between the rugged Sonoma coast and the vineyards of the Russian River valley. The Inn at Occidental, a block up from Main Street, dates from 1867 and was refurbished as an inn in 1988. From the wrap-around porch you enter the living room whose intimate and elegant furnishings are set in front of an inviting wood-burning fireplace. The dining room where breakfast is served adjoins the living room. Breakfast offerings include freshly baked pastries, seasonal fruit, and such tempting delights as orange-thyme pancakes. Beautiful fir floors accented with lovely Oriental carpets are found throughout the public rooms of the inn. The decor of each guestroom is taken from the colors in the original art displayed in the room and feather beds topped with European down comforters assure the guest of a wonderful night's sleep. Recently remodeled, each of the inn's eight rooms now boasts appealing amenities such as a romantic fireplace, hot tub in a private garden oasis, or luxurious Jacuzzi tub. Conference facilities are available in a downstairs room with antique pine furnishings and stone fireplace. I can wax eloquent about how lovely the inn is, yet the element that makes this inn so very special is Jack and his staff. *Directions:* One hour north of San Francisco, take Highway 101 to Highway 116 west to Sebastopol then the Bodega Highway west for 6 miles toward Bodega Bay to the Bohemian Highway and on to Occidental.

THE INN AT OCCIDENTAL
Owner/Innkeeper: Jack Bullard
Assistant Innkeepers: Andy, Jennifer, and Meg
3657 Church Street, Occidental, CA 95465
Tel: (707) 874-1047 or (800) 522-6324
Fax: (707) 874-1078
E-mail: innkeeper@innatoccidental.com
8 Rooms, Double: $145–$245
Open all year, Credit cards: all major
Inappropriate for children, No smoking, Wheelchair friendly
www.karenbrown.com/california/innatoccidental.html

Places to Stay

| ORLAND | INN AT SHALLOW CREEK FARM | Map: 1d |

The Inn at Shallow Creek Farm, a simple farmhouse enjoying the quiet and peace of a rural setting just a few miles off Highway 5, offers travelers a shady respite from the never-ending band of asphalt. Mary and Kurt have decorated their fruit-farm inn with family furnishings and mementos, creating a welcoming and pleasingly informal atmosphere. Breakfast, which not surprisingly features lots of fresh fruit, is often served in the formal dining room or at tables set on the back sun porch. Just off the living room is the Penfield Suite, a large restful room whose windows are dressed with a soft-yellow printed fabric and a sitting area which enjoys the morning sun (this has the only private bathroom in the main house). The other two guestrooms in the main house share a bathroom at the top of the landing, are cozy, set under the different angles and eaves of the old roof line, and have views out to the garden. Off to the side of the farmhouse is a free standing cottage with its own fully stocked kitchen, separate living room, bedroom, and bathroom. The paneling in the living room is original to the cottage and its furnishings are basic and simple. *Directions*: Take the Chico-Orland exit from Interstate 5. Go west 2.5 miles then turn right on Road DD. Go half a mile, cross the low bridge, and turn right into the next driveway on the right.

INN AT SHALLOW CREEK FARM
Innkeepers: Mary & Kurt Glaeseman
4712 Road DD
Orland, CA 95963
Tel: (530) 865-4093 or (800) 865-4093
4 Rooms, 2 with private bathrooms
Double: $65–$85
Open all year, Credit cards: MC, VS
Inappropriate for children, No smoking

PACIFIC GROVE GOSBY HOUSE Map: 5a

Sandwiched between the busier resorts of Monterey and Carmel, Pacific Grove has managed to avoid much of their more touristy ambiance and retains the air of being an inviting Victorian summer retreat. The Gosby House is a perfect place to retreat to, with certainly a lot more fun and frolic than in days gone by when it was the summer home of a stern Methodist family. While the decor is decidedly Victorian in flavor, it has been done with such whimsy and fun that all formal stuffiness has been dispelled: a glass-fronted cabinet in the dining room is filled with antique dolls and teddy bears are posed rakishly on each bed. The bedrooms are scattered upstairs and down, some have garden entrances and several occupy an adjacent clapboard house tucked behind the pretty garden. Over half the bedrooms have fireplaces and all but two have luxuriously appointed bathrooms. Each room is appealingly decorated in soft colors and many benefit from the romantic touch of antique beds. Before you venture out for dinner, enjoy hors d'oeuvres and wine in the living room. When you return, your bed will be turned down and chocolates placed on your pillow—such a sweet way to end the day.
Directions: Take Highway 1 to Highway 68 west to Pacific Grove. Continue on Forest Avenue to Lighthouse Avenue, turn left, and go three blocks to the inn.

GOSBY HOUSE
Innkeeper: Tess Arthur
643 Lighthouse Avenue
Pacific Grove, CA 93950
Tel: (831) 375-1287 or (800) 527-8828
Fax: (831) 655-9621
22 Rooms, 20 with private bathrooms
Double: $90–$160
Open all year, Credit cards: all major
Children accepted in annex rooms, No smoking
www.karenbrown.com/california/gosbyhouse.html

Places to Stay

PACIFIC GROVE — THE GREEN GABLES INN   Map: 5a

The Green Gables Inn is sensationally positioned overlooking Monterey Bay. This romantic, half-timbered, Queen Anne-style mansion with many interesting dormers is as inviting inside as out. The living room and dining room have comfortable arrangements of sofas and chairs placed to maximize your enjoyment of the view. Upstairs many of the bedrooms, set under steeply slanting beamed ceilings with romantic diamond-paned casement windows, offer ocean views. While the Garret room does not have an ocean view, it is the coziest of hideaways. All but one of the upstairs bedrooms share bathrooms. The ground-floor suite has a sitting room and fireplace. The recently renovated rooms in the adjacent carriage house all have fireplaces, sitting areas, and private bathrooms. While a guest at The Green Gables Inn you will certainly not perish from hunger or thirst—beverages are available all day, goodies are readily at hand in the cookie jar, and wine and hors d'oeuvres appear in the evening. Breakfast, too, is no disappointment: a hearty buffet of fruit, homemade breads, and a hot egg dish. *Directions:* From Highway 1 take the Pacific Grove-Del Monte exit. As you go through the tunnel, Del Monte becomes Lighthouse Avenue that you follow into Pacific Grove. Go right one block and you are on Ocean View Boulevard—the inn is on the corner at Fifth Street.

THE GREEN GABLES INN
Innkeeper: Toni McDaniel
104 Fifth Street
Pacific Grove, CA 93950
Tel: (831) 375-2095 or (800) 722-1774
Fax: (831) 375-5437
11 Rooms, 7 with private bathrooms
Double: $110–$195
Open all year, Credit cards: all major
Children accepted, No smoking
www.karenbrown.com/california/greengablesinn.html

PALM SPRINGS — CASA CODY — Map: 7b

Casa Cody, a moderately priced hotel in the heart of Palm Springs, although quite simple, stands out like a gem from its neighbors. The one-story inn has three U-shaped garden courtyards, two with their own swimming pool. There is a nostalgic, old-fashioned comfort to this pink-stuccoed building with turquoise trim. Once owned by Wild Bill Cody's cousin, Casa Cody (the oldest continuously functioning hotel in Palm Springs) had fallen into a state of hopeless-looking disrepair until bought by Therese Hayes (who is French) and Frank Tysen (who is Dutch). After hard work, lots of imagination, and much love, the hotel once again blossomed into an appealing small hotel with a nice choice of accommodations—ranging from a standard double to a spacious two-bedroom, two-bath suite. Many of the rooms have the added bonus of kitchenettes and fireplaces. The interior decor exudes a fresh, clean "Santa Fe" look with a southwest color scheme and handmade furniture. This friendly, comfortable inn is a remarkable value, especially the reasonably priced studio units such as 1, 2, 3, 4, 21, and 23 that have both fireplaces and well-equipped kitchens. However, my very favorite is the 1920s doll-house-like, one-bedroom cottage (with kitchen) tucked in under the trees in the corner of the property. *Directions:* Drive south through Palm Springs on Palm Canyon Drive. Turn right on Tahquitz-McCallum Road, then left on Cahuilla Road.

CASA CODY
Owners: Therese Hayes & Frank Tysen
Innkeeper: Elissa Goforth
175 South Cahuilla Road
Palm Springs, CA 92262
Tel: (760) 320-9346, Fax: (760) 325-8610
23 Rooms, Double: $79–$159
Open all year, Credit cards: all major
Children accepted mid-week, Smoking
www.karenbrown.com/california/casacody.html

Places to Stay

PALM SPRINGS — DESERT HILLS HOTEL   Map: 7b

Stopping to chat with a delightful couple lounging by the pool, I was amazed to learn that this was their 36th season of vacationing at the Desert Hills Hotel. Actually, after a tour of the hotel I was not surprised to find the majority of guests return each year. Along with the scent of flowers, a gentle, friendly ambiance permeates the air, enhanced by the charming graciousness of your hostess, Joanne Petty, who built the hotel with her husband in 1956. The location is excellent—an easy walk to the heart of Old Palm Springs and yet snuggled up against the rugged San Jacinto mountains. The hotel does not have an antique ambiance, but rather a timeless theme of restful, pleasing pastel desert colors. The spotlessly tidy guestrooms (most with kitchenettes) are attractive, with liberal use of rattan furniture, comfortable chairs, excellent lighting, and quality mattresses. The rooms face a lush lawn and well-tended gardens surrounding a pretty pool. From the outside the one-story Desert Hills looks like most of the other hotels of similar vintage on the street—you only realize its specialness when you see that every detail shows loving care. The Desert Hills is not a flashy, trendy hotel that would appeal to those looking for action, but rather the old-fashioned kind of tranquil oasis where you can settle in for an extended time, relaxing by the pool, hearing the wind whisper through the palm trees, and feeling like a friend of the family. *Directions:* Turn west off Palm Canyon on Arenas and go six blocks—the hotel is on the northwest corner of Arenas.

DESERT HILLS HOTEL
Innkeeper: Joanne Petty
601 West Arenas Road, Palm Springs, CA 92262
Tel: (760) 325-2777 or (800) 350-2527
Fax: (760) 325-6423, E-mail: deshils@aol.com
14 Rooms, Double: $70–$160
Open all year, Credit cards: all major
Children accepted over 16
No smoking, Wheelchair friendly
www.karenbrown.com/california/deserthillshotel.html

PALM SPRINGS GIVENCHY HOTEL & SPA Map: 7b

If you want a deluxe hotel reflecting the style of a splendid European spa, the Givenchy is a perfect choice. The hotel is a walled, 14-acre complex of crisp-white buildings enclosing a beautifully manicured garden courtyard. The exterior of the main part of the hotel (which incorporates the reception area, lounges, dining room, and many of the guestrooms) has a formal Grecian flair with tall, slender white columns gracefully stretching up to the roof. Inside, however, the mood changes, the decor exuding the ambiance of a beautiful French country manor. There is an air of spacious grandeur with soaring ceilings, two-story-tall French doors opening out to the garden, and an inviting lounge with comfortable chairs set in front of a fireplace flanked by bookshelves. Opening off the main lounge is a beautifully appointed dining room with elegantly set tables. The spacious guestrooms are individually decorated and continue the ambiance of refinement and good taste. Tucked in the gardens behind the hotel are cottages with large suites. Also facing onto the central courtyard is a deluxe, full-service spa with two indoor pools. In addition, there are two outdoor pools and tennis courts (golf privileges can be arranged at nearby courses). Although the facilities are delightful, one of the most outstanding attributes of the Givenchy Hotel is its charming owner, Rosa Narva, who is on the premises, personally overseeing the contentment of the guests. *Directions*: From Palm Springs go east about 4 miles on Palm Canyon Drive. The hotel is on your left.

GIVENCHY HOTEL & SPA
Owner: Rosa Narva
4200 East Palm Canyon Drive
Palm Springs, CA 92264
Tel: (760) 770-5000, Fax: (760) 324-6104
95 Rooms, Double: $275–$850, Villas to $3,500
Limited operation July to September
Credit cards: all major
Children accepted, Smoking, Wheelchair friendly
www.karenbrown.com/california/givenchyhotel.html

PALM SPRINGS — INGLESIDE INN — Map: 7b

As you enter the large wrought-iron gates of the Ingleside Inn, you have the impression of being the guest on a private estate. This is not surprising, since the Ingleside Inn was once the home of the Humphrey Birge family, manufacturers of the Pierce Arrow automobile. Although the hotel is located in the heart of Palm Springs it is an oasis of tranquillity. The park-like grounds are surrounded by a high adobe wall and the San Jacinto Mountains rise steeply behind the hotel, forming a dramatic backdrop. A pretty pool and gazebo highlight the front lawn. Some of the guestrooms open off an inner courtyard, while others are nestled in nearby cottages. Each room is individually decorated with antiques. All have whirlpool tubs, coffee makers, and refrigerators stocked with complimentary light snacks and juices. Many rooms have the added bonus of wood-burning fireplaces. Breakfast is served either on the verandah, poolside, or on your private patio. The owner of Ingleside Inn, Melvyn Haber, also owns one of the famous restaurants in Palm Springs, appropriately called "Melvyn's," which is located next to the lobby. In the evening the restaurant traffic intrudes somewhat upon the solitude, but it is wonderfully convenient to have such an excellent restaurant so close at hand. *Directions:* Drive through Palm Springs, south on Palm Canyon Drive and turn right on Ramon Road.

INGLESIDE INN
Innkeeper: Melvyn Haber
200 West Ramon Road
Palm Springs, CA 92264
Tel: (760) 325-0046 or (800) 772-6655
Fax: (760) 325-0710
E-mail: ingleside@earthlink.net
30 Rooms, Double: $95–$385
Open all year, Credit cards: all major
Children accepted over 16
Smoking, Wheelchair friendly

PALM SPRINGS — KORAKIA PENSIONE
Map: 7b

Most of the newcomers to Palm Springs are slick, trendy resorts trying to outdo each other in money spent on glitzy glamour. However, the magic of the desert can best be captured on balmy, starlit nights from the bougainvillea-shrouded patios of intimate hotels with the laid-back style and grace of yesterday. A rare example of such perfection is the Korakia Pensione, a Moorish-style villa built in 1924 by Scottish artist Gordon Coutts, just four blocks from the heart of the Palm Springs. The derelict building had immediate appeal to Doug Smith who spent four years on a tiny Greek island where he owns a bar and restaurant, catering to the rich and famous yacht set. Doug (an architect specializing in restoring historic buildings) saw the great potential of the Korakia, which reminded him of the sun-drenched houses of the Mediterranean. After several years of love and labor, his dream of a jewel of a small hotel materialized. With a backdrop of the San Jacinto Mountains, this little inn has the flavor of Europe mingled with the romance of the Greek islands: whitewashed walls, Oriental carpets, handmade furniture, lovely natural fabrics, antiques, Moroccan fountains, fragrant fruit trees, and two pools surrounded by gardens create a stunning ambiance. There are 20 rooms. Doug will soon open an open-air day spa and café. *Directions:* Turn west off Palm Canyon on Arenas, go four blocks, turn south on Patencio Road.

KORAKIA PENSIONE
Owner: G. Doug Smith
Manager: Melissa McDaniel
257 South Patencio Road
Palm Springs, CA 92262
Tel: (760) 864-6411, fax: (760) 864-4147
20 Rooms, Double: $109–$229
Closed in August, Credit cards: none
Children accepted over 16, No smoking, Wheelchair friendly
www.karenbrown.com/california/korakiapension.html

Places to Stay

PALM SPRINGS — VILLA ROYALE — Map: 7b

The Villa Royale is a romantic desert oasis. From the moment you enter this charming small hotel, you step into a magical world reflecting the essence of Spain: softly splashing fountains, walls draped in bougainvillea, decorative mosaic tile work, secluded little nooks, columned arcades, overhanging tiled roofs, and meandering paths. The guestrooms too are very special. Not only do many have their own wood-burning fireplaces and private spas, but each accommodation represents a country, so you can choose your room to complement your mood, with such options in decor as Irish, English, Moroccan, Swiss, Italian, German, Spanish, Dutch, or Greek. There are 3½ walled acres in which the rooms are cleverly arranged for maximum privacy around secluded interior courtyards. Even the least expensive rooms, although small, have style and charm. The main courtyard has a swimming pool with a nearby terrace where tables are set for lunch or snacks. In the evening, dinner is served at the Europa Restaurant either in a romantic dining room reminiscent of the French countryside or outside. The Villa Royale is located on the edge of Old Palm Springs. *Directions:* Drive south through Palm Springs on Palm Canyon Drive and just a couple of blocks after the road makes a bend to the left and becomes East Palm Canyon Drive, turn left on Indian Trail.

VILLA ROYALE
Owners: Amy Aquino & Company
Innkeeper: Greg Purdy
1620 Indian Trail
Palm Springs, CA 92264
Tel: (760) 327-2314 or (800) 245-2314
Fax: (760) 322-3794
E-mail: info@villaroyale.com
33 Rooms, Double: $95–$295
Open all year, Credit cards: all major
Inappropriate for children, Smoking
www.karenbrown.com/california/villaroyal.html

PALM SPRINGS — THE WILLOWS — Map: 7b

Once a sleepy desert town, Palm Springs was discovered in the 1920s by glamorous movie stars that made it their secret hideaway. This balmy paradise also captivated the heart of Samuel Untermyer, a New Yorker and former United States Secretary of the Treasury, who bought a beautiful estate, The Willows, snuggled next to the mountains just a few blocks from the center of town, where in winter he entertained many distinguished friends. The home remained a private residence until opening in 1996 as a deluxe small hotel after total renovation which returned it to its former elegance and successfully captured the ambiance of the 30s. The clay-colored building with wrought-iron trim and red-tiled roof is softened by a profusion of greenery and brightened by a cheerful array of colorful flowers. A pool nestles on the lower garden area—but an equally inviting nook for a refreshing drink is a beautiful flagstone terrace enclosed on one side by a wall of natural rock with a cascading waterfall. Every lovely guestroom has its own personality, with the price basically reflecting its size. The rates are expensive, but you will feel like guests in a private home displaying the opulence of a bygone era.
Directions: Located in the heart of Palm Springs. From either Palm Canyon Drive or Indian Canyon Drive, take Tahquitz Canyon Way west. In a few blocks the street dead-ends. The Willows is at the end of the road on your right.

THE WILLOWS
Owners: Tracy Conrad & Paul Marut
Manager: Connie Stevens
412 West Tahquitz Canyon Way
Palm Springs, CA 92262
Tel: (760) 320-0771 or (800) 966-9597
Fax: (760) 320-0780
E-mail: innkeeper@thewillowspalmsprings.com
8 Rooms, Double: $250–$500
Open all year, Credit cards: all major
Children accepted over 16, No Smoking

PASADENA, SOUTH — THE ARTISTS' INN — Map: 7a

When the last of Janet Marangi's four children left the nest, she fulfilled her dream of opening a small bed and breakfast. Just two blocks from the colorful center of South Pasadena, she found an 1895 Victorian-style farmhouse, built by a settler from Indiana for his family. The house is painted a pretty buttercup-yellow, accented by white trim. A white picket fence and old-fashioned swinging gate enclose a perfectly groomed front lawn. One hundred rose bushes line the fence and border the path leading to the spacious front porch. Janet's goal was to instill a totally comfortable, homey ambiance, re-creating happy memories of visits to grandmother's house. She has succeeded. The furnishings are mostly pieces lovingly collected over the years by Janet while antique browsing. The living room is painted a rich green which sets off the white wicker furniture and rich floral fabrics. The nine bedrooms are appealingly decorated, each representing an artistic period. The Eighteenth-Century English is a cheerful room with king-sized canopy bed, old-fashioned rose-patterned wall paper, antique desk, and white lace curtains. Five new rooms were recently opened in the cottage; three are two-room suites with fireplaces, Jacuzzi tubs, and canopy beds. *Directions*: Fifteen minutes from downtown Los Angeles. Take Highway 110 (the Pasadena Freeway) and exit at the Orange Grove off-ramp. Turn right on Orange Grove, go two blocks, and turn left on Magnolia.

THE ARTISTS' INN
Owner: Janet Marangi
1038 Magnolia Street
South Pasadena, CA 91030
Tel: (626) 799-5668 or (888) 799-5668
Fax: (626) 799-3678
E-mail: artistsinn@artistsinns.com
9 Rooms, Double: $115–$165
Open all year, Credit cards: all major
Children accepted, No smoking
www.karenbrown.com/california/theartistsinn.html

PASADENA, SOUTH — THE BISSELL HOUSE — Map: 7a

Built in the 1880s for the renowned carpet-cleaner family, this is a lovely three-story home with dormer windows and wrap-around porch set on a lush lawn shaded by mature trees just 12 minutes from downtown Los Angeles. On one side of the entry you find the cozy library decorated in dark greens and plaids which looks out onto the swimming pool, and on the other side, through French doors, is the formal living room with its piano and sofas set in front of the fireplace. Central to the living room, the hand-carved wood fireplace opens up at the back so that it also warms the adjacent breakfast room. Just beyond the dining room it is fun to peek into the butler's pantry whose tin roof is original to the home and whose shelves display a lovely collection of Christmas Spode. The Prince Albert Room on the second floor has lovely old wooden floors, queen bed, and private bath. The third floor boasts three romantic accommodations tucked under the eaves. Thoughtful amenities like a communal refrigerator stocked with complimentary refreshments, cookies, and brownies as well as in-room touches such as large fluffy towels, robes, fresh flowers, and a basket of fruit make you feel very welcome and cared for. *Directions*: From either the 134, 210, or 110 freeways, take the Orange Grove Avenue exit. The Bissell House is located on Pasadena's historical Millionaires' Row on the southwest corner of Orange Grove and Columbia. The entrance is on Columbia.

THE BISSELL HOUSE
Innkeepers: Russ, Leonore, & Ivis Butcher
201 Orange Grove Avenue
South Pasadena, CA 91030
Tel: (626) 441-3535, Fax: (626) 441-3671
5 Rooms, Double: $115–$160
Open all year, Credit cards: all major
Inappropriate for children, No smoking
www.karenbrown.com/california/bissell.html

PASO ROBLES — THE ARBOR INN — Map: 6a

The newly built Arbor Inn, with its nostalgic charm of a lovely country English-style home, makes an ideal choice if you want to stop en route between San Francisco and Southern California. Its setting is superb—nestled in a spectacularly beautiful area of gently rolling hills, either covered with vineyards or dotted with oak trees. You enter the long, low, white frame home with its old-fashioned wrap-around porch and overhanging roof through large double doors into a spacious entry hall. To the left is a formal dining room, to the right is a sun-filled living room—bright and cheerful with sofas and chairs covered in colorful English-style fabrics. The guestrooms, all large and individually decorated, have a mood of comfortable elegance. Each bedroom has either a private terrace or balcony that looks out over the vineyards (my personal favorites are the rooms in the rear which have the most expansive views) and a beautifully appointed bathroom. All of the rooms have their own gas log fireplace. The inn is owned by the Treana Winery that has a gift shop and offers wine tasting. However, the Arbor Inn is not only convenient for wine tasting, but also makes a good base for visiting Hearst Castle which is just a short drive away by a scenic road. *Directions*: From highway 101, at Paso Robles take highway 46 west for 1¼ miles. The Arbor Inn is on your right.

THE ARBOR INN
Innkeepers: Denise Mertens & April Ziegebren
Owner: Treana Winery
2130 Arbor Road
Paso Robles, CA 93447
Tel: (805) 227-4673, Fax: (805) 227-1112
9 Rooms, Double: $125–$235
Open all year, Credit cards: MC, VS
Children accepted over 12
No smoking, Wheelchair friendly
www.karenbrown.com/california/arborinn.html

PETALUMA — CAVANAGH INN

Maps: 1c, 2d & 3b

Petaluma is a charming agricultural town situated on the Petaluma River which feeds into the San Francisco Bay. On a pretty residential street, the Cavanagh Inn is within walking distance of the historic downtown area with its multitude of antique shops and the river. Accommodations are in two neighboring neoclassic Victorian homes sharing a lawn shaded by a large Magnolia tree and enclosed by a white picket fence. The main home was built in 1902 as a family residence, and the cottage was added on in 1912 to accommodate the sisters. The main home is lovely, handsome, and rich with redwood floors and walls. Just off the entry are the library and parlor with chairs set in front of an open fireplace and a dining room which opens onto the back porch and garden. Climb a beautiful staircase to reach a stunning, octagonal redwood-paneled landing. Four guestrooms open onto the landing where you will find a library of good books. The guestrooms in the house are very comfortable and homey, all with a private bath or shower. The three rooms in the cottage enjoy a welcoming sun porch and are smaller, more calico than Victorian in décor. The twin-bedded room has a private bath, and the other two share a bath. A gourmet breakfast is offered to all in the dining room of the main house or on the back porch in pretty weather. *Directions:* Traveling Highway 101 north, take Petaluma Boulevard South: Follow it to Western Avenue. Turn left, go two blocks and make another left on Keller.

CAVANAGH INN
Innkeepers: Jeanne & Ray Farris
10 Keller Street, Petaluma, CA 94952
Tel: (707) 765-4657 or (888) 765-4658
Fax: (707) 769-0466
E-mail: info@cavanaghinn.com
7 Rooms, 5 with private bathrooms
Double: $85–$130
Open all year, Credit cards: all major
Children accepted over 12, No smoking
www.karenbrown.com/california/cavanaughinn.html

PLAYA DEL REY   INN AT PLAYA DEL REY   Map: 7a

People simply driving by the Inn at Playa del Rey would probably not be drawn inside by the inn's exterior and location on a busy road. However, this newly constructed Cape Cod-style inn backs onto the Ballona Wetlands, a 350-acre bird sanctuary, and was beautifully designed to complement rather than compete with the setting and natural surroundings. Large picture windows frame a panorama of grassy expanse of wetlands and distant marina. A narrow channel banded by an inviting bike path that weaves a passage through the wetlands, often navigated by tall-masted boats charting a course to the ocean. The decor is light and airy, with pine furnishings matched with lovely fabrics and attractive wallpapers. The guestrooms are each individual in style and floor plan, and maximize any opportunity to incorporate views. The choice rooms are of course those at the back of the inn with unobstructed views of the wetlands. Those at the front are less expensive and enjoy the morning light while dual-glazed and shuttered windows minimize the noise of traffic. Public areas include a front, central outdoor courtyard and a lovely breakfast room and living room running the length of the back of the building, banked by handsome French doors. *Directions:* Exit off the San Diego Freeway (405) onto the Marina Freeway (90) and travel west toward Marina del Rey. The freeway ends at a stoplight at Culver Blvd. Turn left and proceed west 2 miles to the inn.

INN AT PLAYA DEL REY
Owner: Susan Zolla
Innkeeper: Donna Donnelly
435 Culver Boulevard, Playa del Rey, CA 90293
Tel: (310) 574-1920, Fax: (310) 574-9920
E-mail: playainn@aol.com
21 Rooms, Double: $125–$275
Open all year, Credit cards: all major
Children accepted
No smoking, Wheelchair friendly
www.karenbrown.com/california/innatplayadelrey.html

POINT RICHMOND   EAST BROTHER LIGHT STATION   Maps: 2d & 3b

The East Brother Light Station, sitting snugly on its own tiny island, dates back to 1873 when it was built to guide ships through a 2-mile-wide strait connecting San Francisco and San Pablo Bays. Adjoining the tower beacon, a small house with gingerbread trim was built for the lightkeepers and their families. This nostalgic lighthouse was doomed for destruction until a group of concerned citizens banded together in 1979, raised the funds, and rescued it. As a boy, one of the saviors, Walter Fanning, spent many happy hours at the East Brother Light Station, where his grandfather was the lighthouse keeper. Today, a few lucky guests enjoy the island in far more commodious circumstances than the keepers of old. Guests are brought by boat in the afternoon, treated to a champagne tour and delicious four-course dinner with wines, then lulled to sleep by the sound of a foghorn. There are four guestrooms, not large or luxurious, but pleasantly decorated with antiques and all with a view of the bay. The innkeepers, Julie and Gary, live on the island, prepare the meals, and graciously tend to the needs of their guests. Because all the water is caught from the rain and is limited, only guests staying more than one night may use the showers. *Directions:* The East Brother Light Station, located in San Pablo Bay, is reached by boat. When you call for reservations, ask for further information.

EAST BROTHER LIGHT STATION
Owner: US Coast Guard
Innkeepers: Julie Robinson & Gary Sullivan
117 Park Place, Point Richmond, CA 94801
Tel: (510) 233-2385, Fax: (510) 232-5425
4 Rooms, 2 with private bathrooms
Double: $295-$325*
*Includes breakfast & dinner with wine
Open all year, Thursday to Sunday
Credit cards: all major
Inappropriate for children, unless the entire inn is booked by a private party, No smoking

RANCHO SANTA FE   INN AT RANCHO SANTA FE   Map: 7c/d

The known history of the Rancho Santa Fe property dates back to 1845 when an 8,842-acre land grant was given to Juan Maria Osuna. In 1906 the Santa Fe Railroad purchased the land grant, changed the name to Rancho Santa Fe, and planted about three million eucalyptus seedlings with the idea of growing wood for railroad ties. The project failed: the wood was not appropriate, so the railroad decided instead to develop a planned community and built a lovely Spanish-style guesthouse for prospective home buyers. This became the nucleus for what is now the Inn at Rancho Santa Fe and houses the lounge, dining rooms, offices, and a few of the guestrooms. The lounge is extremely appealing, like a cozy living room in a private home, with a large fireplace, comfortable seating, impressive floral arrangements, and a roaring fire. The dining rooms are more "hotel like" in ambiance. The bedrooms, most tucked away in cottages scattered throughout the property, are attractively decorated with traditional fabrics and furnishings and many have fireplaces. The grounds are lovely, filled with flowers and shaded by fragrant eucalyptus trees. The inn's greatest asset is the Royce family, who own the hotel and give what first appears to be a slick commercial resort the warmth and friendliness of a small inn. *Directions:* From San Diego go north for 25 miles on Highway 5, take the Lomas Santa Fe Drive turnoff, and travel 4-1/5 miles to the inn.

INN AT RANCHO SANTA FE
Innkeeper: Duncan Royce Hadden
Linea del Cielo at Paseo Delicias
P.O. Box 869, Rancho Santa Fe, CA 92067
Tel: (619) 756-1131, Fax: (619) 759-1604
75 Rooms, Double: $110–$600*
*Breakfast not included
Open all year, Credit cards: all major
Children accepted, Smoking, Wheelchair friendly
www.karenbrown.com/california/innatranchosantafe.html

RANCHO SANTA FE   RANCHO VALENCIA RESORT   Map: 7c/d

Inland from the Del Mar racetrack, tucked into the foothills, you find an exclusive and quietly elegant resort, Rancho Valencia. The sports aficionado will love it here with the multi-tiered tennis courts and privileges at three distinguished private golf clubs, while the romantic will simply settle into one of the 21 individual casitas and hide away in the luxury of its accommodation. The casitas house 43 sumptuous suites, each with its own wet bar, fireplace, vaulted ceiling with overhead fans, spacious bathroom, dressing room, and private garden terrace. The feeling of the complex is Mediterranean, with warm, soft-peach-stucco buildings, doors and windows trimmed in an attractive forest-green, and roofs decked with rich terra-cotta tiles. Lovely garden paths bordered by an abundance of colorful flowers weave through the property and lead to the central lodge whose handsome pine and wicker furnishings set on terra-cotta floors, large open wood-burning fireplaces, and bountiful flower arrangements beckon you indoors. Central to the lodge is a lovely courtyard patio with a soothing fountain, set with tables amidst terra-cotta pots overflowing with flowering plants. On the far side of the lodge is a restaurant whose lovely expanse of window overlooks the tennis courts and surrounding valley—dining here is an epicurean delight. *Directions*: From the Interstate 5 in Del Mar, take the Via de la Valle Road east to San Dieguito Road and follow signs to the resort.

RANCHO VALENCIA RESORT
Director: Michael Ullman
5921 Valencia Circle
P.O. Box 9126, Rancho Santa Fe, CA 92067
Tel: (619) 756-1123 or (800) 548-3664
Fax: (619) 756-0165, E-mail: ranchov@aol.com
43 Suites, Double: $410–$650*
*Breakfast not included
Open all year, Credit cards: all major
Children accepted, Smoking, Wheelchair friendly

REDDING   TIFFANY HOUSE   Map: 1b

Tiffany House is a pretty soft-blue Victorian set back behind a white picket fence. Off the front porch the lovely entry serves as the reception and is also central to most of the public rooms. From the formal parlor decorated in 1850s furniture and rich hues of dark blue, you can climb the stair to the three guestrooms in the main house. The Victorian Rose Room is dressed in colors of greens, mauves, and blacks, reminiscent of the Victorian period, and a claw-foot tub is staged dramatically in the alcove of the turret with distant but unobstructed views of Mount Lassen. Off the landing to the right is the attractive, light, and airy Oak Room whose colors of red, white, and blue complement the nostalgic Americana theme. The Oak Room, hung with 12 signed Wallace Nutting prints, has an inviting sitting area tucked under the eaves and overlooks the peaceful back garden. The Tierra Room is a pretty and restful room with its white iron bed and delicate blue-and-white prints all set under the delightful angles and eaves of the roofline. Accessed off the back garden patio with its own private entrance is Lavinia's Cottage, a light, airy, and spacious room with lovely pine walls, a romantic high iron bed, and an in-room Jacuzzi. From the corner sitting area one is blessed with an expanse of paned windows through which you can see Mount Lassen. *Directions*: From Interstate 5, travel west on Lake Boulevard for 4/5 mile to Market Street. Go south on Market to Benton Drive then west on Benton Drive for 1/5 mile to Barbara Road.

TIFFANY HOUSE
Innkeepers: Susan & Brady Stewart
1510 Barbara Road, Redding, CA 96003
Tel: (530) 244-3225
E-mail: tiffanyhse@aol.com
4 Rooms, Double: $85–$135
Open all year, Credit cards: all major
Inappropriate for children, No smoking
www.karenbrown.com/california/tiffanyhouse.html

SAINT HELENA — THE INK HOUSE — Map: 2b

Built 114 years ago, The Ink House is a charming yellow and white Victorian accented with light-blue trim. Architecturally interesting, the house enjoys a verandah wrapped all the way around and a cupola that affords a 360-degree vista of the area. We immediately felt The Ink House's relaxing and comfortable atmosphere when we arrived to the laughter and conversation of guests—relative strangers—enjoying wine and hors d'oeuvres in the downstairs parlor. The guestrooms, on the second floor, vary in size—two share a bath, and some are rather small. The side and back rooms overlook vineyards and a large old barn that sits behind the house. Different in each room, the decor is fittingly traditional as it is in the public rooms downstairs. The accommodation can be described as homey, with old Oriental carpets and family furnishings. A full breakfast is served in the dining room on one long table and guests are invited to take their coffee to the verandah. Although the house sits just off the principal road through the wine country, the double-paned windows help buffer the street noise, and the country setting is quiet and peaceful. Diane, with years of expertise (she managed the Wine Country Inn in Saint Helena for seven years), offers a genuine warmth of welcome to her guests. *Directions*: Traveling north on Highway 29, before you approach downtown Saint Helena, turn left on Whitehall Lane. The bed and breakfast is located on the corner of Whitehall Lane and Highway 29.

THE INK HOUSE
Innkeeper: Diane Horkheimer
1575 St. Helena Highway at Whitehall Lane
Saint Helena, CA 94574-9775
Tel: (707) 963-3890, Fax: (707) 968-0739
E-mail: inkhousebb@aol.com
7 Rooms, Double: $99–$189
Closed Christmas
Credit cards: MC, VS
Children accepted, No smoking

Places to Stay

SAINT HELENA — MEADOWOOD NAPA VALLEY   Map: 2b

On 256 sprawling acres, Meadowood, an attractive complex of sand-gray gabled wooden buildings with crisp white trim, is a resort community in a secluded, quiet valley sheltered by towering Ponderosa pines and Douglas firs. Wooded areas open up to a nine-hotel golf course, croquet courts, tennis courts, and swimming pools. Centrally located, the clubhouse—a three-story structure overlooking the golf course—houses The Restaurant, featuring wine-country cuisine in an elegant setting; The Grill, offering meals in a less formal setting; a golf shop; conference facilities; and the inviting reception lodge. There are 13 guestrooms in the Croquet Lodge which overlooks the perfectly manicured croquet lawn. Other bedrooms are found in clusters of lodges scattered about the property. The atmosphere, relaxed, informal, and unpretentious, is accurately described as "California casual." Although expensive, the accommodations are luxuriously appointed and attractively furnished, reflecting an incredible attention to detail. Concern for a guest's comfort and satisfaction is foremost and service is carried out with a friendly and professional flair. Meadowood is a luxurious resort with every amenity, including a full-service, state-of-the-art health spa and a most caring staff. *Directions:* From Saint Helena take Pope Street east from Highway 29 to the Silverado Trail. Cross the Silverado Trail, jog to the left and then right on Howell Mountain Road following Meadowood signs.

MEADOWOOD NAPA VALLEY
Managing Director: Seamus McManus
900 Meadowood Lane
Saint Helena, CA 94574
Tel: (707) 963-3646 or (800) 458-8080
Fax: (707) 963-3532
85 Rooms, Double from $345 to $670*
*Breakfast not included
Open all year, Credit cards: all major
Children accepted, Smoking, Wheelchair friendly
www.karenbrown.com/california/meadowood.html

Places to Stay

SAINT HELENA — HOTEL SAINT HELENA

Map: 2b

With an entry tucked off a small shopping arcade on Saint Helena's delightful main street, the Hotel Saint Helena affords an ideal location for those who want to stay within walking distance of shops and a wide range of interesting restaurants. The attractive lobby, decorated in rich tones of burgundy, mauve, and brown, sets an inviting ambiance that is carried through to the decor in the bedrooms. A few steps up off the lobby is an extremely cozy wine bar whose intimate tables are set against rose-colored walls and dressed with pink cloths. Here you can sample by the glass fine Napa Valley wines and accompany your tasting with tempting appetizers or cheese plates. In addition, the wine bar serves a large selection of imported beers, coffees, and teas. A Continental breakfast of croissants, cereal, fresh fruit, and hot beverages is also served in the wine bar and on sunny days you can carry a tray out into the lovely garden courtyard. The hotel's 17 bedrooms and one suite are located up a narrow flight of stairs decorated with attractive prints on the walls. While the guestrooms are on the small side, most have private bathrooms and all are delightfully decorated and furnished with Victorian antiques including some brass headboards and bent-willow furniture. Members of the Martin family share innkeeping duties in the course of the week and Adam Roberts is there to welcome and offer assistance on a daily basis. *Directions:* Located on the west side of Main Street in downtown Saint Helena.

HOTEL SAINT HELENA
Innkeeper: Elisabeth Martin
1309 Main Street, Saint Helena, CA 94574
Tel: (707) 963-4388, Fax: (707) 963-5402
18 Rooms, 14 with private bathrooms
Double: $145–$195
Open all year, Credit cards: all major
Children accepted, No smoking
www.karenbrown.com/california/hotelsainthelena.html

SAINT HELENA — VINEYARD COUNTRY INN   Map: 2b

Just off Highway 29 at the corner of El Bonita, on the outskirts of Saint Helena, the Vineyard Country Inn backs onto an expanse of vineyards. Newly constructed to resemble a French country manor, the attention to detail and the quality of appointments is impressive. Handsome slate roofs dotted by whimsical brick chimneys top the inn's complex of buildings. A path winds from the main building which houses the lobby and attractive breakfast room past the enclosed pool and Jacuzzi, through patches of flowering garden to the guestrooms. Accommodations are all suites which enjoy a sitting area in front of a wood-burning fireplace, a game table or work area, and then a bedroom furnished with either a four-poster king bed or two queen sleigh beds. The decor is clean and elegant in its simplicity. Bathrooms are lovely in their tile and wallpaper and are beautifully fresh and modern. Under beamed ceilings, the downstairs rooms (with the exception of two) open onto patios and under vaulted ceilings; all the upstairs rooms open onto private decks. The Vineyard Country Inn offers guestrooms that are spacious and priced well in comparison to other luxury accommodation offered in the valley. A bountiful breakfast buffet is offered in the mornings. *Directions:* Just on the south approach to Saint Helena, traveling Highway 29, the Vineyard Country Inn is located on the left-hand side at the intersection of El Bonita.

VINEYARD COUNTRY INN
Owners: Michael & Mary Ann Pietro
Innkeepers: Gene & Ida Lubberstedt
201 Main Street
Saint Helena, CA 94574
Tel: (707) 963-1000, Fax: (707) 963-1794
21 Rooms, Double: $155–$205
Open all year, Credit cards: all major
Children accepted, Smoking, Wheelchair friendly
www.karenbrown.com/california/vineyardcountry.html

SAINT HELENA — THE WINE COUNTRY INN — Map: 2b

The Wine Country Inn is a complex of buildings built of wood and stone, fashioned after the inns of New England, settled on a low hillside and surrounded by acres of vineyards. The inn has twenty-four rooms which have been oriented to enjoy the tranquil and scenic setting: fourteen rooms are housed in the main building, six in the Brandy Barn, and four in the Hastings House. Many of the rooms have private patios, balconies, and fireplaces. Each room, unique in its appeal and character, has its own bath and is individually decorated with country furnishings. Many of the quilts were handmade by the owner. The setting is peaceful, the mood relaxing, and the staff knowledgeable and friendly. Public areas include a lovely lobby which opens onto a large expanse of deck and a pool (now heated all year) on the terraced hillside bounded by a patio and colorful gardens. Room tariffs include a wonderful breakfast and an offering of wine and appetizers in the afternoon. *Directions:* Two miles north of Saint Helena on Highway 29 turn right onto Lodi Lane. The Wine Country Inn is in a quarter of a mile on the left.

THE WINE COUNTRY INN
Innkeeper: Jim Smith
1152 Lodi Lane
Saint Helena, CA 94574
Tel: (707) 963-7077, Fax: (707) 963-9018
E-mail: romance@winecountryinn.com
24 Rooms, Double: $145–$268
Open all year, Credit cards: MC, VS
Inappropriate for children, No smoking
www.karenbrown.com/california/winecountryinn.html

Places to Stay

SAN DIEGO–Coronado　　HOTEL DEL CORONADO　　Map: 7c/d

This guide supposedly features small hotels with charm, so how could we even remotely consider including a resort hotel? Especially one with 692 rooms! The reason is quite simple: there is just nothing else in California to compare with the marvelously whimsical Hotel del Coronado. If you are looking for a secluded hideaway or subdued elegance, this is not your cup of tea. But if you want a hotel with boundless action, plenty of pizzazz, fabulous architecture, and an incredible creamy-white sandy beach, the Hotel del Coronado is tops. Its history dates back to 1887 when Elisha Babcock and H. L. Story purchased Coronado Island and reserved the prime 26 acres of real estate for their extravagant venture, then sold off the remainder of the land to finance the building of one of the world's largest wooden structures. Within a year, their dream came true. The Hotel del Coronado, a white Victorian, gingerbread-hotel—a fantasy of turrets, wrap-around porches, funny little towers, and perky gables—was ready to open. Over the years, two contemporary wings have been added, but the original Victorian building remains much as it was over a hundred years ago (except of course for a computer game arcade and a virtual shopping paradise discreetly tunneled beneath the building). If you want a contemporary beachfront room, opt for the Ocean Towers, but if you value nostalgia, ask to be in the Victorian building (be aware that some of the rooms are very small). *Directions:* Take Highway 5 to the Coronado Bridge. Turn left on Orange Avenue.

HOTEL DEL CORONADO
Manager: Michael Hordisty
1500 Orange Avenue, Coronado, CA 92118
Tel: (619) 435-6611 or (800) 468-3533
Fax: (619) 522-8262
692 Rooms, Double: $205–$2,300*
*Breakfast not included
Open all year, Credit cards: all major
Children accepted, Smoking, Wheelchair friendly
www.karenbrown.com/california/delcoronado.html

SAN DIEGO–Pacific Beach CRYSTAL PIER HOTEL & COTTAGES Map: 7c

The slogan of the Crystal Pier Hotel & Cottages—"Come Sleep Over the Ocean"—aptly expresses just what is so unique and special about this property. Charming white clapboard cottages trimmed in blue and dressed with window boxes are located on both sides and cover the length of this public pier in colorful Pacific Beach, or P.B. as referred to by the locals. Unless the tide is out, the surf washes beneath the cottages and wooden slats of the pier. Cottages all enjoy an expanse of deck and unobstructed views of ocean, surfers, and beachcombers. It is easy to get to know your neighbors while watching the sunset over the ocean as only low white picket fences divide the territories of each cottage patio. The most private units are the two end studio cottages. Recently renovated, the studio units are angled on the deck and afford private patios and spectacular ocean views from the one large bedroom-living room. All the cottages enjoy a little kitchen (stocked with convenient utensils), living room and are described and priced according to whether they are a spacious studio, one bedroom with bath, two bedroom with two baths, and if they are remodeled or dated in décor and bathroom fixtures. Furnishings are comfortable and we find it an ideal spot to base with children. If you are looking for quiet, know that the morning starts early on the pier with fishing at its end, the rumble of cars on the wooden slats as guests come and go and the arrival of beachcombers, lifeguards, and surfers on the beach below. Although locked to the public in the evening with 24-hour security, the pier is open to the public by day. *Directions:* Exit Hwy 5 at Balboa/Garnet Ave. The pier is located at the end of Garnet Avenue on Ocean Front walk.

CRYSTAL PIER HOTEL & COTTAGES
Manager: Jim Bostian
4500 Ocean Boulevard in Pacific Beach
San Diego, CA 92109
Tel: (619) 483-6983, Fax: (619) 483-6811
29 Units, Double: $100–$260, $185–$275 (summer)
Open all year, Credit cards: all major
Children accepted except in studios, No smoking

Places to Stay

SAN FRANCISCO   THE INN AT UNION SQUARE   Maps: 1c, 2d, 3a, & 4a

The Inn at Union Square has a convenient and strategic location, smack in the heart of San Francisco—just steps from Union Square, the theaters, and shopping. Owned by an association, this is a professionally managed hotel. The small lobby is entered off the street and appears more like the entryway of a country home than a lobby in a commercial hotel. An elevator takes guests to the upper floors. As you step off the elevator, each floor has its own little sitting area where chairs are grouped comfortably around a fireplace and where complimentary tea is served each afternoon from 4 to 5:30 pm with sandwiches and cakes, followed in the early evening from 5:30 to 8 pm by wine and hors d'oeuvres. Newspapers are left outside each door in the morning. Guests can either go to the lounge (the same one where tea and wine are served) for Continental breakfast or else they can have a tray brought to their room. (Breakfast is not included in room rate.) The decor in each of the rooms is most attractive, with a traditional mood created by the use of beautiful fabrics and fine furniture. Some of the rooms have their own fireplaces and the penthouse suite has a Jacuzzi tub. Every room, from the least expensive small room to the deluxe suites, is spotlessly maintained and appealing. *Directions*: Located one block off Union Square on Post Street.

THE INN AT UNION SQUARE
Owners: Norm & Nan Rosenblatt
Innkeeper: Brooks Bayly
440 Post Street
San Francisco, CA 94102
Tel: (415) 397-3510 or (800) 288-4346
Fax: (415) 989-0529, E-mail: inn@unionsquare.com
30 Rooms, Double: $160–$350*
*Breakfast not included in rate, No gratuities accepted
Open all year, Credit cards: all major
Children accepted, No smoking, Wheelchair friendly
www.karenbrown.com/california/innatunionsquare.html

SAN FRANCISCO — MARINA INN

Maps: 1c, 2d, 3a, & 4a

The Marina Inn is not a typical country inn: in fact, it is a large, four-story building whose boxy exterior is made more lively by tiers of bay windows. But as soon as you enter, the successful effort to achieve the warmth of a homey inn is immediately apparent. The lobby is small and intimate, with light-pine furniture, a pair of handsome upholstered chairs, green potted plants, and off-white walls. The staff is friendly and eager to be helpful. An elevator leads upstairs to the bedrooms, each similar in decor with two-poster country beds, pastel-print wallpaper, comfortable chairs, light-pine armoires, and forest-green carpeting. In addition to being pleasantly decorated, the rooms offer all the amenities of a proper hotel: television in each room, comfortable queen-sized beds, direct-dial telephones, and modern bathrooms with toiletries and marble sinks. On the second floor a sitting room is provided where in the morning a buffet Continental breakfast is served and in the afternoon complimentary sherry. One of the nicest merits of this hotel is its excellent price—a real value for such a spiffy place. Other pluses: Cribs are provided for babies and children under five are free of charge. The hotel is located just a brisk walk from Fisherman's Wharf, Ghirardelli Square, and the Saint Francis Yacht Club. *Directions:* Take Van Ness Avenue north to Lombard Street. Turn left and go three blocks to Octavia.

MARINA INN
Innkeeper: Kelly Wilson
3110 Octavia
San Francisco, CA 94123
Tel: (415) 928-1000 or (800) 274-1420
Fax: (415) 928-5909
40 Rooms, Double: $55–$115
Open all year, Credit cards: all major
Children accepted, Smoking, Wheelchair friendly
www.karenbrown.com/california/marinainn.html

SAN FRANCISCO PETITE AUBERGE Maps: 1c, 2d, 3a, & 4a

The Petite Auberge is a lovely little hotel on Bush Street sitting next to its sister "Four Sisters" hotel, the White Swan. Whereas the White Swan has an English flavor, the Petite Auberge is like a romantic French country inn snuggled at the heart of the city, just steps from the famous theater district and exclusive shopping and fine dining. The façade is most appealing—a narrow, four-story building with a double column of bay windows bordered by narrow windows decorated with flowerboxes. An antique carousel horse, burnished woods, and soft pastel colors give a warm welcome to the cozy entry. Each guestroom is attractively decorated with delicate colors, all have private baths, and many have fireplaces. Downstairs there is a suite with a private outside entrance and deck. Wine and hors d'oeuvres are available every afternoon for those guests who want a quiet moment after a busy day. A delicious breakfast is served buffet style in the delightful breakfast room with its French marketplace mural and sliding glass doors giving onto a pretty patio where you can sit in pleasant weather. Breakfast includes a selection of teas and coffee, homemade breads, fruit, a hot dish, cereals, and pastries. *Directions:* Take Van Ness Avenue north to Bush Street. Turn right on Bush and go approximately 1 mile. The inn is between Taylor and Mason.

PETITE AUBERGE
Innkeeper: Brian Larsen
863 Bush Street
San Francisco, CA 94108
Tel: (415) 928-6000 or (800) 365-3004
Fax: (415) 775-5717
26 Rooms, Double: $120–$245
Open all year, Credit cards: all major
Children accepted, No smoking
www.karenbrown.com/california/petiteauberge.html

SAN FRANCISCO SHERMAN HOUSE Maps: 1c, 2d, 3a, & 4a

The Sherman House is an oasis of luxury and provides San Francisco with some of its most exceptional accommodation and personalized and attentive service. This French Italianate three-story mansion was built in 1876 for Leander Sherman, founder of the Sherman Clay Music Company and host to a number of famous musicians who performed within its walls. A soaring, three-story music hall is now a stunning salon for hotel guests. The main house contains 11 rooms or suites, while the carriage house, set in the middle of the gardens designed by Thomas Church, offers three spectacular suites. Armoires, mirrors, desks, chairs, paintings, and chandeliers have been carefully selected for each room. Each room, although grand in decor is not necessarily grand in size, has a grand canopy bed, sumptuously draped in luxurious fabrics with feather-down mattresses, and a magnificent private bath finished in black granite with the exception of one in Chinese slate. The restaurant is open only to hotel residents and is spectacular when compared to any of the world's finest restaurants. The chef shops every day to obtain only the freshest and finest ingredients and plans his menu accordingly. *Directions:* From the south, take Highway 101 to Fell Street, bear left onto Fell for one block, then turn right on Webster. After about 35 blocks turn left off Webster onto Green Street. The Sherman House will be in the middle of the block on the right-hand side.

SHERMAN HOUSE
Owner: Manou Mobedshahi
Manager: Christine Berlin
2160 Green Street, San Francisco, CA 94123
Tel: (415) 563-3600, Fax: (415) 563-1882
E-mail: tshrez@mhotelgroup
14 Rooms, Double: $385–800*
*Breakfast not included, 20% service charge additional
Open all year, Credit cards: all major
Children accepted, No Smoking
www.karenbrown.com/california/shermanhouse.html

Places to Stay

SAN FRANCISCO SPENCER HOUSE Maps: 1c, 2d, 3a, & 4a

The Spencer House does not look like a hotel and there is no sign in front of the beautiful old Victorian to give any clue that guests are solicited. Yet within this stately, immaculately maintained mansion is one of San Francisco's most personalized, delightful places to stay. The owners, Barbara and Jack Chambers, have converted a woefully neglected charmer back to its original glory—the attention to detail and the amount of love, labor, and money that must have gone into the project is astounding: the floors gleam again as when first installed, Lincresta Walton wall coverings have been restored to their original perfection, the living room and bedrooms have been padded and "papered" with beautiful fabric to soften any distracting noises, the kitchen looks straight out of *Gourmet*, the original gas lights are still operable. Barbara took advantage of Jack being a commercial airline pilot and flew to London to pick out all of the exquisite fabrics and many of the gorgeous antiques used throughout. It is like being in a private home with each guestroom exuding its own personality, but all, even the smallest, are most inviting. One of the greatest assets of the inn is Barbara, a superb hostess and a fabulous cook. Breakfast is always a memorable, gourmet event and dramatically presented using the finest china and silver. *Directions:* From the south, take Highway 101 to Fell Street. Turn left off Fell onto Baker then three blocks on to Haight.

SPENCER HOUSE
Innkeepers: Barbara & Jack Chambers
Manager: Michael Baker
1080 Haight Street at Baker
San Francisco, CA 94117
Tel: (415) 626-9205, Fax: (415) 626-9230
E-mail: bjc@spencerhouse.com
6 Rooms, Double: $120–$170
Open all year, Credit cards: all major
Children accepted over 16, No smoking
www.karenbrown.com/california/spencerhouse.html

Places to Stay

SAN FRANCISCO   THE UNION STREET INN   Maps: 1c, 2d, 3a, & 4a

For those familiar with San Francisco, Union Street is always a favorite place to dine, shop, and play. The several blocks of Union Street which stretch out at the foot of exclusive Pacific Heights offer charming restaurants and pretty boutiques in quaint Victorian houses. Right in the heart of this attractive area, snuggled into a pretty, off-white Victorian house, is The Union Street Inn. Steps on the left side of the building lead up to the front door which opens into a small reception foyer. To the left is an old-fashioned parlor, comfortably furnished with antiques. Doors from the parlor lead out to the most special feature of the inn—an exceptionally attractive, English-style garden where a brick path meanders through a medley of shrubs, flowers, and shade trees. At the end of the garden, behind a white picket fence, is a cute cottage that has been converted into a guest suite. In the house itself are five more guestrooms, each individually decorated in a traditional style. My favorite is the English Garden Room which has its own small deck overlooking the garden. All of the rooms have a welcome basket of fresh fruit. Continuing the mood of hospitality, wine and hors d'oeuvres are set out for guests each afternoon, and in the morning a full breakfast is served. Your hosts are Jane Bertorelli, who is English, and David Coyle, who is Irish. They oversee every detail of the inn and personally welcome guests. *Directions:* Take Van Ness north and turn west on Union Street. The inn is located on the left between Fillmore and Steiner.

THE UNION STREET INN
Owners: Jane Bertorelli & David Coyle
2229 Union Street
San Francisco, CA 94123
Tel: (415) 346-0424, Fax: (415) 922-8046
E-mail: janeb@unionstreetinn.com
6 Rooms, Double: $135–$245
Open all year, Credit cards: all major
Children accepted, No smoking
www.karenbrown.com/california/unionstreetinn.html

Places to Stay

SAN FRANCISCO — WASHINGTON SQUARE INN   Maps: 1c, 2d, 3a, & 4a

The Washington Square Inn has a great location in the North Beach area, facing historic Washington Square. Within easy strolling distance is a wealth of wonderful little places to eat and a bit farther, but an interesting walk through Chinatown, are the theaters and shops of the Union Square area. From the moment you enter, the ambiance of the French countryside surrounds you—an antique dining table, mellowed with age and surrounded by country chairs, stretches in front of large windows framed with tie-back drapes. Large gilt mirrors, pots of orchids, and a fireplace with an antique wooden mantel add to the country appeal. In the afternoon guests have tea or wine in front of the fire and in the morning an expanded Continental breakfast of juice, fruit, muffins, breads, croissants and hot and cold cereals, is served here (if guests prefer, breakfast will be brought to their room). Two staircases lead to the guestrooms, each individually decorated. From the simplest room to the most luxurious suite, each of the rooms, dressed with beautiful coordinating fabrics, exudes a lovely country charm. A couple of rooms have cozy bay windows accented with inviting sitting nooks. The restaurant next door, Moose's, serves fine cuisine. *Directions:* In North Beach, on Washington Square.

WASHINGTON SQUARE INN
Innkeeper: David A. Norwitt
1660 Stockton Street
San Francisco, CA 94133
Tel: (415) 981-4220 or (800) 388-0220
Fax: (415) 397-7242
15 Rooms
Double: $125–$210
Open all year, Credit cards: all major
Children accepted, No smoking, Wheelchair friendly
www.karenbrown.com/california/washingtonsquareinn.html

SAN FRANCISCO — WHITE SWAN INN

Maps: 1c, 2d, 3a & 4a

The White Swan Inn, a small, London-style hotel with English-country decor, has a splendid location just steps from a wide selection of quaint restaurants and a five-minute walk from San Francisco's fabulous Union Square shopping and theater district. But the appeal of the White Swan is far greater than its setting: From the moment you enter, you will know immediately that this is not a standard commercial hotel. Off the entry a small sitting area and a reception desk greets you, but the heart of the inn is down a flight of stairs where a spacious lounge awaits with one section set up with tables and chairs for breakfast—a hearty meal of coffee, muffins, a hot entree, juices, and cereals. Beyond the eating area is a pretty living room with a fireplace and comfortable lounge chairs. Next door is the library, cricket bat mounted on the wall, another cozy area for relaxing. Although the inn is in the center of the city, French doors open out from a conference room at the back onto a deck and small English-style garden. The bedrooms are beautifully decorated with pretty coordinating fabrics. Each room has a separate sitting area, fireplace (which can be turned on by a bedside switch), small refrigerator, wet bar, direct-dial telephone, and color television. This hotel is an absolute delight. *Directions:* Take Van Ness Avenue north, turn right on Bush and go approximately 1 mile. The inn is between Taylor and Mason.

WHITE SWAN INN
Innkeeper: Brian Larsen
845 Bush Street
San Francisco, CA 94108
Tel: (415) 775-1755 or (800) 999-9570
Fax: (415) 775-5717
26 Rooms, Double: $165–$250
Open all year, Credit cards: all major
Children accepted, No smoking
www.karenbrown.com/california/whiteswaninn.html

Places to Stay

SAN RAFAEL — GERSTLE PARK INN

Maps: 1c, 2d, & 3a

The Gerstle Park Inn, a rambling wood-shingled home on 1½ acres, is a beautiful inn set in a residential district of San Rafael, caters mostly to business travelers and local families, as well as tourists. The inn carries an air of sophistication wonderfully complemented by a homey and welcoming ambiance. Just off the entry are the formal living room whose décor reflects an Asian influence and the enclosed wrap-around porch which serves as an intimate and elegant breakfast room. Each guestroom is individual in its decor and appeal. Upstairs, rooms range from the Redwood Suite, cozy and romantic with its pine-planked, low-angled ceiling and wooded views afforded by a row of windows tucked right at ceiling height, to the San Rafael Suite, spanning the length of one end of the building, with its twin beds and large deck facing the surrounding hills. The separate carriage house has two suites complete with well-stocked kitchens, breakfast nooks, living rooms, and private patios. Two stand-alone cottages also have kitchens and provide wonderful privacy. All the rooms enjoy amenities and conveniences such as two-line telephones with voice mail, televisions, VCRs, hairdryers, and robes. For Judy and Jim Dowling, your gracious and talented hosts, running Gerstle Park Inn is a dream fulfilled. *Directions*: Exit Highway 101 at San Rafael Central exit. Go west on 3rd Street, then left on D Street, right on San Rafael Avenue, and left on Grove Street.

GERSTLE PARK INN
Innkeepers: Judy & Jim Dowling
34 Grove Street
San Rafael, CA 94901
Tel: (415) 721-7611 or (800) 726-7611
Fax: (415) 721-7600
E-mail: innkeeper@gerstleparkinn.com
12 Rooms, Double: $139–$199
Open all year, Credit cards: all major
Children accepted, No smoking, Wheelchair friendly
www.karenbrown.com/california/gerstleparkinn.html

Places to Stay

SANTA BARBARA THE CHESHIRE CAT Map: 6c

The Cheshire Cat is comprised of two lovely beige and white Victorians sitting side by side near the center of Santa Barbara and connected by a tranquil bricked patio (where breakfast is served on all but grim days.) In the foyer a grouping of *Alice in Wonderland* figurines sets the whimsical theme of the inn: Each of the rooms is named for an *Alice in Wonderland* character with the exception of two rooms—Jean's, (named for the owner Chris's mother), the Eberle Suite, (named for the previous owners), and the new cottages. Each guestroom is unique in appeal although consistent in the Laura Ashley coordinated prints and wallpapers which are used in the decor, from plums and creams in the Mad Hatter Room to smoke-blue and cream in the Dormouse's Room. Two wonderful suites, Tweedle Dum and Tweedle Dee, are located above the garage and enjoy the luxury of space, fireplace, Jacuzzi, and their own entrance off the back garden. Named after the prettiest villages in Cheshire, three recently renovated two-bedroom cottages, the Woodford, Prestbury, and Mobberly are elegant in their furnishings afford the decadence of a fully stocked kitchen, living room, log burning fireplace, and a large private redwood deck with a hot tub for an evening of luxuriating under the stars. Loving touches make each guest feel special: fresh flowers in the rooms, individual bottles of Baileys Cream, and delicious chocolates. *Directions:* Exit Highway 101 at Mission Street, go east on Mission Street for five blocks, right on State Street for three blocks, and right on Valerio.

THE CHESHIRE CAT
Owner: Christine Dunstan
Innkeepers: Amy Taylor & Bharti Singh
36 West Valerio Street, Santa Barbara, CA 93101
Tel: (805) 569-1610, Fax: (805) 682-1876
E-mail: cheshire@cheshirecat.com
17 Rooms, Double: $150–$325
Open all year, Credit cards: all major
Children accepted in cottages, No smoking
www.karenbrown.com/california/thecheshirecat.html

Places to Stay

SANTA BARBARA — THE SECRET GARDEN   Map: 6c

Not a new inn to Santa Barbara, the Secret Garden, however, has realized its potential under the wonderful ownership of Christine of the long-recommended Cheshire Cat. This complex of cottages shaded by trees and banded by a beautiful garden is lovely. With her sophisticated eye, Christine has not made dramatic changes, but rather subtle ones to the decor that surprisingly make a huge difference to the appeal and ambiance of the inn. The main building houses an inviting living room, a lovely country dining room, and two of the guest accommodations. The other guestrooms are extremely private, located in individual guest cottages with their own entrance—very romantic, peaceful, and restful. Each room has its own decor and special appeal, such as Hummingbird with a private deck and hot tub and Nightingale with a spacious living room, fireplace, and private deck with hot tub. Central to the cottages at the back of the main house is a lovely, lush garden that surrounds a patio shaded by persimmon, avocado, and mock orange trees. On mornings blessed with sunshine, tables are set here for breakfast. *Directions*: From Highway 101 northbound, exit at Arrellaga Street; from Highway 101 southbound, exit at Mission Street, travel two blocks to Bath Street. Cross streets are Bath and Mission.

THE SECRET GARDEN INN
Owners: Christine Dunstan and Jack Greenwald
Innkeeper: Jack Greenwald
1908 Bath Street, Santa Barbara, CA 93101
Tel: (805) 687-2300 or (800) 676-1622
Fax: (805) 687-4576
E-mail: garden@secretgarden.com
11 Rooms, Double: $115–$225
Open all year, Credit cards: all major
Children accepted over 12 & in Wood Thrush Cottage
No smoking
www.karenbrown.com/california/secretgardeninn.html

SANTA BARBARA   SIMPSON HOUSE INN   Map: 6c

The Simpson House Inn, a handsome, rosy-beige Victorian landmark with white and smoke-blue trim, is located on a quiet residential street only a five-minute walk from the historic downtown shopping attractions of State Street. The lush surrounding gardens of the inn include an acre of lawn banded by beautiful flower beds and mature shade trees. An irresistible feature of the inn is a cheerful back porch under an arbor of draping wisteria with white wicker chairs and comfy pillows: a perfect niche to enjoy the garden. In the main house the sitting room and dining room are quite formal. However, the formality disappears upstairs in the charming guest chambers, each individually decorated with hand printed Victorian wallpapers to suit different tastes—from feminine to a more tailored look. Three cottages in the back garden are beautifully decorated in rich fabrics and intimate with a Jacuzzi tub nestled right into a bay window. The barn also offers spacious accommodations, light and airy, whose pine furnishings are perfect against the exposed beams of the original barn. Each room enjoys niceties such as terry-cloth robes, fresh flowers, and bottled water. In the evenings sherry and local wine are offered with an extensive Mediterranean hors d'oeuvres buffet. Though the Davies's are present daily, an efficient and capable staff assists them with the duties of the inn. *Directions:* From downtown take Santa Barbara Street northeast toward the Mission, then turn left onto Arrellaga.

SIMPSON HOUSE INN
Owners/Innkeepers: Linda & Glyn Davies
Manager: Dixie Budke
121 East Arrellaga Street, Santa Barbara, CA 93101
Tel: (805) 963-7067 or (800) 676-1280
Fax: (805) 564-4811
E-mail: simpsonhouse@compuserve.com
14 Rooms, Double: $170–$400
Open all year, Credit cards: all major
Children accepted over 12, No smoking, Wheelchair friendly
www.karenbrown.com/california/simpsonhouseinn.html

SANTA BARBARA — TIFFANY INN — Map: 6c

The Tiffany Inn is an especially handsome old Victorian separated by a lawn from a rather busy street in Santa Barbara's residential area. Although the traffic in front is a bit distracting, the back garden is very charming and gives a quiet retreat for guests with an attractive, lattice-covered verandah. If you are a fan of beautifully decorated Victorians, you will thoroughly enjoy a stay at the Tiffany Inn. Carol has done a lovely job of decorating, with romantic, old-fashioned antiques accented by well-chosen, colorful fabrics. The living room with its grouping of sofas and chairs around a fireplace is just the perfect place to sit and relax while planning sightseeing adventures. Each comfortable bedchamber exudes its own charm and character and several have the added bonus of a cozy, log-burning fireplace. For those who crave privacy, one of the rooms has its own outside entrance and the added bonus of breakfast delivery each morning. Other guests enjoy a hearty breakfast of an entree, fresh fruits, muffins, and coffee served in the dining room or on sunny days in the peace and quiet of the lattice-covered porch in the back garden. *Directions:* Exit Highway 101 in Santa Barbara at Mission Street, drive east to De La Vina, turn right and the inn is on your right.

TIFFANY INN
Innkeepers: Carol & Larry MacDonald
1323 De La Vina Street
Santa Barbara, CA 93101
Tel: (805) 963-2283 or (800) 999-5672
Fax: (805) 962-0994
E-mail: tiffanyinn@aol.com
7 Rooms, Double: $125–$250
Open all year, Credit cards: all major
Children accepted, No smoking

SANTA CRUZ   THE BABBLING BROOK INN   Map: 5a

The foundations of The Babbling Brook Inn date back to the 1790s when padres from the Santa Cruz Mission built a grist mill on the property, taking advantage of the small stream to grind corn. In the late 19th century a tannery powered by a huge water wheel was constructed. A rustic log cabin remains today as the "heart" of the inn with a homey living room where guests congregate around a roaring fire with tea and coffee and homemade cookies. The historic wheel was recently returned to the brook pond. Most of the guestrooms are in shingled chalets nestled in the garden surrounded by pines and redwoods and overlooking the idyllic little meandering brook. Suzie has decorated the 13 guestrooms in European country style with pretty fabrics and colors. Each has a private bathroom, telephone, radio with alarm, and television. Most have a cozy fireplace, private deck, and an outside entrance—some even have deep, soaking, jet bathtubs for two. The two spacious suites, which can be adjoining, are tastefully decorated and quite private on the top floor. A full buffet breakfast including one hot entrée is served in the dining room, but guests are welcome to retreat to their rooms with breakfast. *Directions:* From San Jose or San Francisco take Highway 17 to Santa Cruz. Turn north on Highway 1 which becomes Mission Street, then left on Laurel for one and a half blocks to the inn.

THE BABBLING BROOK INN
Owners: Dan Floyd & Suzie Lankes
1025 Laurel Street
Santa Cruz, CA 95060
Tel: (831) 427-2437 or (800) 866-1131
Fax: (831) 427-2457
13 bedrooms with private bathrooms
Double: $165–$215
Open all year
Credit cards: all major
Children accepted over 12, No Smoking
www.karenbrown.com/california/babblingbrook.html

Places to Stay

SANTA MONICA   CHANNEL ROAD INN   Map: 7a

The Channel Road Inn dates back to 1910 when Thomas McCall, a Scotsman who made a fortune in Texas oil and cattle, moved to California where he built an elaborate wood-shingled home for his family of six daughters. Although the house was large to begin with, a third story was later added, giving plenty of space for 14 guestrooms. The house has an interesting location: just on the fringe of the elegant suburb of Pacific Palisades yet on a busy street that leads through the somewhat honky-tonk neighborhood to the beach. But, oh what a beach! The wide, sandy stretch of the Santa Monica beach is a wonderful playground. The downstairs lounge and dining areas are sedately decorated, beautifully in keeping with the style of the home. The guestrooms, tucked throughout the large house, are all individually decorated and each has its own personality. My favorite rooms were number 1, one of the less expensive rooms but delightful with a fresh white-and-blue color scheme, and a more expensive room, number 11, with stripped-pine furniture looking so pretty against the dark-green carpet. Kathy can help you pick out a room when you make a reservation. *Directions:* From Highway 405 take 10 west, then Route 1 north about 2 miles. Turn right on West Channel Road.

CHANNEL ROAD INN
Owner: Susan Zolla
Innkeepers: Heather Suskin & Christine Maewell
219 West Channel Road
Santa Monica, CA 90402
Tel: (310) 459-1920, Fax: (310) 454-9920
E-mail: channelinn@aol.com
14 Rooms, Double: $125–$275
Open all year, Credit cards: all major
Children accepted, No smoking, Wheelchair friendly
www.karenbrown.com/california/channelroadinn.html

SANTA MONICA — SHUTTERS ON THE BEACH

Map: 7a

With the opening in 1993 of Shutters on the Beach, a stunning, deluxe, and expensive hotel emerged in the Los Angeles area. The property fronts directly onto the superb Santa Monica beach and although it is of new construction, the hotel has a delightfully nostalgic mood. The attractive, Cape Cod-like whisper-gray, wood-shingled building is enhanced by white gingerbread trim. I am not sure how it is accomplished, but there is an engaging, home-like ambiance throughout—perhaps it is the low ceiling or the cozy groupings of plump, comfy sofas, or the fireplaces. The designer's goal was to create an inn where guests would feel that they were staying at a friend's beach house rather than a commercial hotel: The goal has certainly been achieved. My favorite rooms are in the three-story building that fronts the sea. A garden terrace (where white lounge chairs are grouped around an attractive swimming pool) spans a small street to connect the beach house with a more traditional-looking hotel section. All of the guestrooms are attractive: pastel blues, aquas, beiges, and peach colors accent a predominantly white color scheme. An uncluttered, simple yet elegant mood prevails, enhanced by fine linens and furniture of excellent quality. Every room has heavy wooden, white louvered shutters which give the hotel its name. *Directions*: Go west on Highway 10 (Santa Monica Expressway) to Santa Monica. Take the 4th Street exit south to Pico Boulevard.

SHUTTERS ON THE BEACH
Owner: Edward Thomas Company
General Manager: Klaus Mennekes
One Pico Boulevard, Santa Monica, CA 90405
Tel: (310) 458-0030, Fax: (310) 458-4589
E-mail: sotb@earthlink.net
198 Rooms, Double: $335–$2,500*
*Breakfast not included
*17% service charge additional
Open all year, Credit cards: all major
Children accepted, Smoking, Wheelchair friendly
www.karenbrown.com/california/shutters.html

Places to Stay

SANTA ROSA   THE GABLES   Maps: 1c & 2b

The Gables is a fine example of a bed and breakfast whose owners' love, dedication, and caring enhance the comfort and welcome and make it a very special place to stay. Judy and Mike selected The Gables, an aristocratic Victorian home on the outskirts of Santa Rosa, with a dream of opening a bed and breakfast. Although the Gables enjoys an expanse of 3 acres at the back, with a wonderful old barn that creaks with age, the home sits just off Petaluma Hill Road. A little traffic can be heard from the front guestrooms, but the back rooms overlooking the garden enjoy the quiet of the country meadow setting. The decor throughout the inn is in keeping with the grandeur of the home. Guestrooms are spacious and pretty with a country-Victorian theme. Accommodation is also offered in a dear side cottage which enjoys its own little sitting area, fireplace, kitchenette, Jacuzzi tub, TV, VCR and video library, and cozy upstairs sleeping loft. Judy is quite an accomplished cook and her casual afternoon tea features homemade cookies and brownies. Breakfasts are quite a repast with freshly squeezed juice, fruit, and a main course—a bounty that will take one right through to dinner. Mike is a talented craftsman, and he is responsible for many of the fine finishes throughout the inn, most notably a wonderful birdcage, home to some beautiful finches, which sits on the inn's back deck. *Directions:* From San Francisco travel Highway 101 north to Sonoma County. Exit at Rohnert Park Expressway. Turn right off the exit ramp and travel 2½ miles, turning left on Petaluma Hill Road.

THE GABLES
Innkeepers: Judy & Mike Ogne
4257 Petaluma Hill Road, Santa Rosa, CA 95404
Tel: (707) 585-7777 or (800) 422-5376
Fax: (707) 584-5634, E-mail: innkeeper@thegablesinn.com
8 Rooms, Double: $135–$225
Open all year, Credit cards: all major
Children under 10 accepted in the cottage
No smoking, Wheelchair friendly
www.karenbrown.com/california/thegables.html

SANTA ROSA — VINTNERS INN — Maps: 1c & 2b

For those who would rather stay in a hotel with all the attendant amenities than in a bed and breakfast, the Vintners Inn is a natural choice, centrally located for visiting the Napa, Sonoma, or Russian River areas. Just off the freeway, the Mediterranean-style building is set amid 45 acres of vineyards (be sure to request a room that faces the vineyards). The 44 spacious rooms are housed in 4 buildings that encircle a fountain in the bricked courtyard. The guestroom decor is French country with antique pine furniture, and all the rooms, which have just been redecorated, offer oversized tubs, small refrigerators, robes, televisions, data ports, and patios or balconies. Junior suites with vineyard views have fireplaces, wet bars, and sitting areas. Guests enjoy a deluxe, Continental-style buffet breakfast in the Fireside Dining Room or, in warm weather, on the adjacent wisteria-covered terrace. Added bonuses are the outdoor Jacuzzi and use of a luxury health club five minutes from the inn. There is also a restaurant, John Ash & Co, on the property. Vintners Inn is a comfortable, well-appointed accommodation at the crossroads of the Wine Country. *Directions*: From San Francisco travel 101 north to Santa Rosa. Exit at River Road and take the first left onto Barnes Road. The first driveway on your left leads to the inn.

VINTNERS INN
Owners: Cindy & John Duffy
4350 Barnes Road
Santa Rosa, CA 95403
Tel: (707) 575-7350, Fax: (707) 575-1426
44 Rooms, Double: $168–$225
Open all year
Credit cards: all major
Children accepted, No smoking
Wheelchair friendly

SAUSALITO CASA MADRONA HOTEL Maps: 2d & 3a

Sausalito is a quaint waterfront town with fabulous views across the bay to San Francisco. Alongside the harbor runs one main street from which small roads spider-web up the steep 1885, with marble fireplaces, stained-glass windows, wrought-iron grillwork, and lacy wood trim, which has been converted to a wonderful hotel. The dining room and a few of the guestrooms are in the original home, while the rest of the rooms are in a new building which terraces down the hill. Guestrooms in the original house have been refurbished in Victorian style with all the behind-the-scenes amenities added for modern comfort. The newer rooms, each with its own style of decor, are larger and enjoy bay views, and many have fireplaces and decks. Casa Cabana has a southwest flavor; Misia's Lilac and Lace is all fancy with eyelet and laces; La Belle Provence is very pretty in it's country French style and colors; Summer House is light and airy with light woods and wicker furniture; Artist's Loft is most appealing with a cottagey New England look and a tempting easel set center stage—to mention just a few! The restaurant, with its large glassed-in porch, and gorgeous views, is popular for dinner or Sunday brunch. *Directions:* By ferry from San Francisco or by car on Highway 101 across the Golden Gate Bridge to Alexander Avenue that becomes Bridgeway.

CASA MADRONA HOTEL
Innkeeper: John W. Mays
801 Bridgeway
Sausalito, CA 94965
Tel: (415) 332-0502, Fax: (415) 332-2537
E-mail: casa@casamadrona.com
34 Rooms, Double: $138–$260
Open all year, Credit cards: all major
Children accepted, No smoking, Wheelchair friendly
www.karenbrown.com/california/casamadronahotel.html

SAUSALITO — THE INN ABOVE TIDE

Maps: 2d & 3a

Just beyond Sausalito's yacht club and ferry dock, right on the water's edge, sits The Inn Above Tide, very cleverly converted to an inn from what was originally an apartment complex and then most recently an office building. All of its 30 rooms enjoy million-dollar views of the San Francisco Bay and skyline and are appropriately stocked with binoculars. Twenty-four of the rooms have wonderful little decks whose partitioning wall is of glass, creating the illusion of being right on the water, almost boatside. The remaining six rooms, although without a deck, benefit from being a little more spacious. The rooms are attractive, light, and airy so as not to compete with the view, many have fireplaces, and the decor plays on a nautical theme with porthole windows and blue-and-white prints with little fish. The two suites are both spectacular, spacious rooms with magnificent views of the city and private decks. The buffet in The Drawing Room is set in the evenings with an offering of wine and cheese, and mornings with a Continental breakfast. (Trays are also available should you prefer to enjoy breakfast in the privacy of your guestroom.) If you want to use Sausalito as a base from which to explore San Francisco, you can easily journey back and forth by ferry, avoiding the hassle and cost of a car. *Directions*: From San Francisco cross the Golden Gate Bridge and exit on Alexander Avenue. Alexander becomes Bridgeway. Turn right toward the water after the first stop light, on El Portal.

THE INN ABOVE TIDE
Owner: William H. McDevitt
Manager: Mark D. Flaherty
30 El Portal, Sausalito, CA 94965
Tel: (415) 332-9535 or (800) 893-8433
Fax: (415) 332-6714
E-mail: inntide@ix.netcom.com
30 Rooms, Double: $195–$445
Open all year, Credit cards: all major
Children accepted, No smoking, Wheelchair friendly
www.karenbrown.com/california/innabovetide.html

Places to Stay

SAUSALITO — HOTEL SAUSALITO

Maps: 2d & 3a

The Hotel Sausalito boasts a colorful past. Its early days saw activity as a bordello, and as a speakeasy during Prohibition—located next to the docks; liquor from the trucks that rumbled past its doors conveniently found its way into its parlor. It is now home to a delightful family that hails from Scotland. The Purdie's Scottish brogue will charm you, but it is their warm, professional approach to innkeeping that impresses. A steep flight of stairs (there is an elevator) leads up to guestrooms from the small street-side entry. With a backdrop of walls washed in warm pastel tones, the furnishings are handsome, custom designed and handcrafted by local artisans, and have been selected to enhance the individuality of each guestroom. The size, outlook, and bathroom appointments determine the room tariff. Some of the rooms are snug, yet greatly appreciated by the traveler looking for value. Regardless of location or size, guestroom appointments, such as furnishings, art, the finest linens, desktop phones with data port, voice mail, and cable television, are luxurious and provided to pamper the guest. We enjoyed one of the larger rooms that overlooked the activity of Sausalito's main street, but was buffered from the noise by well-insulated windows. Mornings, a complimentary newspaper will be delivered to your doorstep, and although, breakfast is not served in the hotel, coupons are provided for coffee and pastries next door. *Directions:* Refer to directions for The Inn Above Tide—they are neighboring hotels.

HOTEL SAUSALITO
Innkeepers: Mr & Mrs William (Billy) Purdie
16 El Portal (at Bridgeway), Sausalito, CA 94965
Tel: (415) 332-0700 or (888) 442-0700
Fax: (415) 332-8788
E-mail: hotelsaus@aol.com
16 Rooms, Double: $135–290
Open all year, Credit cards: all major
Children accepted, No smoking
www.karenbrown.com/california/hotelsausalito.html

SHINGLETOWN   WESTON HOUSE   Map: 1b

Located on the western outskirts of Shingletown 18 miles from Mount Lassen National Park, Weston House offers a private oasis nestled on 5½ mountaintop acres with million-dollar views of meadows, valleys, and mountains stretching for miles below. The setting and views are breathtaking and the handsome complex of wood-shingled houses complement rather than compete with the setting. Running the length of the main house is a magnificent lap pool banded by an expanse of deck whose various levels afford intimate settings from which to enjoy the sweeping panorama. There are just five guestrooms. Anna's Room and Evan's Room are accessed off the pool deck on the ground floor and share a spectacular bath. Climb the stair in the tower to Vanessa's Room, my favorite, with a lovely queen bed angled in the corner to maximize the view through the sliding glass door across the small private balcony to some fabulous views, and enjoying a bath and wood stove. Just up from the pool and off a meadow of glorious wildflowers are Helen's and Laura's rooms, very popular two rooms with guests. There are two dogs and two cats on the property. Note: As restaurant options are limited, you might want to consider packing a picnic dinner. A full breakfast is offered. *Directions*: Take Shingletown Ridge Road (on the westside of town) off Highway 44 and then left on Red Rock Road. Signs encourage you along as the road winds, narrows, and changes from asphalt to loose gravel.

WESTON HOUSE
Innkeeper: Angela Weston
Red Rock Road
P.O. Box 276, Shingletown, CA 96088
Tel: (530) 474-3738, Fax: (530) 244-9494
5 Rooms, 3 with private bathrooms
Double: $90–$145
Open all year Credit cards: MC, VS
Well-behaved children accepted, No smoking

SONORA — BARRETTA GARDENS INN Map: 4b/d

On a full hilltop acre above the town of Sonora, the attractive Barretta Gardens Inn, built around 1895, sits off the road in the shade of its own mature and lush landscaped garden. Barretta Gardens benefits from the enthusiasm, dedication, and graciousness of its new proprietors, Mike and Nancy Brandt, who have thoughtfully refurbished the inn to give it its present fresh and tastefully elegant appearance. Just off the formal Victorian living room is an appealing solarium, a plant-filled room set with white furniture, enclosed on each side by a wall of windows overlooking the outside foliage. On the other side of the living room with its an array of family pictures and a handsome grandfather clock is the dining room whose custom table is original to the home. Two guestrooms are found on the entry level. The Krystal room, with its wall of windows looking out to the Sonora hills, is dressed in greens and maroons and enjoys a large Jacuzzi for two and a private bath. Christy, off the living room with windows overlooking the front porch, is set under 10-foot-high ceilings and a crystal chandelier. Beautiful Italian beds have been converted to accommodate a queen mattress. Its private bath is across the hall. Upstairs, the Stephanie room is pretty in a wash of rose, while the Angelina room boasts Nancy's mother's brass king bed. A small parlor sits between the Angelina room and the pretty Gennylee room which together can be rented as a two-room suite or as a one-room suite with just the Gennylee room. *Directions*: Barretta Street is off business Highway 108.

BARRETTA GARDENS INN
Innkeepers: Mike & Nancy Brandt
700 South Barretta Street
Sonora, CA 95370
Tel: (209) 532-6039 or (800) 206-3333
Fax: (209) 532-8257
5 Rooms, Double: $95–$250
Open all year, Credit cards: MC, VS
Children accepted, No smoking

STINSON BEACH   CASA DEL MAR   Map: 3a

The Casa del Mar, a Mediterranean-style villa crowning a maze of lovely terraced gardens, is a pastel-peach, three-story stucco building with a red-tile roof. Refreshingly different from most California bed and breakfasts, there are no fussy frills to the decor of Casa del Mar: it has fresh white interior walls, furnishings of light pine and wicker, terracotta tiled floors, and colorful fabrics. For accent, the owner, Rick Klein, has selected bright and dramatic paintings and sculptures from local talent. The guestrooms are modest in size, with just enough space to accommodate a queen mattress set upon a custom-made wood platform and a corner chair or two. The closet is a functional alcove with a freestanding chest of drawers. Four guestrooms (Passion Flower, Shell, Hummingbird, and Heron) have subtle decorative touches to match their name and balconies where chairs are set for you to enjoy the view—the decor is fitting for a beach and park setting. With the sound of waves in the distance, one can enjoy evening hors d'oeuvres and linger over an incredible morning feast. Just steps from the bed and breakfast is an entrance to the park which accesses hundreds of miles of trails, while two blocks down the road is the justifiably famous white sandy stretch of Stinson Beach. *Directions:* As you drive into town from the south, the first building on the right is a small firehouse. Turn right at the firehouse onto Belvedere Avenue.

CASA DEL MAR
Innkeeper: Rick Klein
37 Belvedere Avenue
P.O. Box 238, Stinson Beach, CA 94970
Tel: (415) 868-2124 or (800) 552-2124
Fax: (415) 868-2305
E-mail: inn@stinsonbeach.com
6 Rooms, Double: $140–$235
Open all year, Credit cards: AX, MC, VS
Children accepted, No smoking
www.karenbrown.com/california/casadelmar.html

Places to Stay

SUTTER CREEK   THE FOXES   Map: 4b

Sutter Creek is a charming Gold Country town whose main street is bordered at either end by New England-style residences surrounded by green lawns and neatly clipped hedges. Occupying one of these attractive homes is The Foxes, an idyllic hideaway put together with great flair and taste by Min and Pete Fox. The symbol of the inn is the fox and the perky little fellow pops up everywhere, yet this is not an inn with a cutesy theme, but an unpretentious, sophisticated inn where everything has been done with exquisite flair. Four suites are found in the main house and three suites have been added to the rear. The lovely Victorian and Anniversary Suites upstairs in the main house have been enlarged and redecorated this year, and a service area for cold drinks and coffee has been added between the two. The Honeymoon Suite, very spacious, is a most elegant bedchamber where a large brick fireplace overlooks a magnificent bed and gorgeous Austrian armoire. Sparkling crystal chandeliers light the enormous bathroom. Each suite has a sitting area with a table for breakfast. Min and Pete discuss with you what you would like for breakfast, and then it is brought to your room with silver service accompanied by a large pot of coffee or tea. The Foxes pamper guests. *Directions:* Sutter Creek straddles Highway 49, 4 miles north of Jackson. The Foxes is at the north end of Main Street on the west side of the street.

THE FOXES
Innkeepers: Min & Pete Fox
77 Main Street
P.O. Box 159, Sutter Creek, CA 95685
Tel: (209) 267-5882 or (800) 987-3344
Fax: (209) 267-0712
E-mail: foxes@cdepot.net
7 Suites, Double: $125–$170
Closed at Christmas, Credit cards: MC, VS
Inappropriate for children, No smoking
www.karenbrown.com/california/thefoxes.html

SUTTER CREEK — GREY GABLES INN   Map: 4b

Grey Gables Inn is a pretty, soft-gray-blue house detailed with a white trim sitting appealingly behind an English Boxwood hedge easy walking distance of the wonderful array of shops and restaurants in Sutter Creek. A red-brick pathway winds to the front entrance and weaves its way through a lovely back garden with fountains, vine-covered arbors, and a patchwork of flowers. Inside this renovated inn (the original part of the house dates back to 1897), the ambiance reflects the owners' heritage—Roger and Sue Garlick hail originally from the Cotswolds, and they have brought a touch of the English countryside to the Mother Lode. Seven of the eight guestrooms are named for an English poet. Browning, Byron, Wordsworth, and Shelley are located on the main floor, just off the entry, while Keats, Brontë, and Tennyson are found on the lower garden level. Garden-level rooms have fewer windows, while secluded away on the top floor is the Victorian Suite. All the rooms are decorated with floral spreads that complement the decor in hues of greens, rose, and mauve. All rooms have fireplaces, most have garden views, and some enjoy claw-foot tubs. Guests settle in the formal dining room and parlor to enjoy a traditional afternoon tea with scones, refreshments with cakes and wine in the early evening, and a bountiful breakfast. *Directions*: Grey Gables Inn is located on the west side of Highway 49 on the north side of town.

GREY GABLES INN
Innkeepers: Sue & Roger Garlick
161 Hanford Street
P.O. Box 1687, Sutter Creek, CA 95685
Tel: (209) 267-1039 or (800) 473-9422
Fax: (209) 267-0998
E-mail: reservations@greggables.com.
8 Rooms, Double: $95–$145
Open all year, Credit cards: all major
Children accepted over 9
No smoking, Wheelchair friendly
www.karenbrown.com/california/greygablesinn.html

Places to Stay

TAHOE CITY — THE COTTAGE INN — Map: 4b

The Cottage Inn, built as a resort in 1938, offers a number of story-book cottages nestled under the trees on the edge of Lake Tahoe. Parking is limited, so unfortunately the drive that weaves through the grounds is hampered by guests' cars. The lovely cottages, all with individual themes, capture the mountain-cabin atmosphere with their exposed knotty-pine walls, rich fabrics, Swedish pine furniture, and a variety of beds (brass, willow, or pine). The Fireplace Room has the added attraction of a wood-burning fireplace. The Pomin House, the original home on the property, contains a reception area, a breakfast room, and a large sitting room with games, books, local restaurant menus, and a small sitting area where wine and cheese are set out in the afternoons before the blazing log fire. In summer you can happily while away the hours sunning yourself on the dock and swimming in Lake Tahoe's cool, clear waters—the inn boasts access to a private beach. The more energetic can take advantage of the lovely bicycle trail that passes in front of the inn and travels the lakeshore drive. Vikingsholm, Emerald Bay, and D.L. Bliss Park are a short car ride south. Ski resorts are between a five-minute and twenty-minute drive. *Directions*: From the Bay Area take Highway 80 to 89 Tahoe City exit, follow the river to Tahoe City, and continue south on 89 following West Lake Boulevard: the inn is 2 miles along on your left.

THE COTTAGE INN
Innkeeper: Susanne Muhr
1690 West Lake Boulevard
P.O. Box 66, Tahoe City, CA 96145
Tel: (916) 581-4073, Fax: (916) 581-0226
E-mail: cottage@sierra.net
15 Rooms, Double: $140–$220
Open all year, Credit cards: MC, VS
Inappropriate for children
No smoking, Wheelchair friendly

TAHOE CITY   RIVER RANCH   Map: 4b

Lake Tahoe is an exquisite, crystal-clear blue lake ringed by pines and backed by high mountains. The only outlet for this enormous body of water is the Truckee River, and standing one of its broad bends some 3 miles downstream is River Ranch. This historic lodge enjoys a marvelous setting, best enjoyed from the circular bar with its picture windows and expanse of outdoor patio opening onto the river. Four of the five bedrooms in the lodge itself have sliding glass doors opening to small balconies and the rushing river. These lodge rooms are decorated with traditional antiques. The remaining bedrooms are decorated in a mountain-lodge style with lodgepole-pine beds (usually king-sized)—be sure to request one with a river view. (There are several rooms without the view that are less expensive.) In the mornings a Continental breakfast is served in a part of the bar that is cantilevered over the river. The restaurant offers California-style cuisine and specializes in steaks, fresh seafood, and wild game. In winter Squaw Valley (5 miles) and Alpine Meadows (3 miles) operate shuttle buses to and from the ranch (discounted tickets are available). In summer you can rent a bike and peddle along the bike path into Tahoe City or hop aboard the rafting bus into town and raft back. In spring and fall room rates are deeply discounted. *Directions:* From the Bay Area take Highway 80 to the 89 Tahoe City exit and follow the river to River Ranch.

RIVER RANCH
General Manager: Bric Haley
Innkeeper: Jane Glynn
2285 River Road
P.O. Box 197, Tahoe City, CA 96145
Tel: (916) 583-4264 or (800) 535-9900
Fax: (916) 583-7237
22 rooms, Double: $130–$140
Open all year, Credit cards: all major
Children accepted, No smoking
www.karenbrown.com/california/riverranch.html

TAHOE CITY   SUNNYSIDE RESTAURANT & LODGE   Map: 4b

From the deck of this comfortable mountain lodge you can look over the crystal-clear blue waters of Lake Tahoe to pines and high mountains—an exquisite view at any time and magnificent when the mountains are capped with snow and pink and purple hues paint a spectacular sunset. Lake Tahoe has long been one of our favorite spots in California and since we found Sunnyside we have a base from which to go skiing in winter, water-skiing, sailing, and hiking in the High Sierra in summer, and revel in the beauty of the area year round. A meal at Sunnyside is a real pleasure for not only do the dining room and deck have magnificent lake views but the food is most enjoyable, with the menu offering fresh seafood, prime rib, chicken dishes, and pasta, followed by a tempting array of desserts. It would be a shame to stay in such a lovely spot and not have a view of the lake and several rooms have wonderful river-stone fireplaces—what could be more romantic on a winter evening? Sunnyside has its own marina offering sailboat rentals and water skiing during the summer. In winter discount tickets for nearby major ski resorts are available. If you are unable to bring your own mountain bike, there is no shortage of places to rent one. Nevada casinos with their gambling opportunities and super-star entertainment are less than an hour's drive away. *Directions*: From Truckee take Highway 89 to Tahoe City. Turn right at the traffic lights and follow the lake shore south for 2 miles to Sunnyside.

SUNNYSIDE RESTAURANT & LODGE
Lodge Manager: Janet Patterson
1850 West Lake Blvd
P.O. Box 5969, Tahoe City, CA 96145
Tel: (916) 583-7200 or (800) 822-2754
Fax: (916) 583-2551
23 rooms, Double: $90–$200
Open all year, Credit cards: all major
Children accepted, Wheelchair friendly

TRINIDAD THE LOST WHALE Map: 1a

The Lost Whale, a gray-wash Cape-Cod house with blue trim set on five acres of windswept coast of Northern California, was designed by Susanne and Lee Miller who manage it with a refreshing, bountiful enthusiasm. The mood is set by the living room with its fir floors warmed by throw rugs, and comfortable sofas arranged to enjoy not only the fireplace but also the magnificent view across the garden, through the towering pine trees to the ocean. Five rooms capture this same glorious view while three overlook the quiet road that runs behind the inn. Whichever room you select, you will find it decorated in a light, airy decor. Several rooms have an extra bed to accommodate a child and two have a sleeping loft. Whereas most inns discourage children, here at The Lost Whale they are made genuinely welcome. Relax on the deck or well-placed chairs in a quiet corner of the garden and listen to the crashing waves and the distant barking of sea lions. Stroll down the cliff path to the two-mile private beach or pop into your car for the short drive up the road to Patrick's Point State Park that offers miles of beaches, walking paths along rocky headlands, and the opportunity to explore a re-created Indian village. The Lost Whale is a homey inn in a spectacular setting. *Directions:* North from Trinidad take the Seawood Drive exit, turn right on Patrick's Point Drive, travel 1-1/8 mile north on Patrick's Point Drive. South from Oregon, exit at Patrick's Point Drive, continue south 1 mile.

THE LOST WHALE
Innkeepers: Susanne Lakin & Lee Miller
3452 Patrick's Point Drive
Trinidad, CA 95570
Tel: (800) 677-7859, Fax: (707) 677-0284
E-mail: lmiller@lostwhaleinn.com
8 Rooms & farmhouse, Double: $140–$170
Open all year, Credit cards: all major
Children accepted, No smoking
www.karenbrown.com/california/lostwhale.html

TRINIDAD TRINIDAD BAY BED & BREAKFAST Map: 1a

The Trinidad Bay Bed & Breakfast is a Cape Cod-style home constructed in 1949, painted barn-red with crisp white trim, located just across the road from the Trinidad Memorial Lighthouse. Although neither the building nor the furnishings are old, this small inn is very inviting. You enter into a cheerful family room with a brick fireplace faced by a sofa and flanked by two wooden rockers. A table is set prettily for breakfast which consists of homemade jams, hot baked bread and muffins, and fresh fruit. Upstairs are two double rooms, each with an alcove in the dormer with views of the coast. Above the garage is a suite with the best view from its long strip of windows overlooking the harbor. The fourth room, a suite on the ground floor, has a wrap-around window, king-sized bed, a fireplace for cozy evenings, its own private entry, and a private area of the garden perfect for soaking up the magnificent view of ocean and rocky headland. Both suites enjoy the luxury of breakfast delivered to the room. There is nothing outstanding in the decor, but then there is no pretense: this is just a homelike inn, but immaculately clean with everything shining with a "just scrubbed" look. The best part of all is the location: overlooking Trinidad Bay, whose old wharf still looks like a proper wharf should and where the trails along the magnificent headlands still maintain their unspoiled splendor. *Directions:* Take the Trinidad exit west off Highway 101 to Trinidad Bay Memorial Lighthouse—the inn is across the street.

TRINIDAD BAY BED & BREAKFAST
Innkeepers: Carol & Paul Kirk
560 Edwards Street
P.O. Box 849, Trinidad, CA 95570
Tel: (707) 677-0840
4 Rooms, Double: $125–$155
Closed December & January
Credit cards: MC, VS
Children accepted, No smoking

TWAIN HARTE — McCAFFREY HOUSE B&B INN

Map: 4b/d

The McCaffrey House B&B Inn is a lovely country home nestled in a grove of giant oak, pine, and cedar trees. In 1996, Michael and Stephanie built this three-story house which sits on the lot where Stephanie's family cabin sat for 35 years. The living room and other common areas are tastefully decorated and inviting for visiting with other guests or reading a book. You will also find over 500 videos for watching in your room. The warmth of the owners is apparent throughout the inn by the family photos hung on the walls and by their love of their three dogs. Because the McCaffreys designed the house as a bed and breakfast, its seven rooms are spacious, comfortable, and well appointed, each with an iron firestove with a self-timer so that you can doze off in front of the fire, and a bathroom with tub and shower. A handmade Amish quilt sets the color scheme for each room, and robes and extra towels are provided for jaunts to the hot tub. Most rooms have a balcony or patio, and some have views down to a creek. The McCaffreys serve a complete breakfast at 9, but are happy to accommodate skiers' schedules by serving earlier. Thoughtful appointments, charming owners, and a picturesque setting make this a winner. *Directions*: From San Francisco take Highway 580 east to 205, go east to 120, then east to 108. When you reach Sonora, travel east for 11 miles, and ½ mile above the East Twain Harte exit, make a right turn off the highway just beyond the 4,000-feet elevation marker.

McCAFFREY HOUSE B&B INN
Innkeepers: Stephanie & Michael McCaffrey
P.O. Box 67
23251 Highway 108
Twain Harte, CA 95383
Tel: (888) 586-0757, Fax: (209) 586-3689
E-mail: innkeeper@mccaffreyhouse.com
7 Rooms, Double: $95–$120
Open all year, Credit cards: all major
Infants not appropriate, No smoking

Places to Stay

VENICE   VENICE BEACH HOUSE   Map: 7a

Immediately south of Santa Monica, Venice Beach is one of Los Angeles' most popular stretches of beach and its Oceanfront Walk draws a colorful crowd. Just a block from the bustle of Oceanfront Walk is a lovely residence offering bed and breakfast accommodation, the Venice Beach House. Sheltered behind its own fence and lovely gardens, the Beach House is inviting with a lived-in ambiance and comfort. You enter from the front porch into an open and pretty sitting room where iced tea and cookies are set out in the afternoons and a full breakfast is served each morning. Fresh flowers dress the room which is warmed on cooler days by a wood-burning fireplace. The welcome by the innkeeper is casual and relaxed, yet gracious and warm. The home has nine guestrooms of varying sizes, five of which enjoy a private bathroom, and are decorated like bedrooms in a private home. Just off the front room the Olympic Suite, which commemorates the 1932 Olympic games hosted by Venice Beach, is lovely, with a large bay window which seems to bring the garden into the room. Favorite rooms upstairs are the Abbott Kinney, small but cozy with its own porch and decorated in a tartan of blues and greens, and the Pier Suite which boasts an ocean view and a wood-burning fireplace. *Directions:* Exit the 405 at Washington Street and travel west to Speedway. The Venice Beach House is located off Speedway between 29th and 30th. Limited private parking is found on the north side of the inn.

VENICE BEACH HOUSE
Innkeepers: Phillip & Vivian Boesch
15 Thirtieth Avenue
Venice, CA 90291
Tel: (310) 823-1966, Fax: (310) 823-1842
9 Rooms, 5 with private bathrooms
Double: $95–$165
Open all year, Credit cards: all major
Children accepted, No smoking

YOSEMITE — THE AHWAHNEE — Map: 4d

The Ahwahnee with 123 bedrooms hardly qualifies for inclusion in a country inn guide. It is a large, bustling resort with a level of activity in its lobby that is comparable to that at many airports, yet it merits inclusion because it is the most individual of hotels, with all the sophistication of a grand European castle, surrounded by the awesome beauty of Yosemite Valley. The lofty vastness of the lounge dwarfs the sofas and chairs and its huge windows frame magnificent views of the outdoors. The dining room has to be the largest in the United States: it is gorgeous with its massive floor-to-ceiling windows framing towering granite walls, cascading waterfalls, and giant sugar pines. In contrast to the surrounding wilderness the dining room wears an air of sophistication in the evening when guests dress for dinner and flickering candlelight casts its magical spell. Bedrooms are in the main building or in little cottages in a nearby woodland grove. There is a small swimming pool just off the back patio and it is not unusual to see deer grazing on the lawn. This is undeniably a grand old hotel but if the price tag is a little rich for your blood, less expensive accommodations in Yosemite Valley are briefly outlined on pages 60 and 61. *Directions:* The Ahwahnee is located in Yosemite Valley just east of Yosemite Village.

THE AHWAHNEE
Innkeeper: Brett Archer
Yosemite National Park, CA 95389
Tel: (209) 372-1407, Fax: (209) 456-0542
Reservations: (209) 252-4848
E-mail: yosemitepark.com
123 Rooms & cottages, Double: $250–$735*
*Breakfast not included
Open all year, Credit cards: MC, VS
Children accepted, Smoking, Wheelchair friendly

Places to Stay

YOSEMITE–Wawona   WAWONA HOTEL   Map: 4d

While the attractions of staying in Yosemite Valley cannot be denied, a more serene, country atmosphere pervades the Wawona Hotel, located within Yosemite Park about a 27-mile drive south of the valley. With its shaded verandahs overlooking broad, rolling lawns and a 9-hole golf course, the hotel presents a welcoming picture that invites one to while away the afternoon beside the pool, fondly referred to as the swimming tank. Bedrooms are in several scattered buildings and private bathrooms are at a premium. Hotel rooms without private baths have bathroom and shower facilities located at the end of each building's verandah. The Annex building was completely refurbished in 1996, and the main dining room renovated in 1997—both in a gracious turn-of-the-century style. This is the kind of wonderful old hotel that attracts lots of families. In the summer rangers give interpretive presentations on such topics as bears, climbing, and photography and there are carriage rides, wonderful Sunday brunches, Saturday-night barbecues, and barn dances. The Wawona now offers two bed-and-breakfast packages: Autumn Golf and Winter Romance, both very good value for money. *Directions:* Wawona is in Yosemite National Park, 27 miles south of Yosemite Valley on Highway 41.

WAWONA HOTEL
Innkeeper: Martha Moses
Yosemite National Park, CA 95389
Tel: (209) 375-6556, Fax: (209) 456-0542
Reservations: (209) 252-4848
E-mail: yosemitepark.com
104 Rooms, 50 with private bathrooms
Double: $81–$114*
*Breakfast not included
Closed January 4 to February 4
Credit cards: MC, VS
Children accepted, Smoking, Wheelchair friendly

YOUNTVILLE MAISON FLEURIE Map: 2b/d

The location of the Maison Fleurie is superb—right in the heart of the quaint town of Yountville, within walking distance of great shopping and a selection of restaurants. The inn (with a look of the French countryside) is a romantic cluster of thick stone and brick buildings, entrancingly draped with ivy. From the moment you enter, the mood is conducive to a carefree holiday. You come into a parlor-like foyer with a corner fireplace, sofa, and chairs. When you begin to wonder if this is a hotel, you notice a discreet reception desk in the room beyond. To the right, a few steps lead down to an inviting lounge where two comfortable sofas (slip-covered with a pretty floral fabric) flank a brick fireplace. The price of the bedrooms depends upon size—the larger are more expensive. None are especially spacious, but all are appealingly decorated and well priced for value received. The friendly, well-managed Maison Fleurie offers many extras: not only is a hearty breakfast served in the morning, but also wine and hors d'oeuvres in the late afternoon. Cold and hot drinks are available all day, along with cookies. The morning paper, bathrobes, turn-down service, and the complimentary use of bicycles are additional amenities. Tucked into the courtyards behind the inn are a swimming pool and a hot tub. *Directions:* Coming north from Napa on Highway 29, turn right into Yountville onto Washington Street. When the road splits, keep to the right onto Yount Street. You will see the inn on your left.

MAISON FLEURIE
Innkeeper: Shelley Claudel
6529 Yount Street
Yountville, CA 94599
Tel: (707) 944-2056 or (800) 788-0369
Fax: (707) 944-9342
13 Rooms, Double: $110–$230
Open all year, Credit cards: all major
Children accepted, No smoking, Wheelchair friendly
www.karenbrown.com/california/maisonfleurie.html

Places to Stay

YOUNTVILLE VINTAGE INN Map: 2b/d

The Vintage Inn is a large hotel complex nestled between Highway 29 and the main street of Yountville. The 80 rooms are housed in an attractive mix of two-story green and blue, wood-sided and red-brick buildings which are connected by meandering paths. We recommend the Vintage Inn as an alternative to bed and breakfast accommodation, if you seek a bit more anonymity, privacy, and the full services of a luxury hotel. A concierge is present for assistance, a limited menu is offered poolside and through room service, and the stretch limousine parked at the front entry is available for hire. Guestrooms are very attractive in their decor, spacious, and comfortable, equipped with television, fireplace (duraflame logs), coffee maker, a complimentary bottle of wine, tub-shower with Jacuzzi jets, and terry-cloth robes. Turndown service is offered each evening and appreciated touches such as a fresh supply of towels and bedside chocolates are thoughtfully provided. In the mornings, an appetizing champagne breakfast buffet of juice, hot beverages, fresh-baked pastries, cereals, yogurt, and fruit is set out in the front lobby and you can sit either inside or at tables on the patio. The Vintage Inn has a capable management team which extends a courteous welcome and strives to please. *Directions:* Take the Yountville exit off Highway 29, turn right at the bottom of the exit, then a quick left on Washington Street. The Vintage Inn is just off Washington Street beyond Vintage 1870.

VINTAGE INN
Innkeeper: Patti Larson
6541 Washington Street
Yountville, CA 94599
Tel: (707) 944-1112, Fax: (707) 944-1617
E-mail: lopez@I-café.net
80 Rooms, Double: $150–$300
Open all year, Credit cards: all major
Children accepted, Smoking, Wheelchair friendly
www.karenbrown.com/california/vintageinn.html

Key Map

Map 5

Map 6

Index

A

A B Seas Kayaks, 25
Afternoon Tea, 8
Agate Cove Inn, Mendocino, 197
Agness, Oregon, 104
Ahwahnee, The, Yosemite National Park, 76, 277
Albion
 Albion River Inn, 112
Alcatraz, 16
Amador City, 82
 Imperial Hotel, 113
American River Inn, Georgetown, 152
Anderson Valley, 96
Andrew Molera State Park, 29
Angels Camp, 81
Año Nuevo State Reserve, 23
Applewood, Guerneville, 162
Aptos
 Bayview Hotel, 114
 Mangels House, 115
 Seascape Resort–Monterey Bay, 116
Arbor Inn, The, Paso Robles, 230
Artists' Inn, The, South Pasadena, 228
Ashland, Oregon, 110
Avalon
 Inn On Mt Ada, 135
Avenue Of The Giants, The, 98

B

Babbling Brook Inn, The, Santa Cruz, 257
Balboa, 41
 Balboa Island, 41
 Balboa Pavilion, 41
 Pavilion Queen, 41
Ballard
 Ballard Inn, The, 117
Bandon, Oregon
 Beach State Park, 109
 Cheese Company, 110
 Driftwood Museum, 109
Barretta Gardens Inn, Sonora, 266
Bathrooms, 5
Bayview Hotel, Aptos, 114
Beach House, Half Moon Bay, 163
Beaulieu Vineyards, 60
Bel-Air, Hotel, Los Angeles, 188
Belle de Jour Inn, Healdsburg, 165
Beltane Ranch, Glen Ellen, 154
Benbow Inn, Garberville, 151
Benziger Winery, 68
Beringer Vineyards, 63
Big Sur
 Big Sur Coastline, 28
 Deetjen's Big Sur Inn, 118
 Nepenthe, 29
 Phoenix Shop, The, 29
 Ventana, 119
Bissell House, The, South Pasadena, 229
Bixby Creek Bridge, 29
Blackthorne Inn, Inverness, 172
Blue Heron Inn, Mendocino, 198
Blue Lantern Inn, Dana Point, 140
Blue Whale, The, Cambria, 126
Bolinas Lagoon, 93
Breakfast, 8
Brigadoon Castle, Igo, 171
Brookings, Oregon, 103
 World War II Bombing Site, 108
Brookside Farm B & B Inn, Dulzura, 142

Buelleton, 32
   Andersen's Restaurant, 32
Buena Vista Winery, 71

C

Cable Cars, 17
Café Beaujolais, Mendocino, 96
Calaveras Big Trees State Park, 80
California Missions, 14
   Carmel Mission, 28
   Mission Dolores, 20
   Mission La Purisma Concepcion, 32
   Mission San Antonio de Pala, 47
   Mission San Diego de Alcala, 44
   Mission San Francisco De Assisi, 20
   Mission San Francisco Solano de Sonoma, 70, 71
   Mission San Juan Bautista, 25
   Mission San Juan Capistrano, 42
   Mission San Luis Obispo, 31
   Mission Santa Barbara, 34
   Mission Santa Ysabel, 47
California Petrified Forest, 66
Calistoga, 65
   American Balloon Adventures, 65
   Calistoga Gliders, 66
   Calistoga Spa and Hot Springs, 65
   Château De Vie, 120
   Christopher's Inn, 121
   Cottage Grove Inn, 122
   Meadowlark Country Inn, 123
   Scarlett's Country Inn, 124
   Zinfandel House, 125
Cambria, 31
   Blue Whale, The, 126
   Squibb House, The, 127
Campbell Ranch Inn, Geyserville, 153
Cancellation Policies, 6
Cannery Row, 26

Cape Blanco, Oregon
   Cape Blanco Lighthouse, 109
   Cape Blanco State Park, 109
Cape Sebastian, Oregon, 107
Capitola
   Inn At Depot Hill, The, 128
Car Rental, 2
Carmel, 27
   Carmel Mission, 28
   Cottage Gallery, 27
   Mission Ranch, 129
   Point Lobos State Reserve, 28
   San Antonio House, 130
   Sea View Inn, 131
   Seventeen-Mile Drive, The, 27
   The Cottage Gallery, 27
   Vagabond's House Inn, 132
Carmel Highlands
   Tickle Pink Inn, 133
Carmel Valley
   Stonepine, 134
Carson City, 88
   Nevada State Museum, 88
Carter House Victorians, Eureka, 101, 147
Casa Cody, Palm Springs, 221
Casa Del Mar, Stinson Beach, 267
Casa Madrona Hotel, Sausalito, 262
Casa Malibu, Malibu, 191
Catalina Island
   Inn On Mt Ada, 135
Cavanagh Inn, Petaluma, 231
Cedar Street Inn, The, Idyllwild, 169
Centerville Beach, 101
Channel Road Inn, Santa Monica, 258
Charm of Inns, 6
Château De Vie, Calistoga, 120
Château du Sureau, Oakhurst, 216
Château Saint Jean, 67
Chaw'se Indian Grinding Rock State Park, 82

Check-in, 6
Cheshire Cat, The, Santa Barbara, 253
Children, 7
Chinese Camp, 78
Christopher's Inn, Calistoga, 121
City Hotel, Columbia, 80, 137
Coloma, 83
    Coloma Country Inn, 136
    Marshall Gold Discovery State Historic Park, 83
    Sutter's Sawmill, 83
Columbia, 79
    City Hotel, 80, 137
    Fallon Hotel, 80, 138
Corona del Mar, 41
Coronado, San Diego
    Hotel del Coronado, 242
Cottage Grove Inn, Calistoga, 122
Cottage Inn, The, Tahoe City, 270
Credit Cards, 7
Crescent City, 102
Cromberg
    Twenty Mile House, 139
Crystal Pier Hotel, San Diego-Pacific Beach, 243
Cuyamaca Rancho State Park, 46
Cypress Inn, Half Moon Bay, 164

D

Daffodil Hill, 82
Daly Inn, The, Eureka, 148
Dana Point
    Blue Lantern Inn, 140
Davenport, 23
    New Davenport Cash Store, 23
Deer Creek Inn, Nevada City, 212
Deetjen's Big Sur Inn, Big Sur, 118
Del Coronado, Hotel, San Diego-Coronado, 43, 242
Desert Hills Hotel, Palm Springs, 222
Disneyland, 36, 38
Domaine Chandon, 57

Donner Lake and Pass, 85
Doryman's Inn, Newport Beach, 41, 215
Drakesbad
    Drakesbad Guest Ranch, 141
Driving Times, 2
Drytown, 82
Dulzura
    Brookside Farm B & B Inn, 142
Dunbar House, 1880, Murphys, 208
Dunes National Recreation Area, Oregon, 110

E

Eagle Mine, 46
Eagle's Landing, Lake Arrowhead, 184
East Brother Light Station, Point Richmond, 233
Eiler's Inn, Laguna Beach, 180
Elephant Seals, 23
Elk, 97
    Elk Cove Inn, 143
    Griffin House, 144
    Harbor House, 145
    Sandpiper House Inn, 146
Emma Nevada House, Nevada City, 213
Eureka, 101
    Carson Mansion, 101
    Carter House Victorians, 101, 147
    Daly Inn, The, 148
    Old Town, 101

F

Fallon Hotel, Columbia, 80, 138
Felton, 24
Fern Canyon, 102
Fern Valley Inn, Idyllwild, 170
Ferndale, 100
    Gingerbread Mansion, The, 100, 149
    Museum, 100
    Repertory Theater, 100
    Shaw House, The, 100, 150

Fess Parker's Wine Country Inn, Los Olivos, 190
Fisherman's Wharf, 18
Flora Pacifica, Oregon, 108
Fort Bragg, 97
    Mendocino Coast Botanical Gardens, 97
    Skunk Railroad, 97
Fort Ross, 95
Foxes, The, Sutter Creek, 268

G

Gables, The, Santa Rosa, 260
Gaige House Inn, Glen Ellen, 155
Garberville
    Benbow Inn, 151
Garden Court Café and Bakery, Glen Ellen, 70
Georgetown, 83
    American River Inn, 152
Gerstle Park Inn, San Rafael, 252
Getty Center, The, Los Angeles, 38
Geyserville
    Campbell Ranch Inn, 153
Ghiradelli Square, 18
Gingerbread Mansion, The, Ferndale, 100, 149
Givenchy Hotel, Palm Springs, 223
Glen Ellen
    Beltane Ranch, 154
    Gaige House Inn, 155
    Garden Court Café and Bakery, 70
    Jack London State Park, 69
Glendeven, Little River, 186
Gloria Ferrer Champagne Caves, 72
Gold Beach, Oregon, 103
    Inn at Nesika Beach, 104
    Tu Tu' Tun Lodge, 104, 157
Gold Bluffs Beach, 102
Golden Gate Bridge, 19, 91
Gosby House, Pacific Grove, 219

Grandmere's Inn, Nevada City, 214
Grass Valley, 83
    Empire Mine State Park, 83
    Murphy's Inn, 158
Green Gables Inn, The, Pacific Grove, 220
Grey Gables Inn, Sutter Creek, 269
Griffin House, Elk, 144
Groveland, 78
    Groveland Hotel, The, 159
Gualala
    North Coast Country Inn, 160
    Old Milano Hotel, 161
Guerneville, 95
    Applewood, 162

H

Half Moon Bay, 22
    Beach House, 163
    Cypress Inn, 164
    Half Moon Bay Feed and Fuel, 23
    Half Moon Bay Nursery, 23
Hanns Kornell Winery, 63
Harbor House, Elk, 145
Haydon Street Inn, Healdsburg, 166
Headlands Inn, The, Mendocino, 199
Healdsburg, 96
    Belle de Jour Inn, 165
    Haydon Street Inn, 166
    Honor Mansion, The, 167
    Inn On The Plaza, 168
Hearst Castle, 30
Hogin House Bed & Breakfast, McCloud, 194
Honor Mansion, The, Healdsburg, 167
Hop Kiln Winery, 96
Humboldt Redwoods State Park, 98
    Rockefeller Forest, 99
Huntington Library, 38

I

Idyllwild, 48
    Cedar Street Inn, The, 169
    Fern Valley Inn, 170
Igo
    Brigadoon Castle, 171
Imperial Hotel, Amador City, 113
Ingleside Inn, Palm Springs, 224
Ink House, The, Saint Helena, 237
Inn Above Tide, The, Sausalito, 263
Inn At Depot Hill, The, Capitola, 128
Inn at Nesika Beach, Gold Beach, Oregon, 104
Inn At Occidental, The, Occidental, 217
Inn at Playa del Rey, Playa del Rey, 232
Inn at Rancho Santa Fe, Rancho Santa Fe, 234
Inn at Shallow Creek Farm, Orland, 218
Inn at Union Square, The, San Francisco, 244
Inn On Mt Ada, Catalina Island, 135
Inn On The Plaza, Healdsburg, 168
Innkeepers
    Professionalism, 8
Introduction, 1
    About Driving Itineraries, 2
    About Inn Travel, 5
Inverness
    Blackthorne Inn, 172
    Manka's Inverness Lodge, 173
    Sandy Cove Inn, 174
    Ten Inverness Way, 175
Itineraries
    Leisurely Loop of Southern California, 36
    Maps, 2
    Overview Map, 3
    San Francisco to Los Angeles via the Coast, 14
    San Francisco to the Oregon Border-& a Bit Beyond, 90
    Wandering through the Wine Country, 52
    Yosemite, the Gold Country, & Lake Tahoe, 74

J

J. Rochioli Winery, 96
Jack London State Park, 69
Jackson, 81
    Amador County Museum, 81
Jamestown, 78
    Jamestown Hotel, 78, 176
    National Hotel, The, 78, 177
    Railtown 1897 State Historic Park, 79
San Francisco, 19
Jarvis Winery, 55
Jerry's Rogue Jet Trips, Oregon, 104
Joshua Grindle Inn, Mendocino, 200
Julia Pfeiffer Burns State Park, 29
Julian, 46
    Eagle Mine, 46
    Julian White House, The, 178
    Orchard Hill Country Inn, 179

K

Karen Brown Website, The, 12
Kenwood Winery, 67
Key Overview Map, 281
Klamath, 102
Korakia Pensione, Palm Springs, 225
Korbel Winery, 95
Kunde Winery, 67

L

La Jolla
    Bed & Breakfast Inn at La Jolla, The, 181
    La Valencia Hotel, 182
    Scripps Inn, 183
    Scripps Institution of Oceanography, 44
La Residence, Napa, 211
La Valencia Hotel, La Jolla, 182
Lady Bird Johnson Grove, 102

Laguna Beach, 42
    Eiler's Inn, 180
Lake Arrowhead, 50
    Eagle's Landing, 184
    Saddleback Inn, 185
Lake Tahoe, 86
    Eagle Falls, 88
    Eagle Lake, 88
    Emerald Bay, 87
    Sugar Pine State Park, 86
    Vikingsholm, 87
Lassen National Park
    Drakesbad Guest Ranch, 141
Le Montrose Suite Hotel, Los Angeles, 189
Leggett, 98
Little River
    Glendeven, 186
Livermore
    Purple Orchid Inn, 187
Lombard Street, 20
Lompoc
    Mission La Purisma Concepcion, 32
Los Angeles, 34, 37
    Disneyland, 36, 38
    Getty Center, The, 38
    Hotel Bel-Air, 188
    Huntington Library, Gallery, Gardens, 38
    Le Montrose Suite Hotel, 189
    NBC Television Studios, 39
    Norton Simon Museum Of Art, The, 39
    Pueblo de Los Angeles, 39
    Queen Mary, The, 39
    Universal Studios, 40
Los Olivos
    Fess Parker's Wine Country Inn, 190
Lost Whale, The, Trinidad, 273

M

Maison Fleurie, Yountville, 279

Malakoff Diggins, 84
Malibu
    Casa Malibu, 191
    Malibu Beach Inn, 192
Manchester
    Victorian Gardens, 193
Mangels House, Aptos, 115
Manka's Inverness Lodge, Inverness, 173
Maps
    Itinerary Maps, 2
    Key Overview Map, 281
    Leisurely Loop of Southern California, 35
    Map 1 - Hotel Locations, 282
    Map 2 - Hotel Locations, 283
    Map 3 - Hotel Locations, 284
    Map 4 - Hotel Locations, 285
    Map 5 - Hotel Locations, 286
    Map 6 - Hotel Locations, 287
    Map 7 - Hotel Locations, 288
    Overview of Itinerary Maps, 3
    San Francisco to Los Angeles via the Coast, 13
    San Francisco to the Oregon Border- & a Bit Beyond, 89
    Wandering through the Wine Country, 51
    Yosemite, the Gold Country, & Lake Tahoe, 73
Marin Headlands, 91
Marina Inn, San Francisco, 245
Marine Mammal Center, 92
Marine World, Africa USA, 54
Mccaffrey House B&B Inn, Twain Harte, 275
McCloud
    Hogin House Bed & Breakfast, 194
    McCloud Guest House, 195
    McCloud Hotel, 196
Meadowlark Country Inn, Calistoga, 123
Meadowood Napa Valley, Saint Helena, 238
Mendocino, 96
    Agate Cove Inn, 197
    Blue Heron Inn, 198
    Café Beaujolais, 96

Mendocino (continued)
    Headlands Inn, The, 199
    Joshua Grindle Inn, 200
    Mendocino Farmhouse, 201
    Stanford Inn By The Sea, The, 202
    Whitegate Inn, 203
Mercer Caverns, 80
Mexico, 44
    Tijuana, 44
Mission Ranch, Carmel, 129
Moaning Cavern, 80
Monarch Butterfly, 26
Monterey, 25
    Aquarium, 26
    Cannery Row, 26
    Fisherman's Wharf, 26
    Old Monterey Inn, 204
    Old Town, 26
    Spindrift Inn, 205
Montrose Suite Hotel, Le, Los Angeles, 189
Moss Beach, 22
    Fitzgerald Marine Reserve, 22
    Moss Beach Distillery, 22
    Seal Cove Inn, 22, 206
Muir Beach, 92
    Pelican Inn, 92, 207
Muir Woods, 92
Mukulumne Hill, 81
Murphy's Inn, Grass Valley, 158
Murphys, 80
    Dunbar House, 1880, 208
    Old Timers' Museum, 80
    Redbud Inn, The, 209

N

Napa
    La Residence, 211
    Oak Knoll Inn, 210
National Hotel, The, Jamestown, 78, 177

Navarro Winery, 96
NBC Television Studios, 39
Nepenthe, Big Sur, 29
Nevada City, 84
    Deer Creek Inn, 212
    Emma Nevada House, 213
    Grandmere's Inn, 214
Newport Beach, 40
    Dory Fleet, 40
    Doryman's Inn, 41, 215
    Oyster Bar & Grill, 40
Niebaum-Coppola Winery, 59
North Bloomfield, 85
North Coast Country Inn, Gualala, 160
Norton Simon Museum of Art, The, 39

O

Oak Knoll Inn, Napa, 210
Oakhurst
    Château du Sureau, 216
Oakville, 58
    Oakville Grocery, 58
Occidental
    Inn At Occidental, The, 217
Old Coast Road, 29
Old Faithful Geyser, 66
Old Milano Hotel, Gualala, 161
Old Monterey Inn, Monterey, 204
Old Stonewall Mine, 46
Opus One, 58
Orchard Hill Country Inn, Julian, 179
Oregon
    Agness, 104
    Ashland, 110
    Bandon Beach State Park, 109
    Bandon Cheese Company, 110
    Bandon Driftwood Museum, 109
    Brookings, 103
    Cape Blanco Lighthouse, 109

Oregon (continued)
    Cape Blanco State Park, 109
    Cape Sebastian, 107
    Dunes National Recreation Area, 110
    Flora Pacifica, 108
    Gold Beach, 103
    Inn at Nesika Beach, Gold Beach, 104
    Jerry's Rogue Jet Trips, 104
    Paradise Lodge, 104
    Port Orford, 109
    Rogue River, 103
    Samuel H. Boardman State Park, 107
    Tu Tu' Tun Lodge, Gold Beach, 104, 157
    World War II Bombing Site, Bookings, 108
Orick, 102
Orland
    Inn at Shallow Creek Farm, 218
Overview Map of Driving Itineraries, 3

P

Pacific Beach, San Diego
    Crystal Pier Hotel, 243
Pacific Grove, 26
    Gosby House, 219
    Green Gables Inn, The, 220
    Monarch Butterfly, 26
Pacific Lumber Company, 99
Pala, 47
    Mission San Antonio de Pala, 47
Palm Springs, 48
    Aerial Tramway, 49
    Casa Cody, 221
    Desert Hills Hotel, 222
    Givenchy Hotel, 223
    Ingleside Inn, 224
    Korakia Pensione, 225
    Living Desert Outdoor Museum, 49
    Villa Royale, 226
    Willows, The, 227

Palomar Observatory, 47
Paradise Lodge, Oregon, 104
Pasadena, South
    Artists' Inn, The, 228
    Bissell House, The, 229
Paso Robles
    Arbor Inn, The, 230
Patrick's Point State Park, 101
    Agate Beach, 101
    Yurok Village, 101
Pebble Beach Golf Course, 27
Pelican Inn, Muir Beach, 92, 207
Petaluma
    Cavanagh Inn, 231
Petite Auberge, San Francisco, 246
Pfeiffer Big Sur State Park, 29
Phoenix Shop, The, Big Sur, 29
Pier 39, 18
Pigeon Point Lighthouse, 23
Pismo Beach State Park, 32
Placerville, 82
Playa del Rey
    Inn at Playa del Rey, 232
Pocket Canyon
    Applewood, 162
Point Lobos State Reserve, 28
Point Reyes National Seashore, 93
    Drakes Bay, 94
    Johnson Oyster Company, 94
    Lighthouse, 93
    Morgan Ranch, 93
Point Reyes Station, 94
    Station House Café, 94
Point Richmond
    East Brother Light Station, 233
Port Orford, Oregon, 109
Princeton, 22
Purple Orchid Inn, Livermore, 187

Q

Queen Mary, The, Los Angeles, 39

R

Rancho Santa Fe
    Inn At Rancho Santa Fe, 234
    Rancho Valencia Resort, 235
Red and White Fleet, 21
Redbud Inn, The, Murphys, 209
Redding
    Tiffany House, 236
Redwood National Park, 102
    Information Center, 102
Reservations, 8
Residence, La, Napa, 211
Responsibility, 9
Rim of the World Highway, 50
River Ranch, Tahoe City, 86, 271
Roaring Camp Railroad, 24
Robert Louis Stevenson Park, 62
Robert Mondavi Winery, 58
Rogue River Mail Boats, Oregon, 104
Rogue River, Oregon, 103
Room Rates, 9
Russian River, 95
Rutherford Hill Winery, 61

S

Saddleback Inn, Lake Arrowhead, 185
Saint Helena, 62
    Culinary Institute of America, 62
    Greystone Restaurant, 62
    Hotel Saint Helena, 239
    Ink House, The, 237
    Library and Museum, 62
    Meadowood Napa Valley, 238
    Vineyard Country Inn, 240
    Wine Country Inn, The, 241

Samuel H. Boardman State Park, Oregon, 108
San Antonio House, Carmel, 130
San Diego
    Balboa Park, 42
    Coronado, 43
    Crystal Pier Hotel, Pacific Beach, 243
    Heritage Park, 43
    Hotel del Coronado, Coronado, 43, 242
    La Jolla, 44
    La Jolla Bed & Breakfast Inn, La Jolla, 181
    La Valencia Hotel, La Jolla, 182
    Mexico, 44
    Mission San Diego de Alcala, 44
    Museums, 43
    Old Town, 43, 45
    Scripps Inn, La Jolla, 183
    Sea World, 45
    Seaport Village, 45
    The Embarcadero, 43
    Wild Animal Park, 45
    Zoo, 42
San Francisco, 15
    Alcatraz, 16
    Asian Art Museum, 19
    Beach Chalet, 19
    Cable Cars, 17
    California Historical Society, 21
    Chinatown, 17
    Coit Tower, 18
    Conservatory of Flowers, 19
    De Young Museum, 19
    Fisherman's Wharf, 18
    Fort Point, 19
    Ghiradelli Square, 18
    Golden Gate Bridge, 19
    Golden Gate Park, 19
    Hyde Street Cable Car Turnaround, 18
    Hyde Street Pier, 18
    Inn at Union Square, The, 244

San Francisco (continued)
    Lombard Street, 20
    Marina Inn, 245
    Maritime Museum, 19
    Mission San Francisco De Assisi, 20
    Museum of Modern Art, 20
    Museum of Natural History, 19
    Palace of The Legion of Honor, 16
    Petite Auberge, 246
    Pier 39, 18
    Sausalito, 21
    Sherman House, 247
    Spencer House, 248
    Steinhart Aquarium, 19
    Stores, 22
    The Cannery, 18
    Theater, 21
    Tiburon, 21
    Union Square, 21
    Union Street, 22
    Union Street Inn, The, 249
    Visitor's Bureau, 16
    Washington Square Inn, 250
    White Swan Inn, 251
    Yerba Buena Gardens and Galleries, 21
San Juan Bautista
    Mission San Juan Bautista, 25
San Juan Capistrano, 42
    Mission, 42
San Luis Obispo, 31
    Mission San Luis Obispo, 31
San Rafael
    Gerstle Park Inn, 252
San Simeon
    Hearst Castle, 30
Sandpiper House Inn, Elk, 146
Sandy Cove Inn, Inverness, 174

Santa Barbara, 33
    Cheshire Cat, The, 253
    County Courthouse, 34
    Mission Santa Barbara, 34
    Secret Garden Inn, The, 254
    Simpson House Inn, 255
    Tiffany Inn, 256
Santa Cruz, 24
    Babbling Brook Inn, The, 257
    Boardwalk, 24
    Roaring Camp Railroad, 24
    The Babbling Brook Inn, 257
Santa Monica
    Channel Road Inn, 258
    Shutters On The Beach, 259
Santa Rosa
    Gables, The, 260
    Vintners Inn, 261
Santa Ysabel, 47
    Dudley's Bakery, 47
    Mission Santa Ysabel, 47
Sausalito, 21
    Casa Madrona Hotel, 262
    Inn Above Tide, The, 263
    Sausalito, Hotel, 264
Sausalito, Hotel, Sausalito, 264
Scarlett's Country Inn, Calistoga, 124
Schramsberg Vineyards, 64
Scotia, 99
Scripps Inn, La Jolla—San Diego, 183
Sea View Inn, Carmel, 131
Seal Cove Inn, Moss Beach, 22, 206
Seascape Resort–Monterey Bay, Aptos, 116
Secret Garden Inn, The, Santa Barbara, 254
Seventeen-Mile Drive, The, Carmel, 27
Shakespeare Festival, Ashland, Oregon, 110
Shallow Creek Farm, Inn at, Orland, 218
Shaw House, The, Ferndale, 100, 150
Sherman House, San Francisco, 247

Shingletown
    Weston House, 265
Shutters On The Beach, Santa Monica, 259
Simpson House Inn, Santa Barbara, 255
Skunk Railroad, 97
Smoking, 10
Socializing in Inns, 10
Solvang, 32
Sonoma, 70
    Barracks, 70
    Cheese Factory, 70
    French Bread Shop, 70
    Lachryma Montis, 71
    Mission San Francisco Solano De Sonoma, 70
    Toscano Hotel, 70
Sonora
    Barretta Gardens Inn, 266
Spencer House, San Francisco, 248
Spindrift Inn, Monterey, 205
Squibb House, The, Cambria, 127
Stanford Inn By The Sea, The, Mendocino, 202
Sterling Vineyards, 64
Stinson Beach, 92
    Casa Del Mar, 267
Stonepine, Carmel Valley, 134
Sunnyside Restaurant & Lodge, Tahoe City, 272
Sutter Creek, 82
    Foxes, The, 268
    Grey Gables Inn, 269

T

Tahoe City, 86
    Cottage Inn, The, 270
    Fanny Bridge, 86
    Gatekeeper's Cabin, 86
    River Ranch, 86, 271
    Sunnyside Restaurant & Lodge, 272
Ten Inverness Way, Inverness, 175

Tiburon, 21
Tickle Pink Inn, Carmel Highlands, 133
Tiffany House, Redding, 236
Tiffany Inn, Santa Barbara, 256
Tijuana, 44
Tomales, 94
    Bakery, 94
Tomales Bay, 94
Trefethen Vineyards, 56
Trinidad, 101
    Lost Whale, The, 273
    Seascape Restaurant, 101
    Trinidad Bed & Breakfast, 274
Truckee River, 86
Tu Tu' Tun Lodge, Gold Beach, Oregon, 104, 157
Twain Harte
    McCaffrey House B&B Inn, 275
Twenty Mile House, Cromberg, 139

U

Union Street Inn, The, San Francisco, 249
Universal Studios, 40

V

V. Sattui Winery, 62
Vagabond's House Inn, Carmel, 132
Valencia Hotel, La, La Jolla, 182
Venice
    Venice Beach House, 276
Ventana, Big Sur, 119
Victorian Gardens, Manchester, 193
Villa Royale, Palm Springs, 226
Vineyard Country Inn, Saint Helena, 240
Vintage Inn, Yountville, 280
Vintners Inn, Santa Rosa, 261
Virginia City, 88
Visitors' Bureau
    San Diego, 42
    San Francisco, 16, 21

Volcano, 82
    Saint George Hotel, 82

W

Washington Square Inn, San Francisco, 250
Wawona Hotel, Yosemite National Park, 77, 278
Weather, 4
Website
    The Karen Brown Website, 12
Weston House, Shingletown, 265
White Swan Inn, San Francisco, 251
Whitegate Inn, Mendocino, 203
Willits, 97
    Skunk Railroad, 97
Willows, The, Palm Springs, 227
Wine Country Inn, The, Saint Helena, 241
World War II Bombing Site, Brookings, Oregon, 108

Y

Yosemite National Park, 76
    Ahwahnee, The, 76, 277
    Cathedral Rock, 77
    Clouds Rest, 77
    El Capitan, 77
    Glacier Point, 78
    Half Dome, 77
    Mariposa Grove, 78
    Wawona Hotel, 77, 278
    Yosemite Lodge, 76
    Yosemite Valley, 76
Yountville, 56
    Adventures Aloft, 57
    Maison Fleurie, 279
    Vintage 1870, 56
    Vintage Inn, 280

Z

Zinfandel House, Calistoga, 125

Become a Karen Brown Preferred Reader

Name _____

Street _____

Town _____

State _____ Zip _____ Country _____

Tel _____ Fax _____

e-mail _____

We'd love to welcome you as a Karen Brown Preferred Reader. Send us your name and address and you will be entered in our monthly drawing to receive a free set of Karen Brown guides. As a preferred reader, you will be the first to know when new editions of Karen Brown guides go to press, and receive special promotions and updated information on hotels & B&Bs.

Please send to: Karen Brown's Guides, Post Office Box 70, San Mateo, California 94401, USA
tel: (650) 342-9117, fax: (650) 342-9153, e-mail: karen@karenbrown.com, website: www.karenbrown.com

SHARE YOUR DISCOVERIES WITH US

Outstanding properties often come from readers' discoveries. We would love to hear from you.

Please list below any hotel or bed & breakfast you discover. Tell us what you liked about the property and, if possible, please include a brochure or photographs so we can share your enthusiasm. We keep a database of all of reader recommendations for future consideration. Note: we regret we cannot return photos.

Owner _____ Hotel or B&B _____ Street _____

Town _____ Zip _____ State or Region _____ Country _____

Comments:

Your name _____ Street _____ Town _____ State _____

Zip _____ Country _____ Tel _____ e-mail _____ date _____

Would you be willing to share your discovery with other Karen Brown readers?
Do we have your permission to electronically publish your review(s) on our website? Yes ____ No ____
If yes, would you like commentary anonymous, Yes ___No ___, or may we use your name? Yes___ No___

Please send report to: Karen Brown's Guides, Post Office Box 70, San Mateo, California 94401, USA
tel: (650) 342-9117, fax: (650) 342-9153, e-mail: karen@karenbrown.com, website: www.karenbrown.com

SHARE YOUR THOUGHTS ON PLACES YOU STAY

We greatly appreciate firsthand evaluations of places in our guides. Your critiques are invaluable to us. To stay current on the properties in our guides, we keep a database of readers' comments. To keep our readers up to date, we also sometimes share feedback with them via our website.

Please list your comments on properties that you have visited. We welcome accolades, as well as criticisms.

Name of hotel or b&b _____ Town _____ Country _____

Comments:

Name of hotel or b&b _____ Town _____ Country _____

Comments:

Your name _____ Street _____ Town _____ State _____

Zip _____ Country _____ Tel _____ e-mail _____ date _____

Do we have your permission to electronically publish your comments on our website? Yes ____ No ____

If yes, would you like commentary anonymous, Yes ___ No ___, or may we use your name? Yes___ No___

Please send report to: Karen Brown's Guides, Post Office Box 70, San Mateo, California 94401, USA
tel: (650) 342-9117, fax: (650) 342-9153, e-mail: karen@karenbrown.com, website: www.karenbrown.com

VISIT OUR WEBSITE

karen@karenbrown.com

- View color photos of a selection of hotels and B&Bs
- Link directly to places featured in Karen Brown's guides
- Learn about our latest discoveries—before they go to press
- Access up to the minute news on Karen Brown properties
- Share readers' comments on hotels and B&Bs
- Order Karen Brown's guides—at special prices

UNITED AIRLINES

is the

Preferred Airline

of

Karen Brown's Guides

KB Travel Service

Independently Owned and Operated by

Town & Country Travel

Quality * Personal Service * Great Values

- Staff advised by Karen Brown to help plan your holiday
- Reservations for hotels, inns, and B&Bs in Karen Brown's Guides
- Countryside mini-itineraries based on Karen Brown's Guides
- Special offerings on airfares to major cities in Europe
- Special prices on car rentals—ask about free upgrades

For assistance and information concerning service and fees, contact:

KB Travel Service / Town & Country Travel
16 East Third Avenue
San Mateo, California, 94401, USA
tel: 800-782-2128, fax: 650-342-2519, e-mail: kbtravel@aol.com

auto europe

Karen Brown's

Preferred Car Rental Service Provider

for

Worldwide Car Rental Services
Chauffeur & Transfer Services
Prestige & Sports Cars
Motor Home Rentals

Seal Cove Inn

Located in the San Francisco Bay Area

Karen Brown Herbert (best known as author of the Karen Brown's guides) and her husband, Rick, have put 22 years of experience into reality and opened their own superb hideaway, Seal Cove Inn. Spectacularly set amongst wild flowers and bordered by towering cypress trees, Seal Cove Inn looks out to the distant ocean over acres of county park: an oasis where you can enjoy secluded beaches, explore tidepools, watch frolicking seals, and follow the tree-lined path that traces the windswept ocean bluffs. Country antiques, original watercolors, flower-laden cradles, rich fabrics, and the gentle ticking of grandfather clocks create the perfect ambiance for a foggy day in front of the crackling log fire. Each bedroom is its own haven with a cozy sitting area before a wood-burning fireplace and doors opening onto a private balcony or patio with views to the park and ocean. Moss Beach is a 35-minute drive south of San Francisco, 6 miles north of the picturesque town of Half Moon Bay, and a few minutes from Princeton harbor with its colorful fishing boats and restaurants. Seal Cove Inn makes a perfect base for whale-watching, salmon-fishing excursions, day trips to San Francisco, exploring the coast, or, best of all, just a romantic interlude by the sea, time to relax and be pampered. Karen and Rick look forward to the pleasure of welcoming you to their coastal hideaway.

Seal Cove Inn • 221 Cypress Avenue • Moss Beach • California • 94038 • USA
tel: (650) 728-4114, fax: (650) 728-4116, e-mail: sealcove@coastside.net, website: sealcoveinn.com

KAREN BROWN wrote her first travel guide in 1976. Her personalized travel series has grown to thirteen titles which Karen and her small staff work diligently to keep updated. Karen, her husband, Rick, and their children, Alexandra and Richard, live in Moss Beach, a small town on the coast south of San Francisco. They settled here in 1991 when they opened Seal Cove Inn. Karen is frequently traveling, but when she is home, in her role as innkeeper, enjoys welcoming Karen Brown readers.

CLARE BROWN began her career in the field of travel in 1969 when she opened her own travel agency. Her specialty was countryside itineraries in Europe for her clients. The focus of her job remains unchanged, but now her expertise is available to a larger audience—the readers of her daughter Karen's guides. Clare lives in Hillsborough, California, with her husband, Bill, who shares her love of travel.

JUNE BROWN'S love of travel was inspired by the *National Geographic* magazines that she read as a girl in her dentist's office—so far she has visited over 40 countries. June hails from Sheffield, England and lived in Zambia and Canada before moving to northern California where she lives in San Mateo with her husband, Tony, their daughter Clare, two German Shepherds, and a Siamese cat.

BARBARA TAPP, the talented artist who produces all of the hotel sketches and delightful illustrations in this guide, was raised in Australia where she studied in Sydney at the School of Interior Design. Although Barbara continues with freelance projects, she devotes much of her time to illustrating the Karen Brown guides. Barbara lives in Kensington, California, with her husband, Richard, their two sons, Jonothan and Alexander, and daughter, Georgia.

JANN POLLARD, the artist responsible for the beautiful painting on the cover of this guide, has studied art since childhood, and is well-known for her outstanding impressionistic-style watercolors which she has exhibited in numerous juried shows, winning many awards. Jann travels frequently to Europe (using Karen Brown's guides) where she loves to paint historical buildings. Jann lives in Burlingame, California, with her husband, Gene.

Travel Your Dreams • Order your Karen Brown Guides Today

Please ask in your local bookstore for Karen Brown's Guides. If the books you want are unavailable, you may order directly from the publisher. Books will be shipped immediately.

_____ *Austria: Charming Inns & Itineraries* $18.95

_____ *California: Charming Inns & Itineraries* $18.95

_____ *England: Charming Bed & Breakfasts* $17.95

_____ *England, Wales & Scotland: Charming Hotels & Itineraries* $18.95

_____ *France: Charming Bed & Breakfasts* $17.95

_____ *France: Charming Inns & Itineraries* $18.95

_____ *Germany: Charming Inns & Itineraries* $18.95

_____ *Ireland: Charming Inns & Itineraries* $18.95

_____ *Italy: Charming Bed & Breakfasts* $17.95

_____ *Italy: Charming Inns & Itineraries* $18.95

_____ *Portugal: Charming Inns & Itineraries* $18.95

_____ *Spain: Charming Inns & Itineraries* $18.95

_____ *Switzerland: Charming Inns & Itineraries* $18.95

Name _____ Street _____

Town _____ State _____ Zip _____ Tel _____ email _____

Credit Card (MasterCard or Visa) _____ Expires _____

For orders in the USA, add $4 for the first book and $1 for each additional book for shipment. California residents add 8.25% sales tax. Overseas orders add $10 per book for airmail shipment. Indicate number of copies of each title; fax or mail form with check or credit card information to:

KAREN BROWN'S GUIDES
Post Office Box 70 • San Mateo • California • 94401 • USA
tel: (650) 342-9117, fax: (650) 342-9153, e-mail: karen@karenbrown.com

For additional information about Karen Brown's Guides, visit our website at www.karenbrown.com